# THE PAST IS ANOTHER COUNTRY

# THE PAST IS ANOTHER COUNTRY

*Representation, Historical Consciousness,
and Resistance in the Blue Ridge*

STEPHEN WILLIAM FOSTER

UNIVERSITY OF CALIFORNIA PRESS
BERKELEY   LOS ANGELES   LONDON

Grateful acknowledgment is made to Ronnie Taylor for permission to reprint the lyrics of "Memories of My Mind"; copyright © 1985 by Ronnie Taylor, all rights reserved.

The poem "Mountain Fertility Rite" by Billy Edd Wheeler reprinted by permission of the publisher from *Voices from the Hills: Selected Readings of Southern Appalachia,* edited by Robert J. Higgs and Ambrose N. Manning; copyright © 1975 by the Frederick Ungar Publishing Company.

Portions of Chapter One of this work originally appeared in "The Exotic as a Symbolic System," *Dialectical Anthropology* 7, no. 1 (1982): 21–30, and are reprinted here by kind permission of Martinus Nijhoff Publishers, Dordrecht, Holland.

All photographs by the author.

University of California Press
Berkeley and Los Angeles, California

University of California Press, Ltd.
London, England

© 1988 by The Regents of the University of California

Library of Congress Cataloging-in-Publication Data

Foster, Stephen William.
    The past is another country: representation, historical consciousness, and resistance in the Blue Ridge / Stephen William Foster.
        p.    cm.
    Bibliography: p.
    Includes index.
    ISBN 0-520-06251-5 (alk. paper)
    1. Ashe County (N.C.)—Social life and customs.    2. Blue Ridge Mountains—Social life and customs.    3. New River (N.C.–W. Va.)
I. Title.
F262.A7F67    1988
975.6'835—dc 19                                              88-2462
                                                             CIP

Printed in the United States of America

1 2 3 4 5 6 7 8 9

*For*
*My Parents*

*The past is a foreign country:*
*they do things differently there.*
                    —L. P. Hartley,
                    *The Go-Between*

# Contents

# List of Figures

# Preface

My interest in Appalachia originated with a concern for the coal-mining families of eastern Kentucky. But in the spring of 1975, I visited an anthropologist in western North Carolina who introduced me to people who had lived their entire lives in Ashe County, located in the northwestern corner of that state. They were engaging and accommodating people who took an immediate interest in my desire to do research in the area. This corner of Appalachia is not a coal region, and conditions differ markedly from those in Kentucky. Ashe County is a preserve of small farms, tiny towns and hamlets, and wooded hillsides. The countryside of the Blue Ridge was to me idyllic, the county had not been previously studied by an anthropologist, and there was no urban population. As in Kentucky, the politics of culture and representation in Ashe County touch directly upon the residents' prospects for pursuing their chosen way of life. A few months after my initial visit, I therefore returned to Ashe County to learn about its people and their culture.

Who these people are and how their situation can be understood are questions addressed in the pages that follow. This book is an investigation of the cultural experiences of Appalachians living in the Blue Ridge mountains. It is not a history book, but it is about history as a local construct, critically examined. In choosing this perspective, I follow the well-established position in anthropology suggesting that an understanding of social life must begin with the study of cultural meaning. Appalachians' definitions of their identity and their situation are at once innovative and tied to the past, and I have tried to place these definitions in the contexts of politics, history, sociology, and ecology. But this study is an ethnographic report in only a limited sense. I make no attempt to cover all aspects of Appalachian culture or even a wide range of topics. The literature on the area is rich and extensive, and there is no need to repeat the often excellent descriptions already available. Instead, the major thrust of my study is interpretive. As Geertz (1973, 19) suggests, "Anthropological interpretation consists in: tracing the curve of social discourse; fixing it into inspectable form."

Interpretation thus requires more than situating meaning within appropriate contexts. One must also come to understand politics, history, sociology, and ecology not merely as givens or as external conditions for meaning and for action but as constructions just as surely as is social life itself. For the people I studied, these elements emerge in social discourse, sometimes implicitly, sometimes explicitly, as individuals forge and modify relationships among themselves, as they create understandings of those relationships and rearticulate their understandings.

Meaning is embedded in action, as is action in meaning. But it is by expressing themselves through symbols that people view their society, manage and communicate about their relationships, and chart their courses through social and personal relationships. Symbols and representations thus embody a mediated reality that must have a central place in the anthropologist's struggle (as indeed it is) to set forth the nature of social life in a given community.

The social discourse that I examine in this study is not an abstraction so much as a sampling of the history of a people and a place. It is but a segment of the ongoing process of continuity and change in the way people converse, interact, and adapt. It is a sampling of that process in a special and distorted sense, since it is derived from my participation in that life, my reaction to it, and my interpretation of it. I cannot claim a perfect correspondence between my experience of the people and their own experiences separate from my interpretations.

What becomes inspectable here is how the people of Ashe County understand their world. Descriptive accounts too often present a picture of "what is" without indicating how "what is" can be grounded in relationships among persons—including the anthropologist—and in the modes of representation and significa-

tion arising from them. Ethnographic "truths" are posed as definitive, but they are relational truths; they remain embedded in the
social discourse of which they were a part. Abstracting them out
of discourse is a matter of convenience or necessity, and must remain, in part, rhetorical.

My dissatisfaction with customary ethnographic reportage resides in its omission of the anthropologist, who too often remains
an invisible yet omnipresent specter (Crapanzano 1977). This ge-
neric convention surely introduces biases, rather than removing
them, and obscures the ethnographic process itself. As a consequence, it produces neither good description nor adequate interpretation. I have struck out in a somewhat different direction. In
eschewing purely "objective" observation, indeed in denying its
existence, I have no choice but to render the sense the people have
of their experience through that of my own. How can a participant
avoid a personal view? If, for instance, I seem to wax adamant over
some of the political issues, it is not only because Ashe County
people were themselves often adamant about them.

Although the population of Ashe County is not without diversity, the cultural uniformity of this population is impressive. Unless otherwise noted, my informants were native to Ashe County,
and most could trace their forebears back a number of generations
without referring to anyone born outside the county. That my informants were uniform in this cultural and historical sense was not
by plan, but indicates the relative demographic and social stability
of the county up to the time of my research. Historically, emigration has been more significant than immigration, though this trend
has recently begun to change.

In studying this population, I remained faithful to the anthropological canon of interviewing, "participant observation," and
survey research. My emphasis was on collecting life-history materials and extensive samples of "discourse," an approach that is in
accordance with the cultural style of these people. Nonetheless,
throughout this work my skepticism and ambivalence regarding
these methods and many of the customary assumptions about the
significance of fieldwork data will become apparent (Clifford and
Marcus 1986).

An additional factor that no doubt structured my biases and my
regard for the people of Ashe County is my own cultural back-

ground. Some of my ancestors lived in the Appalachian region, and my informants thought they could detect this in my physical appearance. My surname was familiar to Ashe County residents, and my Episcopalian upbringing correlated with the social background of some of my informants. I shared with them a notion that we shared some cultural characteristics. Yet I am an urbanite; I do not underestimate the considerable differences between my informants and myself. At times, we deceived ourselves in thinking that mutual understanding could be immediate or easy. The surface similarities often made my initial rapport with informants seem effortless, but did not over time make our differences and disagreements invisible or easy to overcome. The usual clear-cut cultural differences between ethnographer and informants were for me absent. Similarities and differences were instead subtle and elusive, a problem for research. I had also to deal with my critical attitudes toward my own culture—a situation that introduced some interesting complexities and contradictions.

For me, Appalachia was thus both foreign and familiar, and doing ethnography in America rather than abroad had both drawbacks and advantages. Because I worked in English, I was able to explore nuances and shades of meaning in rich and broad samples of discourse—a task not always possible for investigators whose knowledge of their informants' language is incomplete. But "otherness" was more problematic for me because it was less obvious than had I been farther from home. I was forced to reflect at length upon the nature of cultural difference, and I was challenged to make my own society appear exotic in my own eyes. Because of my own cultural background, both the conventional anthropological presumption of the social whole as the primary unit of analysis and the notion of culture as a unitary system had long seemed to me open to question. While such concepts may be usefully applied to the societies most often studied by anthropologists, in Ashe County the status of culture and that of the social whole ("community") are increasingly uncertain. My fieldwork thus provided an opportunity to examine critically how an "exotic" social ideology both induces and inhibits constructing and participating in the social whole.

My interpretations and those of my informants have parallels as well as points of contrast. During the period of my research, they and I had similar experiences, shared comparable historical particulars, lived through broadly similar (American) ideological forms, and were moved by some of the same sentiments. My participation in the history of the people I was studying makes it *our* history. We compared notes. Sometimes we used different words, but we struggled to evolve a fragile rapport, interpreting each other and ourselves to ourselves. As they do with other outsiders, Ashe County people reformulated and rhetorically presented their culture to me as it fit their understanding of our relationship and as it promoted whatever social objectives they had in mind. I did anthropology as they told me about their lives. In so doing, I told them directly and indirectly about mine. We came to a working understanding as they posed an identity that I could compare to my own. The fragile, haltingly constructed semantic terrain that I shared with them necessarily suggested to me a need for self-reflection and a measure of self-disclosure.

As an anthropologist writing about the people of Ashe County, I hope this study will claim the interest of a variety of readers in addition to students of culture. The northwestern corner of North Carolina, bordering on Virginia and Tennessee, has become far less remote as modern transportation and communication collapse geographical distances. Since World War II, Ashe County people have increasingly become involved with people and institutions outside the county and even outside the region. This study thus has implications about the nature of social life not only for those living in rural settings in the United States, but also for Americans at large.

In particular, I discuss the relation of Ashe County residents to groups and institutional structures outside the region during a political dispute over a proposed hydroelectric dam. Because broadly similar debates constantly arise in various locations across the United States, this study also speaks to those concerned with the social ramifications of public-policy formulation and implementation. It may also interest those concerned with environmental issues and relations between minority populations and the larger society, relations that are in many ways complicated and unsettling. How these relations are negotiated and through what institutional channels partly premise social and cultural change in small-scale communities and in urban centers as well.

Finally, I hope this book will be meaningful to the people of
Ashe County and to other Appalachians. While I lived there, some
of the many people with whom I worked asked me directly to
write for and about them. Although I have tried to keep their
charge seriously in mind, I certainly cannot guarantee that local
people will approve of everything that I have to say. But I do think
that much of this book will appeal to people who are interested in
the region's heritage, both its past struggles and especially its still
vibrant culture.

Whenever possible, I have changed the names of individuals
whose words appear in the text. I have changed the name and
exact location of the rural community discussed in Chapter Two. I
have not altered the names of persons who acted in a public capacity and who became well known for their participation in a political dispute that was widely reported in the media (Chapter Three).
In order to ensure the privacy of persons mentioned in this study, I
have made some changes in the details of personal background information. No photographs of the people appear in this volume; it
was enough for them to give their voices.

The research upon which this study is based was funded by a
dissertation research grant from the National Science Foundation
(#SOC–13976) and a predoctoral fellowship from the National
Institute of Mental Health (#MH05422–01). I am grateful for
their support. Field research was conducted in 1975 and 1976 in the
Blue Ridge district of western North Carolina.

I wish to acknowledge the help of the following individuals
who played a part in shaping this study and making it possible:
Gail Langley Newbold lived in the mountains and sparked in me
an interest in the region's people. David M. Schneider did much to
frame my approach to the project. Frederick H. Schultz facilitated
my entry into Ashe County. Patricia D. Beaver and Judy Cornett
provided hospitality, encouragement, and consultation at crucial
junctures. Vincent Crapanzano and Robert N. Bellah read and
commented on the manuscript. Hildred Geertz also provided support. Special thanks go to Paul Rabinow. Jane and Martin Foster
put up with having a writer in their home and have witnessed my
excitement and discouragements ever since I was ten, when my interest in anthropology began as an obsession with ancient Egypt.

Alfred M. Brown helped in many ways. Naomi Schneider at the University of California Press played an important role.

And, of course, I deeply thank all the people of Ashe County who welcomed me to the mountains and shared with me something of their lives. They offered me their trust even when I was unable to make clear to them exactly why I was there. The joy I found in my work comes from my respect for these people and their character.

# Introduction

Like other Americans, Appalachians talk of their past as a time when people were able to exercise their choices untrammeled by the strictures of contemporary bureaucratic society. The people with whom I lived in the Blue Ridge mountains were often quick to point out this cleavage in their history. The differences between how they conducted social life in the past and how they live in the present were a constant and prevalent theme in their talk about community life. They idealize the past and celebrate individualism through their interpretations of history.[1]

There is, I believe, a certain poetic accuracy in these perceptions, and these observations are relevant not only to Ashe County, North Carolina, but, with minor modifications, to other regions of America as well. The crosscurrents of change—economic, political, and social—since World War II have made it increasingly difficult to implement various aspects of American ideology, and the experience of Ashe County people has been notably affected by this transformation. Ideology—the concepts, images, and ideals that people use to think about themselves and their world—has become less of a lived reality for these Appalachians than in the past, or so they argue.[2] In consequence, ideology has increasingly become a set of rhetorical forms that no longer describe social life as it is lived, but instead suggest how people might wish to live and how they think they lived once upon a time. As I will argue, Appalachians at times employ this sort of rhetoric—as do other local populations—in their attempts to differentiate their culture from the encompassing American milieu.

Culture, identity, and the construction of social life have become problems at the local level, some of which can be traced to the modern crisis of individualism. Alexis de Tocqueville had the clairvoyance to discern the centrality of individualism in American social ideology and to anticipate its potential difficulties. His "ethnography" of the American character, *Democracy in America* (first published in 1835–1840), asked whether individualism pushed too far could become the isolation and alienation of the individual. Behind this threat lurked the total deconstruction of the social whole. In *Habits of the Heart* (1985, viii), Robert N. Bellah and his team of researchers diagnose the particulars of this crisis in the late twentieth century, suggesting that individualism today "may be destroying those social integuments that Tocqueville saw as moderating its more destructive potentialities."

In Ashe County the increasing presence of legal-rational agents and methods of managing resources and people has led to a struggle against the encroachment of these "technologies." The relation of technocracy to individualism is crucial: technocracy makes formidable organizational demands upon small-scale social systems oriented toward individualism. In this context the negative aspects of individualism come to the fore, and the use of local culture to give shape and substance to the social whole becomes problematic. This uneasy mix of technocracy and individualism has thus challenged Ashe County people to reformulate culture and identity in order to reconstruct the social whole in locally satisfying ways. The reformulation process has brought about heated arguments about the significance of culture, identity, local autonomy, and outside intervention. Tocqueville would not have been surprised.

Thus individualism, a major element in American and Appalachian social ideologies, has grown in symbolic stature in discourse just as its implications for social life have seemed to become less certain; individualism is posed against bureaucratic hierarchy.[3] (Individualism is also part of the stereotype outsiders have of Appalachians, inaccurate to be sure, but pertinent to how Appalachians relate to Americans living outside the region.) Appalachians see individualism and the valued notions commonly associated with it—freedom of choice, self-determination, and private property—as having been circumscribed, limited, and profoundly modified in their relevance for action. The cultural understanding of the person, of what it means to be a person and the experience it promises, once viewed as a given aspect of being American, has ceased to be a stable reference point for action and has become a political issue, a social drama, and, at times, a personal quest fraught with uncertainty. Struggles over how to negotiate responses to these circumstances have taken on epic proportions for the people of Ashe County. They view their communities as having once been more or less autonomous and self-sufficient (the individual writ large)—but all that has changed. Today it is impossible to understand these people without studying the complicated relationships that exist between them and the rest of American society.[4]

Individualism has premised personal initiative as well as grassroots social and political movements. The burgeoning of bureaucratic authority and administrative technologies in both government and private enterprise is an aspect of late capitalism in which hierarchy rather than the individual has become the locus of decision making. These developments have constrained the efficacy of individual action and the realization of individual choices regarding the nature of social realities. Yet persons well placed within the hierarchy continue to insist upon self-sufficiency and individual autonomy as descriptive of contemporary society. From these contradictions, opposition and alienation are generated for people like those living in Ashe County—and they are by no means alone among Americans in this—who value "deciding for themselves" about everything from what to plant in their fields to when, if, and to whom they will sell their farmland.

The responses of Ashe County residents to the impinging technocracy have oscillated between hope and despair, between political activism and worries about creeping authoritarianism, and between the inflation and erosion of the meaning of the person and of understandings of the person's place in the social whole. From some viewpoints, the construction of that social whole has been assured as complex organizations have been elaborated and merged. From other viewpoints, a sense of wholeness has been precluded by the activism and fragmentation of contending societal subgroups, ethnic populations, religious denominations, political interest groups, cults, collectives, and voluntary organizations through which individuals struggle to shape their lives and to effect social change. This latter process and the social movements associated with it are manifestations of dissent: people working in frank opposition to the lines of emerging social structures. The dissidents argue for the priority of cultural self-determination while drawing upon the symbolic and rhetorical resources of American traditions. This dialectic is not new, but perhaps its scope has widened; its operation is keenly felt by competitors for power from the top to the bottom of the social hierarchy.

Appalachians are but one of many populations caught up in these complex transformations. Some of them have been vociferous in their expression of disaffection. Some have argued eloquently for the continued relevance and viability of traditional cultural forms and social ideologies for shaping the present as they have chosen it—rather than as others have tried to choose it for them. As uncertainty, debate, contention, and disenchantment have become more prevalent in mainstream America, the assimilation of images of affluence has been accompanied by opposition to these images and by efforts to articulate alternate trajectories for change. Public discourse on these matters has become cacophonous and strident within and without the Appalachian region.

Among Appalachians as well as Americans in general, identity is one of the most important issues in these debates. Since John C. Campbell (1921) published his now classic portrayal of Appalachian life, it has been clear that the meaning of Appalachian identity is not exhausted by its associations with geography and localism. What it means to be a person from the Appalachian region and from the Blue Ridge particularly, especially in a time of pervasive change, is a problem for cultural analysis. In the critical study of a culture in which social relations are premised on individualism, identity as culturally constituted necessarily becomes a cardinal subject.

There is considerable variability among cultures as to the representations that embody social conceptions and serve as the locus of value and social order. The person-oriented ideology of Ashe County people eschews an idea of social structure as the basis of social order. The meaning and coherence of relationships are not seen as deriving from institutional frameworks external to the individual. Instead, social experience is given structure and meaning in terms of character or personality or, in the language of the present study, *identity*. In this view the person is a major figure in local social ideology and an important "site" at which the construction of meaning takes place.[5]

For people in Ashe County, the meaning of their experience is integral to the social activities of everyday life. They do not usually abstract or differentiate social ideology from practical matters. The system of meaning to which they refer events is embedded in action and experience. To make this system explicit, I have necessarily situated the problematics of identity and change within local ideology. But what constitutes social ideology from an outsider's perspective is "knowledge" in the view of Ashe County people themselves: it is what they know, what is (or should be) unshakably true about social life. Hence, I use *social ideology* and *knowledge* as names for the same thing viewed from different perspectives.

Simply put, the ideology of Ashe County people incorporates models of and for society that are increasingly at odds with the models brought in by outsiders. As local knowledge comes increasingly under question, Ashe County people have become more involved in debating politics and change. In doing so, they rearticulate local knowledge ideologically, but themselves view their rhetorical practice as straightforward assertion, rather than as a transformation. For example, ethnicity has become more problematic as it has become more evident rhetorically because ethnicity contradicts the customary local canons of inclusiveness and goes against an ideology based on individualism. The people of Ashe County have attempted to surmount this contradiction in part by making ethnicity and identity into political issues.

The politicizing of such aspects of ideology has also come in response to increasing pressures of change in the form of unfamiliar cultural elements that Appalachians regard as polluting their local culture. These pressures, partly a consequence of outsiders' misunderstandings of local styles of life and their attempts to obviate them, have produced a disconcerting struggle between Ashe County people and outsiders to negotiate a mutually satisfying mode of interaction and coexistence. From the novels of Thomas Wolfe to the disciplined community studies of the region, through tracts by political writers, commentaries by humorists, and the works of regional poets, Appalachians have become a familiar figure in American social rhetoric, social discourse, and cultural commentary. James Agee, Harry Caudill, and Robert Coles have become particularly well known as writers sympathetic to the situation of people in Appalachia and the deep South. Agee's *Let Us Now Praise Famous Men* (1939) focuses on Alabama but set the stage for a serious analysis of social conditions throughout rural America during the Depression. Caudill (1962, 1971, 1976) became a spokesman for Appalachia in particular, recounting its history of exploitation by outsiders and detailing aspects of its current condition. He casts Appalachian history in appropriately dramatic terms and does not hesitate to vent his anger regarding the conditions in the coal-mining areas. Coles (1967) provides an overview of the region and its people, authenticated by his insistence upon letting Appalachian people speak through him for themselves. These authors are noteworthy for highlighting Appalachians' responses to outsiders' presuppositions and impositions and for emphasizing what Appalachians think of as meaningful social life in contrast to what outsiders have had in mind for the development of the region.[6]

In contrast, some social scientists have legitimated negative stereotypes of Appalachians. Caldwell (1930) disparages the Appalachian dialect and illiteracy. Ball (1968) views southern Appalachia as an ideal type for the subcultures to which planners should direct their efforts; decrying Appalachians' failure "to improve the quality of social life," he alleges that their responses to change are "nonrational." Similarly, Cain (1970) posits that a persistent traditionalism in Appalachia has repeatedly thwarted attempts to base "development" in the region on a model of industrial urbanism. (That such failures reflect the inapplicability of imposed models of development rather than the backwardness of local social ideology was not an issue for him.)

Such interpretations mirror outsiders' stereotypes of Appalachians and fail to recognize the alternate forms that rationality may take as local populations try to negotiate viable definitions of their culture and themselves. Whisnant (1973a, 1980) correctly traces the attitudes of such writers to an assumption that an urban-industrial way of life is modern and as such ought to be the model for Appalachians, whereas other (rural) ways of life are backward, antiquated, unproductive, and therefore less desirable. His radical commentary on the meaning of change in Appalachia helps us to understand that the imputed "backwardness" or "primitiveness" of the region's people is the result of outside intervention rather than constituting an appropriate reason for intervening.

Other criticisms that can be made of the social science literature on the region include insufficient attention to the relation of Appalachians to the larger society and a frequent failure to integrate material pertaining to ideology and meaning into the analysis of social forms. Communities are described as relatively autonomous, even isolated, social units detached from any cultural substrate of social practices. In some studies, autonomy is stressed at the expense of understanding the interdependences among communities and dependences on regional and national socioeconomic institutions. Fortunately, a series of recent interpretations has begun to rectify these difficulties by relating historical trends to emerging political movements, social rhetoric, and cultural representation (Batteau 1983a; Beaver and Purrington 1984; Beaver 1986).

Appalachians have attempted to respond meaningfully to change by creatively reworking established cultural knowledge. For example, genealogy not only serves to denote the history of social groups but also is used to adapt to the present. Thus Schwarzweller, Brown, and Mangalam (1971) document the persistence of broadly based networks of kin relations among Appalachians, despite a steady migration to industrial centers in the north. As these authors make clear, Appalachians customarily utilize kinship as a social resource in adjusting to rapidly changing social and economic conditions, and specifically to geographical displacement. Philliber and McCoy (1981) also describe this dynamic, but they largely ignore the cultural and political ramifications of this social practice (Foster 1982a).

Similar problems appear frequently in the ethnographic literature on the Blue Ridge. This literature concentrates on social structure, at the expense of indigenous systems of meaning and ideology, in communities subjected to rapid change (e.g., Stephenson 1968). Change means that social structures as well as meaning are "up for grabs," but how people reconstruct social life in response to these conditions has to be understood in the context of how they create new symbols, representations, and rhetorical forms in order to make change "make sense." For the creation of discourse and action are bound up with cultural definitions of "persons" as well as of their situation (cf. Varenne 1977).

While Hicks (1976) does little to integrate the cultural aspect into his interpretation, he does give considerable attention to the relation between the local situation and society beyond the Blue Ridge. He notes the ambivalence with which Appalachians greet government officials who have responsibilities in the area. He considers the significance of tourism and technological developments in industry for the nonfarm employment prospects of the Blue Ridge population. He also remarks upon the many problems that outsiders must confront when they present themselves as agents of change, whether they be missionaries, educators, or government agents.

Conjoining an interpretation of meaning, ideology, and representation with an investigation of change as it is tied to the problematic relations between Appalachians and outsiders is a principal task of the present study. In emphasizing a *cultural* interpretation, I concentrate on the conceptions of social situations that Ashe County people form and reform in the course of their everyday lives. Conception and meaning are fundamental to interpretation because the cultural representation of social life constitutes an important environment for action. At the same time, indigenous ideology defines such environments or *contexts;* ideology, as applied to particular events, is interpreted anew and thereby changed. The framework of my interpretation rests on the following assumptions:

1. Identity and ethnicity are understood and expressed in terms of an idiom or discourse of significant symbols. Such symbols also represent units in a system, however loosely and implicitly defined, of conceptions of the social world (Mead 1956). These conceptions bear on identity in that they specify what it means to live meaningfully, how to do so, and relative to what strictures. Kinship, politics, and religion are major concentrations of such conceptions. Together, cultural elements from these domains give people a sense of appropriate being and action, may secure for them a meaningful continuity among events (a history), and are woven into a larger fabric of meaning that integrates individual pursuits with collective expectations and social orientations.

2. As elements of social ideology, identity-orienting symbols give definition to the person in part through links with various social settings. In other words, the person as culturally constituted is

embedded in a social field. Identity is defined in large part through the person's placement in a social situation or in a complex array of social situations; the social interactions in which a person participates imply something of what it means to possess a given identity. But indigenous social ideology views identity rather differently. For Ashe County people, individualism means that the person comes first, historically and operationally, and interaction is derivative. The person is constituted as such, and interactions and networks are contingent on the character of the person. In indigenous ideology, identity is not derived from interaction or social placement but is thought to exist in its own right. This premise is belied by the experiences local people have had with outsiders, particularly in the political domain. Thus a tension is evident between indigenous notions of the person and the importance of interaction, particularly with outsiders, in defining and determining the meaning of identity and social experience as well.

3. The formation of identity is also encompassed by the cultural meaning of time as *history*. As interaction derives ideologically from the definition of persons, so identity derives from history—personal history, family history, regional history, and finally history in a general sense. As Schutz (1967, xxi) suggests, social action may be defined as "behavior to which subjective meaning is attached." For people in Ashe County, action must be understood in the context of the cultural meaning of the individual as the basic unit of social space and of history as the primary cultural understanding of time.

4. When identity formation occurs within a society undergoing change, transformations of meaning, specific arrangements of social contexts, as well as differing conceptions among actors may generate contradictory meanings for the same representations. In other words, the ideological field, which is a fundamental context of social action, cannot be assumed to be uniform or consistently ordered—it is not a system in an absolute sense. This lack of uniformity, the disagreements among people as to what social ideology and society itself ought to be, must be placed in the larger context of how Ashe County fits or does not fit into American society. Disagreements and debates as to key meanings in the culture can be interpreted in terms of the structure of the relationship of Ashe County people to other Americans.

5. The meaning of identity for people in Ashe County thus involves divergent conceptions of change and assimilation. These conceptions premise directly or indirectly people's conceptions of possible action and possible social and political relationships. Because contemporary events are challenging them with difficult choices in the areas of group and regional identification as well as in family affairs, identity and ethnicity have become issues to be debated rather than attributes to be assumed. Identity and culture are molten, such that their constituent elements conflict, become entangled, rhetorical, enmeshed in the political process of change.

6. Under these conditions, the capacity of terms like *ideology, culture,* and *discourse* to represent social values and social facts remains in flux. The problem for interpretation and for social practice is how to deal with this instability. Discourse may be rhetorically posed to outsiders as serious speech acts.[7] But from the perspective of the county native, the authenticity of this discourse may be more problematic. Ideology may be modified on the basis of a wager regarding the autonomy of local culture. Culture ceases to have a particular "content" (if it ever did) and becomes a representation within discourse with which a variety of meanings may be strategically associated. Discourse must be recognized as speech production that is constrained by its political context but that also strives to escape those constraints. Paul Rabinow's (1986) claim that representations are "social facts" suggests that interpretations that emerge from specific political arenas are at the same time a kind of social intervention or practice. Through the representations that discourse orchestrates, local residents attempt not only to understand but also to force a change: to create a "community" in contradiction and resistance to that which they oppose.

A detailed analysis of the social ideology prevalent in Ashe County is essential for interpreting this dynamic through which social forms are generated and for delineating the relation between local forms of representation and the wider sociocultural milieu of contemporary America. Such an analysis leads naturally into a cultural critique. Interpretation is not an end in itself; it is a means through which the character of the experience of Ashe County people may be made clear. Thus for readers familiar with the literature on the Appalachian region, the present work may provide a perspective on specific forms of cultural organization, on how meaning is arranged and encompassed by these forms, and on the cumulative effect of living through them.

Part I of this book sets forth a baseline overview of the ideology and social circumstances prevailing in the county. In Chapter One my descriptive preview of Ashe County includes brief sketches of a few of the people I met there and suggests the sort of relationships I had with them. I thereby begin to answer the complex question: Who are the people of Ashe County? In addition, I analyze the stereotypes outsiders have of Appalachians, treating stereotypes as a symbolic system that constrains local social meanings and the process of identity formation. This portion of the interpretation sets the stage for a later consideration of how the quest by Ashe County people for self-determination becomes a struggle with outsiders over power, knowledge, and cultural meaning. In this struggle, outsiders' stereotyping of Appalachians plays a key role. These stereotypes impoverish the identity of Appalachians and lead outsiders to ignore or underestimate the innovative powers of local people and to dismiss or undervalue local social forms that run counter to those outsiders envision for the region. To the degree that Ashe County people themselves internalize these stereotypes, cultural domination by outsiders becomes increasingly feasible. The struggle for self-determination for the people living in this part of the Blue Ridge thereby becomes an internal grappling with self-concepts as well as a political conflict.

Chapter Two provides an outline of local social ideology and practice. Identity is seen as arising from the symbolics of kinship, politics, and religion; each of these domains is investigated in turn, along with the parallels and similarities among them. Because the parallels are considerable, each aspect of social life sheds light on the others and suggests the possibility of social ideology providing an integrated and unified definition of social life for Ashe County people. The degree to which this possibility is actualized depends on the political dynamic between local people and outsiders and on the effectiveness of the local cultural rhetoric. Thus in discussing the prospects for an emerging cultural identity in Ashe County (as throughout the Appalachian region) and its basis in social ideology, I use *identity* to cover both individual identity and collective cultural identity.

History is a symbolic form, a figure in ideology, through which identity and ethnicity take shape, particularized in genealogies, in family histories, and in approaches to upbringing. A norm of diffuse, enduring solidarity is associated with such historically derived identities and relationships, tying together various domains of social experience and generating a comprehensive and integrated image of the sort of social life local residents hope to attain. Despite the patterns of interdependence in which they participate, Ashe County people at times insist on thinking of themselves as individually and collectively autonomous. Thus in Part II, I turn more specifically to a consideration of the exigencies of change that Ashe County people have encountered. While Part I sketches an "ethnographic present," a slice of the county's recent history, Part II emphasizes the "moving target" that Ashe County presents to the researcher in the context of change and uncertainty.

In Chapter Three, I assess the nature of shifts in the meaning of identity, primarily from the Ashe County viewpoint. I analyze a political dispute during which Ashe County people faced, as they still face, the challenge of outsiders whose interests, largely economic, and political power posed a serious challenge to the cultural identity of Ashe County people. The dispute involved the question of whether the New River, which flows northward through the county, would be dammed so that a large power conglomerate would be able to provide increased electric power to areas of North Carolina, Virginia, and Tennessee. Proponents of the dams argued for the priority of an increased energy supply, while opponents of the construction cited ecological, economic, and personal losses, especially to the people of Ashe County, that would result from flooding the county's most fertile farmland. In the course of the dispute, local systems of representation and meaning were threatened; the politics of culture and the culture of politics were in a sense juxtaposed. Which culture was to prevail and which forms of knowledge and power were to achieve ascendancy—those of outsiders or of local residents—became a matter of debate and the form in which the substantive issues were rhetorically cast. Culture itself became an element in the rhetoric of the dispute and a more explicit, yet more problematic, concept than it had been prior to the dispute. In Chapter Three, I interpret the rhetorical process and symbolic structure of this confrontation.

Damming the New River, obstructing its flow and flooding fertile farmlands in the interest of outside industry, is a compelling image of the cultural situation of Ashe County, particularly given an economy historically based on small family farms. Damming the river became a central image in the discourse of the controversy; it provided a compact, conceptual framework—a single set of terms—for interpreting in detail the ecological and ideological implications of a major crossroads in the county's history. The particulars of the New River dispute as a historic event readily became a potent metaphor for the dilemmas of change besetting the county. The river became a symbol of time, a symbol of the historical continuity of a way of life that extended back to the colonial period. Many county residents saw the proposal to obstruct the river's flow as a vivid representation of the discontinuity imposed by the increasing presence of outsiders. The dam threatened extant ecological patterns; a discontinuity in history made uncertain the viability of existing social and cultural forms in the present and in the future as well. This confluence of event and symbol offers a striking analogy for the problem of maintaining local culture in its confrontation with monolithic "civilization" (Diamond 1974). This analogy was not lost on local activists. The semantic reverberations of "damming the river" as representation had immediate appeal because of the charged meanings of land, locality, and landscape for many Ashe County people. This dramatic imagery was appropriated and exploited in raising cultural integrity to the level of a political issue.

While the interpretation in Chapter Three is the centerpiece of this book, the zone of uncertainty and controversy is broader than this one political dispute. In Chapter Four, I therefore set forth an interpretation of the broader shifts in meaning that have accompanied the imposition of "civilization." The various cultural elements that brought "civilization" into this part of the Blue Ridge are viewed as constituting a form of domination through which meanings are appropriated, co-opted, and subtly altered. Change is addressed locally through the politics of representation; local discourse addresses the problematics of representation brought about by change through a rhetoric of culture. As outsiders have increasingly sought to dictate the terms of experience to Appalachians, local populations have tried to assert and legitimize a cultural identity of their own.

Paradoxically, the significance of ethnicity in the Blue Ridge is being promoted in part through people's appeal to transcendent national symbols. They point out the inadmissibility of their forced alienation from their land and the nonviability of discontinuities in history as exemplified by the New River dispute. They broach self-determination in life-style and culture as essential and pose their culture and its various aspects as an art form. Yet domination, which some local people recognize as an exploitative form of colonialism, continues through the decomposition of history as an existential given and through the appropriation and re-presentation of indigenous culture as a marketable commodity.

# Part I

*Chapter One*

# Granny's Tooth Necklace

An evening drive from Boone, North Carolina, into Ashe County is a matter of half an hour on two-lane roads. The countryside is dotted with forests, small farms, orchards, and meadows; mountains are everywhere. Traffic is rarely heavy, although at times a slow-moving truck appears, carrying cattle to the livestock market in West Jefferson, or hay, or in late autumn, apples, beans, and tobacco. The landscape is a delight to the eye in all seasons, particularly at the time of day when its contours are accentuated by shadows. In the distance, mountains shade into clouds. Clusters of mailboxes congregate on either side of the road, labeled with family names that are often repeated on other boxes farther along. Lights from the kitchen windows of farmhouses glow invitingly. Cows head toward the barns. Children go inside for the evening meal, to do their homework, or to watch television.

Traffic on the roads becomes heavier between five and six o'clock, as people who make their living outside of Ashe County return home, but it thins out with the approach of the dinner hour. There are the incessant sounds of rural living: barking dogs, roosters crowing at the wrong hour, hot rods taking curves at high speeds, cows lowing. By sundown silence has replaced the buzz of small sawmills in the woods. As the road dips down into the valley of the New River's south fork, one can see Shetland ponies grazing, and a grand alluvial meadow opens out on either side. The river flows east where the road crosses it, but soon turns northward to run parallel to the western slopes of the Blue Ridge mountains.

Beyond the bridge, the road narrows somewhat and begins to twist and turn through the hills. Mountain laurel (rhododendron) abounds, and in the spring exudes a melodramatic splash of color, which gradually gives way to the blackish leafage of fall and winter. There are ponds and brick houses. In Beaver Creek, St. Mary's Church rears up beside the road.

Here the sugarloaf of Mount Jefferson rises above the surrounding landscape as though it had been planned as the symbolic center of the county. The mountain lies within the boundaries of a state park that attracts a growing number of tourists. Jefferson and West Jefferson, the "twin cities," are sheltered by the mountain and give it their name.

The road reaches the crest of a hill. Then it drops down into West Jefferson, passing the substantial brick offices of Ashe County's weekly newspaper, *The Skyland Post.* The lights come up suddenly, radiating jewellike along the town's rudimentary grid. North of town, above the mobile-home emporium, a tall radio tower winks. The shadows of the mountains spill out into the evening gloom. Within the heart of the town, stop lights cycle aimlessly, for in early evening few cars are in the streets and the sidewalks are deserted.

In the center of town, the road branches. One can turn right, continuing on U.S. Route 221, and go on toward Jefferson (incorporated in 1800), a mile or two northeast of West Jefferson. From there, the road winds up over the crest of the Blue Ridge toward Wilkesboro and ultimately on into Winston-Salem, about seventy miles farther to the east. With a population of some 132,000, Winston-Salem is the metropolitan area closest to the center of Ashe County. Or instead of turning right in the center of West Jefferson, one may continue north and then west through Warrensville to Creston, then crossing the state line into Tennessee, or north from Warrensville through Lansing into Grayson County, Virginia.

Ashe County is in some ways a microcosm of rural America.[1] Like rural regions elsewhere, it seems to have about it an aura of stasis or stability—some would say stagnation. But the contingencies that delimit continuity and change in the region are themselves being transformed. And so too, the life-styles of the people living in Ashe County, as those of people living in many parts of the world, are fraught with change, sometimes welcomed, but as often a source of confusion, anxiety, and alienation.

The storied landscape of the Blue Ridge, the oriental bounty of mountains, woodlands, and streams, seems to promise a mythic, biblical, even utopian kind of life. It does not, therefore, come as a surprise to find an influx into the county of "back-to-the-landers," younger people from the cities, as well as vacationers and retirees. Natives of Ashe County, "mountaineers," as they sometimes call themselves, often find it necessary to contend with outsiders: representatives of state or federal governments, agents of corporations, tourists, and even an anthropologist. How people living in the county deal with what they regard as intrusions—insertions of anomalous elements into their meaningful universe—is a key to understanding relations between small populations, or local cultures, and a social system that is national and to some extent even global in scope.

Ashe County, created by an act of the North Carolina General Assembly in 1799, is the northwesternmost county in the state. The county is located on the western slopes of the Blue Ridge mountains, with Tennessee on its western border and Virginia on the north. According to Arthur Fletcher's *Ashe County, A History* (1960, 34), "The county was named for Samuel Ashe, Revolutionary War patriot, who had served as Superior Court Judge for three terms and had been elected Governor [of North Carolina] in 1795 and re-elected in 1796 and 1797." In the 1800s, Ashe County was considered one of North Carolina's "lost counties." Inadequate roads over the Blue Ridge made access from the east difficult. The county remained remote and, outsiders thought, "uncivilized." As late as the turn of the twentieth century, it often took more than a week to reach Winston-Salem; it now takes less than two hours. Especially since the end of World War II, roads have become increasingly important as a determinant of the county's economy and autonomy—from the portico of the Jefferson Memorial in the nation's capital to Jefferson, North Carolina, is less than a six-hour drive.

The county today remains a largely agricultural region. Though there is some light industry and considerable occupational diversity, unlike counties farther west, there are no coal fields and no mining. From the center of the county, the metropolitan areas of

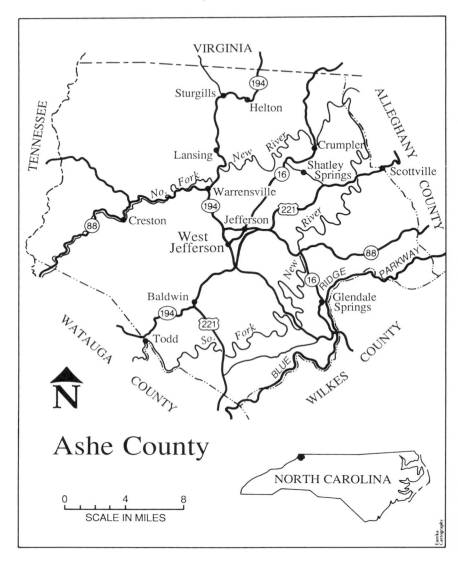

Ashe County

SCALE IN MILES

NORTH CAROLINA

Winston-Salem, North Carolina, and Johnson City, Tennessee, can be reached easily by car. But the county's geographic and cultural affinities are with neighboring counties in Virginia and Tennessee, and even eastern Kentucky and southeastern West Virginia, rather than with the North Carolina of the Piedmont and the Atlantic coast. According to the 1980 U.S. census, the population of the county was 22,325, making for a density of 52 persons per square mile. Although the population declined by about 13 percent between 1940 and 1970, by 1980 it had returned to its 1940 level.[2]

Broadly speaking, Ashe County is considered a part of the southern Appalachian region.[3] Those residents of the county who were born and raised there or in other rural Blue Ridge counties differentiate themselves clearly from "southerners" and from the "outsiders" who have come into the area. Ashe County people do not frequently call themselves "mountaineers" except when speaking to the anthropologist or other outsiders to whom they wish to euphemize themselves. This term is used rarely if at all for identifying one another.

The county has an overwhelmingly rural character, but scattered signs of suburbanization are beginning to appear. There are as yet no large towns in Ashe County; the two principal towns, which orbit about each other in the center of the county are microscopic by urban standards. Jefferson and West Jefferson have a combined population of about 2,200, about 10 percent of the county's total. Jefferson, the county seat and the larger of the two, prides itself on being the first town in the United States to be named after Thomas Jefferson. As though the third president's name belonged at the apex of the county's genealogy, this designation serves as a reminder of the county's inclusion within a broader national identity.

West Jefferson is economically the most important town in Ashe County. It is nestled securely between Mount Jefferson on the east and Paddy Mountain to the west. In the late afternoon, the tall, tapering Paddy Mountain casts a long shadow over the town and the western slopes of Mount Jefferson so that dusk comes rapidly. Paddy Mountain is said to be named for a man who was hanged at its base but, like every other historical "fact" about the county, there are conflicting reports on the matter. One informant stated that a man named George "Paddy" Bowers once lived near the mountain, but "he wasn't hanged, and the mountain wasn't named for him. He was named for the mountain to distinguish him from another George Bowers who lived over in Jefferson."

West Jefferson grew up around the railroad station, which was built in 1914 (Fletcher 1960, 250). The railroad was not extended to Jefferson because the populace voted against putting up the ten thousand dollars necessary to build the additional track extension. Just as Jefferson is the seat of the county government, West Jefferson is notable for its large number of hardware stores and banks (one, locally owned, had assets of over $25 million in 1976). The county's only movie theater is also located in West Jefferson. It serves the citizenry a regular fare of grade-B westerns, horror films, thrillers, and now and then a major Hollywood production.

There are no bars or liquor stores anywhere in dry Ashe County, and no alcoholic beverages can be sold legally. A few bootleggers sell beer and liquor at a considerable markup, but their business is not what it was in the past, when the roads were more difficult to travel. Nowadays, many people drive into the next county eastward, where alcohol is available from state-run outlets. There are also private clubs in the county that serve as a cover for drinking, good fellowship, and politics.

Near the center of West Jefferson, the road branches, and U.S. Route 221 passes in front of the monument works, which features an imposing pink granite statue of a bare-breasted Pocahontas. At the statue's base an inscription records the years of her birth and death. Will Reeves, who owned the marble works before his death, saw the statue while visiting New Orleans and it so struck his fancy that he brought it home and installed it where no one could avoid seeing it. Across the street from the monument works is Flora's. For years, Flora has run a general store out of what was once a gas station. Outside there are still gas pumps, but inside, where the garage work was done, one can find just about any food or household item. Flora keeps the unheated store open very late into the night even in wintertime, thus providing an alternative to the nearby Seven-Eleven store.

The county's Ford Motor agency, the shopping district, Sears, Hardee's Hamburger, and the A&P supermarket dominate West Jefferson. Near the laundromat is the post office, which is the locus of morning traffic jams as residents arrive to check their mailboxes. (The post office recently initiated in-town delivery.) Here too is the always-fragrant livestock market (auctions each Wednesday). Adjacent to the "stock market" is the Stockyard Grill, which is run by two matrons who cook breakfast and lunch before closing up to go home to their families. Top-quality country cooking and a generous menu of current gossip make the Stockyard Grill a center of activity in this part of town. Another such institution is the Rancho, over on the other side of Jefferson, where again excellent food provides an excuse for its habitués to gather for regular news conferences.

The Phoenix plant of the Thomasville Furniture Company is across Jefferson Avenue from the stockyards. It employs approximately two hundred workers in two daily shifts. On a sunny day, the workers toss horseshoes during the afternoon break. The plant was originally owned by the Bear (later Barr) family of West Jefferson. Before the family sold the plant to the Thomasville Company, they had also built houses for the employees. This cluster of company houses, located near the plant and southwest of the town park and cemetery, came to be known as Beartown and is still known by that name today.

A few blocks from the furniture plant is the train yard, dominated by a white, half-abandoned building, once the train station but now a shipping office. Passenger trains no longer come to Ashe County. On Thursday mornings, a freight train arrives to unload coal, machines, building supplies, and the wood that the Thomasville workers turn into chairs. Across the street is a row of warehouses. At the coal yard alongside the track, coal is dumped from the train and later distributed primarily for heating homes during the winter.

Across the train tracks from the shipping office is the West Jefferson town park and cemetery. There are picnic tables, tennis courts, a small creek traversed by bridges, and a baseball diamond. The new Ashe County Library, under construction in one corner of the park, is being built with funds raised largely by private subscription to replace the cramped county library located in the courthouse in Jefferson. Some people object to the new library's site because the new driveways and parking lot will reduce the open space of the park itself.

Beyond the park on the slopes of Paddy Mountain are a number of comfortable brick homes, composing West Jefferson's best residential district. One house even boasts an elevator. Here too is the Bowie mansion, a gigantic, brooding brick house with generous porticoes, sequestered in a wood, surrounded by a high wall, and shrouded in mountain laurel. Such a setting could be fertile ground for a Faulkner or a Thomas Wolfe. Everyday life in Ashe County easily takes on epic proportions in the eyes of its residents, many of whom are fine storytellers.

Saturday is the big shopping day in West Jefferson. Although some people make intermittent expeditions to the shopping mall in Johnson City, Tennessee (sixty miles away), or to Winston-Salem, many people living in Ashe County come into West Jefferson to shop. Jefferson Avenue, the main street through town, is crowded with large cars and pickup trucks, and the sidewalks are jammed. On the street corners and in front of store entrances, friends and relatives meet and form small groups to exchange news of their families, the status of the bean crop or the tobacco, their views on new cars or events at the courthouse.

Near the coal yard someone has parked a pickup truck, lining up watermelons on the tailgate to sell, and piling up squash, apples, tomatoes, grapes, and ears of corn in bushel baskets. The women go about their business at the Five-and-Dime or in the shoestore, then drop a load of wash off at the laundromat or go to the drug-store to buy ice cream sodas for the children.

The shack that houses the office for the coal yard and the soft-drink machine just outside are the site of perpetual gossip sessions. Here, as well as in front of the hardware store and in the barber-shop, the men gather to exchange news. They speculate about the crops, discuss weather predictions, argue politics, or complain about their wives. They drink sodas, smoke, or spit out a chewed-out tobacco plug. Behind them, just across the tracks, stands an ancient water tower, which is festooned with icicles on winter days and serves as the nesting place for the town's much-maligned pigeon population.

There is no doubt that work is being done during these Satur-day conversations. People are enjoying themselves, but they are also in earnest. In a social environment in which information is in-fluence and knowing someone is power, the groups of men talking over local affairs in front of the hardware store or in the barber-shop are not merely engaging in a traditional ritualistic pastime. These activities are part of each speaker's effort to negotiate, articu-late, and formulate a viable economic and social position for him-self and his family. It is an exercise in social placement. They may discuss possible jobs in the county for a son or a nephew; they may ask about who has the expertise to repair the radiator of a tractor, or who is likely or unlikely to marry whom and where they are likely to settle. Saturday afternoons provide a more fluid atmosphere for gossip than church meetings do, and allow more countywide information to be exchanged than do casual encounters of neighbors in the rural communities. As such, they are important social events, not to be taken merely as random encounters.

Businesses in West Jefferson are now beginning to compete for customers with the newly opened Ashe Square shopping center, located on the "four-lane" between Jefferson and West Jefferson and helping to create a suburban interstitial between the two towns. "Originally said to be two miles apart, West Jefferson and Jefferson have practically grown together. Main Street, West Jefferson, may be regarded as an extension of Main Street, Jefferson, and it is inevitable that eventually the two will grow together and become one" (Fletcher 1960, 251). Yet from many places in either town, one can view cattle grazing on the nearby slopes of Mount Jefferson.

Mount Jefferson State Park and the Blue Ridge Parkway, which runs along the summit of the Blue Ridge mountains and which was constructed as part of a federal work project during the Depression and is now administered by the National Park Service, attract the largest number of tourists during the fall, when the colors of autumn leaves rival those of New England, and during the spring, when the woods are studded with wild flowers and the spectacle of mountain laurel in bloom. But in Ashe County tourism has not yet become the large-scale operation it is in neighboring counties to the south (Watauga and Avery), where a diversity of ski areas, country clubs, resort hotels, summer homes, and tourist attractions abound. Ashe County has its share of seasonal residents, many of whom are "Floridians," as they are called locally, and who are generally regarded with ambivalence and initial caution.

South of West Jefferson on U.S. Route 221 is Beaver Creek, an unincorporated area that is primarily residential, although there are a few general stores (one owned and operated by a pair of delightful old women who are identical twins), a Kentucky Fried Chicken, gas stations, and the county's Pontiac dealership. Beaver Creek is also home to one of the county's three high schools, the others being located north of Jefferson in Nathan's Creek and near

Warrensville, farther to the west. In many respects Beaver Creek approximates what is commonly known as suburban sprawl, though its development is somewhat restricted by Mount Jefferson, which crowds it from the northeast, and by the generous acreage of the Ray Farms on the south. According to the will of Dr. Donald Ray, the farms must be retained as a unit in perpetuity and used for agricultural purposes. This property may be the largest single parcel of highly desirable agricultural land in the county. Given its location, it is possibly the one ripest for development.

Smaller settlements are scattered throughout the rest of the county, the foremost among these being Lansing, Warrensville, Todd, and Glendale Springs. Grassy Creek is also given a dot on the map as are Chestnut Hill, Creston, Tuckerdale, and Fleetwood. These are at most hamlets with a service station, in some instances a general store, and perhaps a church or two. Only some of these settlements, including Grassy Creek, have small post offices, the continuing existence of which is being hotly debated. In many cases, these settlements lack the social cohesion that frequently prevails in the smaller, more strictly rural communities characteristic of the county.

These rural communities dot the landscape, congregating about the courses of creeks and streambeds. They are situated on secondary or tertiary roads (for the most part paved or partially paved) identified by road signs: Mill Creek Road, Buck Mountain Road, Black Bear Inn Road. Family residences are clustered along a section of roadway, each house situated on acreage once or still used for farming, orchards, grazing, and vegetable gardening. These communities are commonly delimited by a steep ridge and are seen by their residents as semidiscrete social units. Today they are by no means self-sustaining or socially autonomous, if they ever were. Decade by decade, the clearly discrete settlement pattern has become less representative of the social patterns that, it is said, once made them relatively self-contained. Some communities possess a church, though attendance does not correlate neatly with residence in the same community. Indeed, social institutions beyond the family-based domestic group are increasingly rare. Churches, post offices, and businesses have generally become more centralized than in the past, located on main roads or in town. If these rural communities are a manifestation of what Lévi-Strauss (1963a) calls archaism or if they have become anachronistic rather than growing and thriving, they are neither regressive nor merely vestigial. Their persistence must be situated historically and understood in terms of larger-scale environing social units that have not always existed in their present form. As for the internal cohesion of these rural communities, Beaver (1976, v; 1986, 55) rightly observes that on occasion they mobilize as functionally unified groups but usually show a variable measure of social cohesion, although their persistence as a social form may at times be at odds with increasing countywide interdependence. (The rural community is characterized in detail in Chapter Two.)

A pervasive and intimate symbiosis continues to develop between the residents of the rural communities and the establishments and institutions in the towns, neighboring counties, and regional urban centers. Improved roads have made commuting to town and even to jobs or colleges in other counties increasingly feasible, if not commonplace. There is no public transportation into or out of the county, and none within it, apart from hitchhiking. Road systems in parts of the Appalachian region, particularly where roads have been improved only when they facilitate the quick removal of coal by truck, deserve their deplorable reputation. But the road system in the rural counties of North Carolina has not suffered such neglect or abuse. Maintained largely by state funds, Ashe County roads have been significantly improved in the last forty to fifty years. As Fletcher (1960, 267) notes, "Even secondary roads are well kept and may be considered as all-weather roads. They are . . . always passable and quickly repaired." Ashe County plans to supplement its transportation system with an airport, to be located north of Jefferson. However, the airport is intended primarily for private planes and will not be in operation for some time. The original construction company hit unexpectedly rocky ground, and cost overruns forced the firm into bankruptcy. Now an explosives company has been hired to blast and clear an area for a runway.

Not all rural residents, people living "on the land," cultivate or otherwise exploit their acreage, though many grow vegetable gardens and small plots of tobacco.[4] Some work on salary in town or elsewhere in the county, even commuting fifty or more miles to work. Historically, agriculture was the foundation of household economics, but after 1900 and particularly after World War II rural families largely reliant on agriculture gradually began to diversify in order to gain some economic and monetary flexibility. This practice still prevails for a minority of farming families, while many others now depend on paychecks supplemented in varying degrees by earnings from their land.

One informant who had considerable farming knowledge, if not practical expertise, thought it appropriate to call himself a "peasant" because he was living in a rural community. This self-ascription, however, was most likely a conceit—an ironic comment for the benefit of the anthropologist—since "peasant" is not an epithet in regular use among rural residents. In the case of Ashe County, the term is a rather crude metaphor that dramatizes the precariousness of the rural residents' traditional economic adaptation and their ambivalent feelings about town and city. But in fact there are no hard-and-fast distinctions between the rural style of life and that which prevails in the towns and villages. Agricultural production in Ashe County, far from becoming intensified, is decreasing. Although family farms are frequently subdivided to provide homesites for adult children who remain in the county, many young people leave to make their lives elsewhere, and farms are rarely subdivided to create new independent farms.[5]

The many paradoxes of land use, land ownership, and land exploitation in Ashe County are in large measure dictated by outside economic, demographic, and political exigencies. As in the time of Dan'l Boone, when the frontier was no farther west than the Blue Ridge itself, local concepts of history and social identity, an understanding of the land and the meaning people invest in it, remain fundamental to an understanding of the shape and texture of the social experience and the construction of cultural identity among Appalachian peoples. One resident said of the land, "It's God's country 'cause the Devil wouldn't have it" (Beaver 1976, 103)—an epigrammatic illustration of the ambivalence with which people regard this fundamental "commodity." (The significance of land as a symbol in social ideology is discussed in Chapter Four.)

Ashe County is not merely a geographical or political division, but a social and cultural unit, and a symbol of identity and community. People most often designate themselves as "residents of Ashe County," rather than naming the rural community or town in which they make their home. This designation reflects the prevailing social and economic patterns. Residents of the rural communities constantly interact with family, affines, and friends living in town or in other rural communities in the county. Although marriages between neighbors and people within a rural community are frequent, they are less common than in the past, when roads made travel difficult and before the high schools became important scenes of socialization and courtship. At the beginning of my fieldwork period, my idea was to work in just one rural community. But it soon became clear that interaction outside the community was frequent enough to make the study of one such community as a social unit rather artificial. Despite geographical contiguity, for the most part the rural community lacks any thoroughgoing social integration. Instead, there is a routine and intense pattern of countywide social interaction.

The situation is similar for residents of West Jefferson, Jefferson, and Lansing. Although they make their homes "in town," they have regular contact with people who live outside town or in the rural communities. They may own land or a home that was the family farm, but these rural properties are now used by another member of the family or rented during the summer. There are friends to visit outside town, or church services to attend, and even Jefferson is small enough so that getting out of town is effortless and unavoidable. A distinction between countywide interaction and localized interaction may have been important before the road system was improved, but today few Ashe County residents are strictly isolated—except for a dwindling number of old-timers who rarely come into town.

Thus Campbell's (1921, 87) classification of Appalachians into three groups—urban and near-urban folk living in incorporated communities of more than a thousand, rural folk with fairly large land holdings, and isolated poorer people—is not in the main applicable to the distribution of interaction, kin networks, or economic resources in Ashe County today. The crucial distinction is not between the towns and the rural communities, but between Ashe County residents and people from the big cities beyond the county borders.

Who are the people of Ashe County and what is their cultural style of asserting an identity? One approach to this topic is the study of life history, an indigenous cultural mode of self-presentation and

self-understanding through which the residents themselves interpret, frame, and otherwise manage the ups and downs of everyday
life. The following portraits use this approach to articulating identity and indicate something of the form and variation of county
residents' social experience. The sketches also suggest some of the
problems and prospects of living in the Blue Ridge.

Henry Reeves lived in the room next to mine at the house of
Edna Price James. He is about sixty years of age and no longer
works. After an undistinguished career in the armed forces during
World War II, he worked for many years at a General Motors assembly plant in Michigan. Then he returned to his native Ashe
County, where the members of his family still reside. He rarely
mentions his years in Michigan, but he talks freely about his time
in the service.

Henry keeps to himself. He is fastidious about his personal appearance despite his small wardrobe; his gray hair is always slicked
back and combed into an elaborate pompadour. Above average in
height with rather long legs, he carries himself gracefully and
erect, and he has perfect and delicate manners. A few personal be-
longings are locked in a suitcase in his room.

Many aspects of Henry's life are governed by strict clockwork
patterns. He always goes out early to the Kozy Kitchen or Jefferson Avenue to have breakfast. He exchanges greetings with his ac-
quaintances and talks politely about the weather. Then, crossing
the railroad tracks, he walks the few blocks back to the house. In
the early afternoon, he usually walks over to the soda fountain in
People's Rexall Drugstore to sit and dream over a bowl of soup
and a sandwich.

Henry seldom goes out in the evenings; he'll watch television
for a while until bedtime or hope for a phone call from a relative.
One noontime, a second cousin arrived from Winston-Salem to
see him, and they talked together for a long time. Henry recently
sold a large piece of family land located near the Blue Ridge Parkway. He took care of his aged mother and father single-handedly
for many years before they died.

He talks about being in Germany and in France during the war.
About Paris he says, "Oh, my! What a beautiful city that was, and
how beautiful the women were!" One of his favorite stories from
this period is about buying some grapes from a Paris street ven-

dor. Neither he nor the woman he was with was fluent in French, nor did they have an adequate understanding of the French monetary system. When they paid the vendor, he disappeared rather suddenly, leaving Henry to realize that he had just purchased the entire cartload.

Henry talks about the New York beer halls that had their heyday during the war and about going with a pretty Spanish girl on the subway to Coney Island. "Those were the days," he says, speaking of the period when he was stationed at Fort Dix, New Jersey. Once in a while, he speaks wistfully of traveling again. He says that he has "a girl" in Wilkesboro, but it has been months since he has visited her. (He does not own a car.) He also talks of going to California to spend the winter with a cousin who lives there.

He notes how many people are coming back to the land these days, particularly young people, and appreciates the younger generation's attraction to the land. He enjoys discussing politics, that is, party politics: who is most likely to be elected to what office and why. Then he speaks of women, complaining about how long it takes for a woman to make up her mind about anything. In talking with a friend who had recently lost his wife to another man, Henry comments that being inconsistent is a woman's nature. "It's just part of them," he says. He states that he never married, but having "lived with enough women" in his time, he has learned that "women will go off and do whatever they want right behind your back. You can never trust a woman. A lot of what they say is bullshit anyway." Of course, in expressing his distrust of women, Henry also seems to be foregrounding an important aspect of his social identity and attempting to establish, in talking with another man, the scope of his experience—which may have been more limited than he might have wished. In Goffman's (1959) terms, Henry's self-presentation could be viewed as motivated by a desire to reaffirm his masculinity: strong opinions on political matters and on the subject of women are customary topics of masculine discourse.

Elizabeth Shepard is a young woman with a ten-year-old son. She lives with her parents in West Jefferson. After her marriage, she moved to New York City with her husband and was employed for several years in a large corporate office in Manhattan. After their divorce, she returned with her son to Ashe County, temporarily, she thought, in order to reorient her life. She completed a master's degree and then obtained employment in Boone, in the county south of Ashe. Her provisional household arrangements will change in the near future when she finds a separate residence for her son and herself.

When Elizabeth was in New York, she never imagined that she would even think about returning to live in Ashe County. Now there is nowhere else she would rather live. The "chaos and confusion" of New York are "too much," she says, and the city is not a good place to raise a child. The county is a beautiful place, she explains, there is plenty to do, and she is surrounded by friends. An amateur theater group keeps her busy when she is not working or taking care of her son. Her mother helps out considerably with her grandson's upbringing. Elizabeth also is involved in various programs at St. Mary's Church in Beaver Creek. She teaches Sunday Bible classes for the children.

The pattern of emigration and return, which is a motif in Elizabeth's narrative, summarizes a frequent experience of younger Ashe County people. A period of apparent neglect of ties to people in the county is followed by a period of improvisation and movement and then a rediscovery of the "comforts of home." Elizabeth suggested that being "at home" in the county means to her that she need not constantly maneuver to situate herself, which she says was part of her experience of being "on foreign soil." Knowing who you are is associated with knowing where you are and what can be expected of the people you are apt to meet.

Pearl Seagram Evans, a handsome, dark-haired woman in her early forties, works in the tax records office at the county courthouse. Pearl lives in Warrensville with her mother and fifteen-year-old son; her husband died eight years ago. Her son has a strong interest in auto mechanics and, as she said, "loves to get greasy." She notes that auto mechanics is a good, practical trade. She just throws her son's greasy overalls into the washer: "If they get clean, then they get clean. And if they don't, they don't."

As I looked over some of the tax records, she brought me a cup of coffee. After I finished writing down a few figures, we began to talk. We quickly established a common ground by discovering that one of my informants, Frank Grimes, is "Uncle Frank" to her, since her grandmother, Bernice Graybeal, is Frank's neighbor out on Sugar Run, a rural community not far from Warrensville. She also knows my landlady, Edna Price James, who used to work in the county courthouse. Just as Henry Reeves used an idiom of sexual stereotyping to foreground one aspect of shared identity (masculinity), Pearl emphasized another shared context (neighbor and kin).

When Pearl's husband died, there was only thirty-two dollars in the bank to pay the funeral expenses and all other debts. Her husband had had a life insurance policy, but when she went to the bank to claim it she discovered that the banker, who had had a nervous breakdown, had failed to process the life insurance policy as her husband had wished. The new banker facilitated matters, and Pearl eventually received the benefits due her.

I had told Pearl that I was a student, so she described some of her own experiences as a student, referring to yet another area of shared experience. Within a few months after her husband's death, she managed to pay off the debts and expenses and earned enough to return to college at Appalachian State University, located within commuting distance in the next county. She obtained a scholarship one term, but the rest of the time she paid "like everyone else." She got two hundred dollars a month from Social Security, and in those days "money went somewhere," but she did not complete her degree.

She talked about her job and was soon telling me something about the labyrinth of local politics. In the county, politics—specifically a person's affiliation with a particular political party—provides a symbol of identity. One informant told me, "You'll find that everything here is politics." Pearl said, "You know, all of us over here are Democrats, but on the other side of the hall [of the county courthouse] they are all Republicans." She said that she reckoned she did not have to tell me that Frank Grimes was also a Democrat. She said that most likely he had already told me that himself, and I would surely not have gotten much out of him had I been a Republican. "Well," she said, "we get along all right with the people across the hall, and I reckon they're good people, but we're better." She spoke of the people across the hall as though the hallway itself were a frontier, the boundary between friendly territory and a hostile people. She went on to tell of a confrontation between a son and his father over the party membership of the son and his wife. "The son said, 'Well, we're going to vote all right, but you won't like how we're going to do it. We're going to vote as Democrats.'" The father was incredulous, because the children had been "brought up" Republican. "'Yes,' the son replied, 'but we have to work for a living. The Republicans just keep letting the rich get richer and the poor get poorer.'" In his view, the Democrats did a little better job of looking after the welfare of "the little man."

Frank Grimes has always lived on Sugar Run, a rural community scattered along a creek in the western part of the county. He is in his late seventies and lives with his wife, who is a few years older and has had trouble with her health in the last few years. She is not very active and talks often of her pellagra.

Frank carries on a busy daily regimen, early to bed and early to rise. He was too young to fight in World War I, was elected constable of nearby Creston township, and later appointed deputy sheriff in Ashe County. As a boy he learned carpentry from helping his father build coffins, and Frank has built a number of houses in the county, including his present residence. In the early 1930s, he was paid 10 to 12-1/2 cents an hour for his labor. A few years later he earned 75 cents an hour for carpentry—"That was really progress for you!" He has always done some farming, has always had a tobacco patch and a vegetable garden. Nowadays, he supervises the tending of the tobacco, but his grandsons, who both have families of their own, do much of the actual work. Frank suspects that they keep up the tobacco not only for the money it brings but also to please him. In a few years, he predicts, they will no longer want to bother with tobacco or farming. He knows his grandsons have an interest in living in the country, but he says they really know little about the details of farming and hardly bother to plant a garden. They sometimes rent the meadows to neighbors for grazing and each year buy a steer to graze for a few weeks to fatten up before slaughtering it and filling their freezers with meat for the winter. Frank supervises all these activities with a dour countenance, always approaching his grandsons' activities with a critical eye. In response, they joke and tease him.

Frank also works for the county hospital, driving to homes throughout the county one or two days a week to collect on past-due hospital bills. In the evenings, he reads the newspaper and, with his wife, watches the color television. On Sundays and sometimes on Wednesday evenings, he changes his coveralls for his best clothes, slicks back his hair, and drives down the road to the little Methodist church for the services and to meet his many friends. One Wednesday evening, I drove by the church with his grandson, Walter Huntington, and his wife, Jane. Frank's bright red Chevrolet was parked on the lawn right next to the church entrance. Jane laughed and noted that of course Frank parked his car in the "place of honor." Frank is the informally recognized patriarch of the community, having earned a reputation as the best-informed, most hard-headed, yet most magnanimous of the elder male residents on Sugar Run. He has lived there his entire life and is said to know more of the community's history than anyone now living there. He is also respected for his exemplary neighborliness, routinely using his connections outside the community to get a better break for people living down the road, who are as often as not related to him. Despite a "weak heart," he continues to spend as much time as possible outdoors and does his best to keep track of all that occurs in the community.

Frank is quick to point out the seeming discontinuities between the past and the present. As a young man, he farmed his land, some sixty to seventy-five acres, and hauled goods by horse cart to Wilkesboro (more than forty miles away) for a merchant who lived just "over the hill." He continued to make this trip every Monday for the next sixteen years, going perhaps five miles the first day on the dirt roads. He took produce into the town, and brought back dry goods and other products to stock his employer's general store. At that time, Wilkesboro had only two stores; today, some six thousand people live in Wilkesboro and North Wilkesboro.

Frank's father, Ben Grimes, had a mill on the creek. He worked two days a week at the mill all year round, grinding mostly corn and rye and being paid one gallon for every ten gallons of grain he ground. The millstones now serve as markers that flank the stairs to Frank's house. Frank's grandson, Walter, says one of them will probably become Frank's tombstone.

Walter is now in his middle twenties and lives in a world dramatically different from the one Ben Grimes would have known. Walter has lived in two other states and in one foreign country while in the armed forces. He and his wife are completing college on veterans' benefits. They live rent-free in a small house on Frank's property and commute to Appalachian State University. Walter and Jane have been married for five years and have a three-year-old son.

Walter's version of the family genealogy does not extend back to his great-grandfather Ben. Yet to Frank, Ben is in a sense more real than are his grandsons; Frank conceptualizes the present essentially in terms of the past and not in terms of the future, which he says he cannot readily think about in sensible terms. For Ashe County people such as Frank, history is a representation that provides a matrix of meaning for the present. In response to almost any question, Frank, like many others of his generation, proceeds to delineate "how it was" in the past and then how it all changed to become what it is today. The simplest and clearest way for Frank and others to understand the anthropologist is not as a student of present-day culture or even of family organization, but as a researcher in local history. At least for Frank, studying the history of Ashe County makes good sense, for studying local history is in his conception equivalent to understanding local culture in the present.[6]

Edna Price James has lived all her life in the Blue Ridge. She is just over fifty years of age, though she looks younger. Much of her time is spent maintaining her large home in West Jefferson, raking leaves, waxing floors, or changing the sheets in the rooms of her boarders. Her Aunt Amy, who recently had her eightieth birthday, often drops by. They discuss the details of Amy's will, exchange local gossip, and make decisions about how to distribute the furniture from the old Price homestead, located in a hollow near the north fork of the New River. On other occasions, Edna tells Aunt Amy that she is just too busy to talk and simply continues on her way, to show one of her apartments to a prospective renter or to do an errand at Sears or at the hardware store.

Her husband, Dr. Charles James, died only six months after their son, Tim, was born, so Edna raised her son alone. She has worked as a traveling saleswoman and for fifteen years as county accountant. In the autumn she helps keep the books at the Bean Market just north of West Jefferson, and in late winter and spring she fills out income tax forms at the H & R Block office in Jefferson. Some years ago Edna married her second husband, a wealthy physician. She lived with him for a few years in a neighboring county, but their marriage did not last. She told me that she had to wait on him in every sense of the word, and that he was rather a "stick-in-the-mud." He never wanted to go anywhere and wanted a wife only to display the jewelry and furs he bought for her. But it also seems likely that she felt out of her element in another county while her mother, who later died in Edna's house, kept the home fires burning.

In addition to her home, a large split-level, brick-and-glass affair in the better part of town, Edna owns a building on Jefferson Avenue. A beauty shop occupies the street level of this building, and upstairs are now two apartments where her first husband, who was a general practitioner, once had his medical offices. She also owns and rents out a small house on the lot next to her residence. This smaller house was the one Dr. James bought when he married Edna. She built the larger house that she now lives in about fifteen years ago. She also owns a log cabin on the banks of the New River, on land once part of her parents' farm. Her son spends much of his time there during his infrequent visits from San Francisco, where he has lived since his discharge from the army, and Edna rents out the cabin during the summer.

Edna's modernistic home in West Jefferson has six bedrooms in addition to her own, which was built as the storage room for canned foods and has no heating outlet. The house also includes a self-contained one-bedroom apartment and two kitchens. Edna rents all the bedrooms and the apartment. In December, when the tobacco buyers arrive from the Piedmont to buy locally grown tobacco, she is assured of having a full house. The buyers rent all the rooms and cook sumptuous feasts, thanks to their generous expense accounts.

Edna cuts a figure similar to Eliza Gant, the mother in Thomas Wolfe's *Look Homeward, Angel* (1929). Like her fictional counterpart, Edna is preoccupied with business affairs, real estate, and financial involvements. Edna keeps her house as clean as a hospital yet finds little time and energy for herself: unlike the rest of the house, Edna's room is usually the scene of careless disorder, drawers hanging open, magazines thrown about on the floor, jars and bottles of makeup and powder scattered about at random. Edna shares Eliza's habit of depriving herself of comforts for the sake of the dollars that can be saved by doing so, living in the storage room in order to make another room available to rent.

Now and then Edna decides to take a break from her domestic regime. She goes out to the dance club, to a square dance, or with friends to a play in Winston-Salem. She enjoys a party and has an abiding interest in the attentions of men. From time to time, a lady friend arranges a date or dinner for Edna with an older man of her acquaintance. A sheep rancher from eastern Oregon rented a room at Edna's house while visiting his Ashe County relatives, being himself a native of the county. He ate meals at the Rancho and told people there about his plan for Edna to return to Oregon with him. She did not realize, or perhaps chose not to realize, how serious he was until she heard these stories after he departed. He later phoned from Oregon and sent her a sheepskin rug with greetings written on the back. Edna loves to tell about these adventures, though she seems rarely to think seriously about seeing them through to their conclusion.

Despite her extensive properties, Edna's income is limited and unstable. None of her seasonal jobs provides a substantial income, and the apartments and rooms in her house are not all regularly occupied. Her small house was rented by Agnes, who has two sons but no husband, drives a school bus, and pays her rent but owed Edna for oil and some of her initial deposit. About Agnes, Edna often waxed indignant. Edna's electricity bill was $132 one month (the house is electrically heated). She often complains about high taxes. She sends Tim a healthy sum each month, although he has some income from the G.I. bill for his education.

Edna feels that she has justifiable financial worries and articulates them in terms of elaborate money-making schemes. She talks excitedly about "pyramid power" or about the profits one could make by starting an answering service in Ashe County. She went to West Virginia to apply for jobs in the coal mines, having read in the newspapers that women are being hired as regular mine workers. But after hearing about a mine disaster, she decided that the high wages were not worth dying for and did not follow up her applications.

Minnie Bell, a friend of Edna's who lives in a neighboring county and runs a souvenir shop, suggested to Edna that perhaps they could go into business together, taking over a large tourist concern nearby that was going out of business. They could work on a percentage basis, paying the rent and overhead, and could still make a profit. They planned to carry tourist goods, mountain crafts, quilts, pottery, and wood carvings and also to run a restaurant on the premises. Edna asked me if I thought I would like to work as a part-time cook. They were to have a meeting with the owner the following week. As far as I know, this meeting never took place.

When I went to Ashe County in August 1975, my plan was to live in a rural community for the duration of my fieldwork period. But after repeated attempts to procure housing in a rural part of the county, I rented a room in Edna's house. I remained there from August 1975 through the remainder of the research period, which ended in 1976.

From the beginning, Edna seemed to enjoy introducing me to other people, always telling them a little about my background, usually saying that I was engaged in research on "mountain people." I sometimes talked with her in the evenings, hearing the local gossip, discussing politics, or bemoaning the state of the world. Occasionally, I helped with work around the house or accompanied her to her cabin or apartment to help move heavy furniture or carry a carpet. After a few months, and particularly after I returned from a brief visit to California where I met her son, Edna began to present me to other people as her "second son." Many anthropologists have described this experience of being "adopted into" a family, clan, or tribal group. In this case, Edna's categorization of me and her construction of my identity as "son," if not as kin in a strict sense, allowed her and those around her to assimilate an outsider in terms familiar to them. I was both a son in a general sense and, more particularly, an analogue of some type of Edna's son, Tim, with whom they were already acquainted. This labeling allowed me to regard my own identity in a new light, indeed to restructure it to an extent. Edna often said to me, "You don't look like Tim, but you think like him." Once when she was reading me a letter that had just arrived from Tim, she remarked that our handwriting was similar.

Regardless of my lack of blood ties, my living under Edna's roof, together with her sense of my similarities to Tim in personal attributes, brought about a symbolic association, made it conceivable, comprehensible, preferable, and finally routine. My new and metaphoric social identity gradually became real and increasingly operational. As a result, my social experience with the community at large gained in richness and breadth. As Edna's "son," I acquired a more comprehensive and diffuse identity than the one afforded by my identity as an anthropologist, a functionary with a rather obscure job to do. As a "son," I could situate myself and be situated by others within a comprehensible, even intimate, set of social networks; relationships between myself and others in the community then developed easily.

For Edna, my presence enabled her to take up once again in some approximate fashion her relationship with her own son. For me, the analogy of Edna as "mother" provided a measure of security that anthropologists, especially in the early stages of field research, typically find helpful. From this standpoint, it becomes unclear just who adopted whom.

In spring 1975 I had made a short trip to western North Carolina to visit an anthropologist working in Boone, at Appalachian State University. There I met students who lived in Ashe County and to whom I expressed my interest in Appalachian research. Jane and Walter Huntington invited me to visit their home on Sugar Run and suggested that Ashe County, which had not been previously studied by an anthropologist, would be a fertile territory for my investigations.

Jane and Walter Huntington were born and raised in Ashe County and participated extensively in countywide networks. It was partly through the Huntingtons that I was able to gain entry into these networks. Through their undergraduate courses, Jane and Walter had acquired an understanding of the anthropologist's work, and they provided a lively counterpoint to my interpretations as well as giving me opportunities to participate in the rural life of the county.

After I began living in Edna's house, I learned that her son had been Walter's closest childhood friend. As Tim said later, "I just about lived at their house." Walter grew up in town, moving into Sugar Run only after his marriage. Thus at the beginning of the research period, I already had formed connections that reflected the pattern of my informants' own social experience of ties between the town and the rural community.

The Huntingtons' home became a place where I was always welcome, where I could spend the night and enter into the exchange of family and community gossip. I met members of both Walter's and Jane's families, whose homes were scattered throughout the county. They also introduced me to some of the other residents of Sugar Run. Many afternoons were spent drinking beer, cutting and grading tobacco, talking over how severe the winter would be as judged by the position of the stripes on the backs of the furry caterpillars, worrying over local and national politics or the advantages of planting and canning by the signs (Wiggington 1972, 208 and 212).

At Edna's too, there was always someone to talk with. In addition to Edna herself and Henry Reeves, a whole parade of diverse people passed through the house during the year: Clifford drank and smoked too much, suffered from emphysema, and talked of his days teaching high school mathematics; Jim worked as a ranger in the state park, was converted by Billy Graham, and spent most of his evenings and weekends preaching in churches throughout the county; Janet worked in bookkeeping at the Bean Market and lived in Edna's apartment with her two young children; and Carl Luke Jackson, originally from Kentucky, had a "nervous problem" resulting from his experiences in World War II and saw his wife finally run off with another man. Edna often suggested that even if I restricted my study to the residents of her house, I would still have plenty of material to "write my book."

From these initial contacts, I widened my networks to cover a broad range of Ashe County residents. When first meeting people, I would tell them about the nature of my work and arrange an interview schedule. I often used the term "conversation" rather than "interview," for the latter seemed to strike many people as somehow "official" and intimidating. Some of my work with informants was tape recorded, but some people were uncomfortable in the presence of a tape recorder. Most of my material derives from these interviews.

My informants, both by my own intent and as a result of my initial contacts, were natives of Ashe or neighboring counties in the Blue Ridge district. Diverse categories of non-native persons also live in the county. Their numbers made them visible but not an overwhelming cultural influence. Summer residents from other states, particularly Florida, rarely saw themselves as natives. Others who had taken up residence in the county ("back-to-the-landers") at times posed as natives, but were not consistently accepted as such by long-term residents.

In addition to interviews, which ranged from fairly formal scheduled meetings to informal conversations, my research included a limited amount of archival work at the Ashe County Library, at Appalachian State University, and with private documents obtained from informants. I had access to the usual demographic records, tax records, and court transcripts. I devoted extensive periods to learning the county's geography from U.S. Geological Survey maps and from travel on county roads. I participated in the social life of the county, attending church meetings and revivals, visiting informants at home and sometimes at their places of employment, going to the funeral home in West Jefferson and Saturday night dances. Much of this time I was with families, in family groups, doing what families do.

In a large journal I recorded all these encounters in detail along with interview transcripts, geographical descriptions, various sorts of historical and statistical materials, and passages of analytic speculation and personal musings. The present study has been shaped from this large body of material and is based on the themes that I identified as timely and significant for Ashe County. Much of this book is intended to articulate the relationship—personal, cultural, and conceptual—that I had and have with these people.

To me, fieldwork is not very different from other sorts of interpretive work that people undertake as part of their everyday lives, although ethnographic interpretation attempts a greater degree of abstraction and closure than individuals usually demand in coming to an understanding of their social experience. Wagner (1975, 35) rightly draws a parallel between anthropological work and cultural activity in general. He suggests that in focusing on cultural difference and comparison, anthropologists not only refer to different societal "types" but also imply different styles of creativity (Wagner 1975, 26). Thus ethnographic description, in transcribing "what is there," represents in part a style of creativity embedded in an experience of cultural difference. As an anthropologist, I do not

present an unmediated reality in my writing, but set forth an outcome and continuation of my dialogue with people who inhabit a
social world other than my own.

In appropriating cultural materials and integrating them into
my discourse, I necessarily situate them in a nonindigenous cultural context. These materials are thereby subjected to a new array
of meanings and transformed in the process. The anthropologist
interprets a people's culture for them, and my interpretations may
have reentered my informants' discourse on community life. This
process is by no means unique to ethnographic interpretation. The
interplay of local culture and a dominant culture may be seen as an
exchange or a negotiation. But "negotiation" may also be a euphemism for control. Once the residents of Ashe County consented
to talk with me as anthropologist, they assumed the role of informants and surrendered a measure of control over the presentation
of their cultural materials and social identity (cf. Clifford 1983).
How would I rework and re-present their situation?

While maintaining my role as anthropologist, I also tried to establish a local social identity, however metaphorical or fictional, as
"kin" or friend and familiar. (All this in too short a time.) These
were feasible identities, comprehensible to my informants in a way
that "being an anthropologist" simply was not. But marginality
can never be entirely overcome. A "reporter at large," I remained
in part a functionary, an observer, someone from the city, and perhaps even something of a tourist throughout my fieldwork. Ashe
County residents sometimes worried over the seemingly clinical
aspect of my work. One informant, with whom I also met informally, told me that it would be good for me to visit the county
again at a time when I would not be doing research. Another informant particularly enjoyed telling others that I was from an Ivy
League university and that I recorded our conversations on tape.
Some informants acquired a sense of self-importance from working with me, but one delightfully self-assured woman said that she
was afraid to say anything when I was around because I might go
home and write it down in my journal. Many people made a point
of telling me that they wished to read what I would write about
them, no doubt in order to get a look in the mirror (however distorted) but also in order to remind me that my work would be
scrutinized; I had a responsibility to them.

Like the outsiders who find them exotic or quaint, Ashe County residents invent stereotypes and other symbols to articulate the differences they perceive between themselves and persons of other cultural backgrounds. Such are the means through which people maintain and assert their own identity. Similarly, anthropologists first create cultural barriers by taking cultural differences seriously and then embarking upon fieldwork designed to mediate and to describe these differences. But axiomatic suppositions about the nature of culture, cultural difference, and cross-cultural communication now seem to me to be rhetorical devices—useful fictions.

Because the construction of culture and of difference was especially problematic in the case of my fieldwork in Ashe County, these rhetorical aspects became particularly evident. By conventional anthropological standards, Ashe County is not very remote, very different, or very exotic for an American anthropologist (Foster 1982b). Ashe County people speak English, live for the most part in nuclear-family households, and participate in the other institutions of American society.[7] The culture of the Blue Ridge did not at first seem so different from my own. But these judgments are in a sense shallow and fortuitous, even defensive. It seems that constructing cultural difference is mandated by the culture of anthropology and is implicit in the idea of fieldwork. Like the stereotype, ethnographic description establishes cultural difference as a commonplace even though it is not simple or self-evident. I could not approach difference conceptually until I had tried to explicate Ashe County culture. To understand the people of Ashe County I first had to come to terms with my implicit and explicit assumptions about the cultural similarities and differences between these people and myself and other Americans.

Outsiders' conceptions and stereotypes of Appalachians, I believe, pose impediments to Appalachians' construction of a viable identity for themselves and their ongoing struggles with change. The partial internalization of outsiders' stereotypes constrains Appalachians' efforts to bring about ideological and social changes, indeed constrain and impoverish that group's innovative attempts and self-concepts.

Schneider and Smith (1973) explore the interrelation of class and kinship in America, and Herlinger (1972) interprets Ozark concepts of kinship and ethnicity. But neither study compares local concepts of identity, kinship, and culture to outsiders' stereotypes; nor do these analyses clarify how stereotypes traverse social (ethnic or class) boundaries to become part of indigenous conceptual systems and to act as elements for articulating ethnic or personal identity. Sartre's (1948) study is noteworthy in showing how differing conceptions of ethnic identification arise when groups associate comparable identity-orienting symbols with contradictory social meanings. Clearly, outsiders (an indigenous term) view identity and society differently than do the people of Ashe County. Both groups refer to the same symbolic forms—person, family, and community—but the meanings of these symbols are governed in part by somewhat divergent ideological systems. Because the social ideologies of these groups are in many ways similar, the differences are often denied, obscured, distorted, stereotyped, defended against, or made absolute.

Outsiders have looked upon Appalachian people as hillbillies; as poor white trash; as typically racist, politically conservative, and dogmatic; as the last frontiersmen; and as an extreme embodiment of individualism. Before I began my fieldwork, one anthropologist half-jokingly said to me, "Appalachians are probably too stupid to have a symbology."

One stereotype sees the Appalachian man as tall and gaunt, perhaps stooped, with a deeply lined face and drawn features, hollow eyes, and a thin, set mouth. His dusty coveralls are patched, and his hair is an undefined color between brown and gray. His wife has stringy hair, unhealthy-looking skin, and appears old for her age; her weight suggests poor dietary habits or too many pregnancies. This couple's herd of offspring runs wild about a homestead that consists of a broken-down wooden house with a leaning porch. In this image of American Gothic gone stale, the family collects its welfare check each month. Afternoons the man and his buddies sit in the shade, pass the jug of corn licker round, and watch the road: "I could see the cars going by on the highway if I bothered to turn my head."

Hillbillies are sometimes presumed by outsiders to be lazy and inarticulate, ignorant and illiterate, incestuous and therefore genetically flawed, poor and anarchistic, and generally savage—not unlike the famous "primitive." They indulge their penchant for

violent family feuds, go coon hunting, and chew tobacco. As Mc-
Coy and Watkins (1981), both natives of the region, note, the
prevalent caricatures in jokes told by outsiders concern hillbillies'
lack of cleanliness and their questionable morality. Ignorance of
civilization and a lack of sophistication are other connotations of
pejorative terms such as *briar-hopper* and *ridgerunner.*

Such stereotypes form the backbone of James Dickey's characterizations of Appalachians in his novel *Deliverance* (1970). The
male characters are mentally defective, given to violence, caprice,
and perversion—more like animals than humans. Their culture, if
one can call it that, is associated with nature as a barbaric wilderness untouched by cultivation or civilization. Another aspect of
what to many outsiders is typical of the mountain life-style is
chronicled by Tom Wolfe in a provocative ethnographic report,
"The Last American Hero" (1965): moonshine and an obsession (if
only to transport the moonshine) with automobiles or, rather,
hot rods.[8]

One of the synecdoches for *hillbilly* that Appalachians most re-
sent is Li'l Abner. In this comic-strip world the Appalachian is
a buffoon who dashes about in jalopies or broken-down trucks
on bad roads, trafficking in moonshine. He wears tattered clothing, slouch hats, and coveralls, and he eats great quantities of
country ham.

When Appalachians use *hillbilly* in reference to one another, the
term signifies endearment, merriment, pride, and shared ancestry
as components of in-group identification and solidarity. The term
is a reference to the hills, to the land that, as Herlinger (1972) and
others suggest, grounds local identity by couching it in its geographical particulars. But as Kahn (1973) indicates in *Hillbilly
Women,* when a non-Appalachian uses *hillbilly* in reference to an
Appalachian, the connotation is often demeaning and insulting,
implying a distinct difference in status, social sophistication, and
"culture." According to Coles (1967) and Montgomery (1972),
outsiders view hillbillies as lower class in every sense, a stereotype
that derives from urbanites' experience with "impoverished" Appalachian migrants. Whereas the Blue Ridge conceptual scheme
stresses ethnicity over class hierarchy in defining the person, at
least in relation to outsiders, outsiders stereotypically stress class
over ethnicity. And whereas these rural people see in the land a

symbol of nurturance, for urbanites the countryscape often seems distant, peripheral, and even threatening—a moral and physical wilderness.

*Ethnicity* is used in the present study to indicate Appalachians' self-identification as members of a category of persons who regard themselves as having certain characteristics in common, characteristics that they claim distinguish them from outsiders. The subjective existence of Appalachian ethnicity is assured by the distinctions these people make between themselves and outsiders, as well as those that outsiders make between themselves and Appalachians. This cognitive boundary is maintained by the stereotypes that outsiders formulate of Appalachians as much as by the stereotypes Appalachians have of outsiders. From such stereotypes, usually negative caricatures, arise generalizations about the relation between local culture and "civilization" (an indigenous term).[9]

Stereotypes reflect an effort to categorize and label persons and groups from other societies or societal subgroups, to define the identity and the arrangement of those groups, and particularly to typify how the social world of one group is entered and appropriated by another. Thus by implication, stereotypes articulate and address situations of change. Through stereotypes, social, spatial, and temporal boundaries are drawn; in the context of encountering and delineating cultural differences, ethnicities are defined. In the uneasy dialogue between the people of Ashe County and outsiders, the stereotype is a major element in the rhetoric of cultural distinctiveness and in the struggle for cultural self-definition.

The ethnic boundary between Appalachians and other Americans is also indicated by irreducible differences in cultural orientation that are emblematic of the non–melting-pot aspects of American society. Stereotypes are a distorted expression of these differences and, like cultural differences in general, these cultural constructions are a social commentary on the structure of society and the nature of the social experience within it. The term *hillbilly* is a case in point: When someone is called a hillbilly, he or she is often quick to recognize the term as euphemistic and may respond with an objection.

The euphemistic tone of the stereotype obviates debating its "accuracy": "The reality of life in Appalachia has never approached matching the stereotype for the simple reason that survival would be impossible if it did" (Whisnant 1974, 105). What Evans-Pritchard (1964, 221) says of kinship terms also holds for the ethnic stereotyping of Appalachian people: When used as modes of address, such terms "emphasize social relationships and serve to evoke the response implied in the particular relationships so indicated." Although *hillbilly* is perhaps more often used as a term of reference than as a term of address, through the media Appalachians have become acutely aware of how outsiders speak of them. In light of television shows such as "Hee-Haw" or "The Beverly Hillbillies," it is no wonder that, for example, "mountain children have, until very recently, been taught to be ashamed of their speech and their cultural heritage" (Purrington 1972, 9). Mass media thus not only reinforce the stereotypes for outsiders but also transmit the stereotypes to the group being typed (Newcomb 1979) and thereby influence members' articulation of a self-concept. My informants frequently prefaced their remarks with, "Well, I haven't had much education, but"—qualifying the cultural context and their personal attributes in stereotyped terms.

We may consider "The Beverly Hillbillies" as one such channel for disseminating the imagery of Appalachian stereotypes and dramatizing their meanings.[10] One episode portrays Granny as the country curer, a role many Appalachian women fulfilled before there were university-trained physicians in the region (cf. Wiggington 1972, 230–48). Granny claims to have an effective remedy for the common cold, the "secret ingredient" of which is "corn squeezins'." Since modern medicine scoffs at such home cures, Granny easily becomes the brunt of ridicule and derogatory remarks. As she tries to give one physician a lesson in "practical treatment," he tells her that she ought to wear a bone through her nose and get a shark's-tooth necklace, an obvious reference to the hillbilly as primitive. Granny points out that she merely wanted to share with him "the fruits of her medical research."

Near the end of the episode, she succeeds in setting up her own medical practice. A pharmaceutical salesman mentions antibiotics, but Granny—fulfilling the stereotype of the hillbilly as grossly ignorant—thinks he is describing an ailment. At last Dr. Clyburn, her own physician, arrives to stop her from practicing, only to discover that she has just obtained distribution rights for her cold remedy. The tables have been turned, Granny gets the last laugh, and the stereotype is revivified even in being gently critiqued.

Another television series, "Hee-Haw," was a loosely structured mélange of corny skits, musical presentations, and stock scenarios organized around a stereotyped version of Appalachian life-styles.[11] There are scenes of women at a quilting bee, men gossiping at the barbershop or in the general store. The program relied heavily, though not exclusively, on rural imagery ("I'm just a country boy") and again on the notion of hillbillies as ignorant and even idiotic. An exception is Johnny Cash singing "Look at Them Beans," in which he glorifies the land and its fertility. The men wear coveralls, tell inane jokes, and laugh loudly so that the audience can only laugh with them. Many of the jokes have sexist overtones or betoken a dogmatic, patronizing attitude toward presumed sex-role divisions. Speaking of women, one man says to another, "I thought your idea was to love 'em and leave 'em? Now you're married." The other man replies, "Well, one day I didn't leave fast enough [laughs uproariously]."

In another sequence, a tourist arrives at a gas station in his Porsche and asks for directions. He is told to go whatever way he wants. "Well, just go to the right, and if it doesn't work, go the other way." Musical interludes are provided by The Rustics, who also serve as a sort of chorus, cueing the audience to the proper responses by laughter, side comments, and gestures. The program concludes with allusions to "old-timey" religion. Lulu, the local fat lady, sings a poignant version of "Amazing Grace." Through the repetition of highly elaborate examples of this sort, the stereotypes become part of an idiom for outsiders premising relationships with Appalachians in both talking or thinking about them and in their actual encounters with them.

When a stereotype is used in a speech event in which neither the sender nor the receiver is a member of the stereotyped group, it usually has a derogatory meaning, a premise readily applicable in the case of the "hillbilly." As Goffman (1959, 170) suggests, "When the members of a team go backstage where the audience cannot see or hear them, they very regularly derogate the audience in a way that is inconsistent with the face-to-face treatment that is given the audience." The situation is similar but more extreme when a stereo-

type having negative connotations is used in the presence of a
member of the stereotyped group by a sender who is not a member of that group. The meaning of the usage is again derogatory, if
not derisive, and the receiver is in effect treated as not being present, that is, a nonperson.

Stereotypes such as hillbilly are rarely subjected to any kind of
serious reality testing; instead, they are derived from the sociology
of the situation and involve an exaggeration of selected cultural
characteristics of the stereotyped group. Whatever grain of descriptive accuracy may be contained in the stereotype is distorted
by the implied negative valuation; any seed of veracity is lost in
mythic imagery. The more favorable traits of Appalachians recognized by outsiders are frequently perceived as exceptions to the
general truths the stereotype is thought to enshrine.

Stereotypes of Appalachians define social categories by clarifying for outsiders who they are and the nature of their own cultural
attributes through a dramatic statement of what and who they
themselves are not. The stereotype meaning of "who Appalachians are" alludes to the ethnic categorization of persons; "their
cultural attributes" alludes to the cultural construction of the person in its various ethnic versions, that is, to the meaning of being a
member of one such category or group from the viewpoint of persons both within and without it. In this way outsiders' stereotypes
play a role in deciding and clarifying for Appalachians something
of what their identity is to be. Casting self-definition in terms of
"what we are not" and what we as stereotyped people typically are
supposed to be suggests clearly the exclusionary connotations of
these representations.

Stereotypes thus provide a basis for categorizing persons and
for formulating identity as well as a reason for rejecting and opposing such categorizations and formulations. Appalachians simultaneously internalize and reject aspects of outsiders' stereotypes, thus
inducing them to reject aspects of themselves. On the one hand,
they believe or "buy into" the stereotypes; on the other, the stereotypic labels provide a substantive point of departure for their
objections and their discourse of political dissent and resistance
(see Chapter Three). The constellation of meanings suggested by
the hillbilly stereotype provides a point of reference, and through
a dialectical movement generates the cultural differences that Ap-

palachians perceive between themselves and outsiders. It also re-inforces on both sides of the boundary the sense of in-group soli-darity based on a conception of shared substance (blood, land, and cultural characteristics). Stereotypes point to both collective and personal identity without encompassing or entirely exhausting the meaning of either. They have emotional overtones and indicate the construction of cultural differences and the presumption of shared substance to be two sides of the same coin.

This two-sided, ambiguous aspect of the hillbilly stereotype is exemplified in conversations among Ashe County people in which one of them calls another a hillbilly. Here, the speaker acknowl-edges both the negativity of the connotation that outsiders give the term and its implication of solidarity among local people. A similar dynamic obtains when blacks call one another "nigger" or Americans of Italian origin use the epithet "wop." Radcliffe-Brown (1965) labels such in-group usages "joking relationships" and ob-serves that they pose an approach-avoidance situation for both actors involved. In Ashe County routine joking and teasing rela-tionships between adult men and their fathers or grandfathers may be seen as representing an attempt to diffuse the contradiction be-tween a principle of intergenerational hierarchy and authority and a rule of egalitarianism among adult men. The parallel use of "hill-billy" among Appalachians denotes egalitarianism within the group and domination by the larger society without.

The major import of the stereotype is thus to be found in its usage in interchanges across the ethnic boundary. The stereotyp-ing of Appalachians by outsiders is, apart from the reciprocal ste-reotyping of outsiders by Appalachians, clearly asymmetrical. Unlike joking relations among Appalachians, outsiders' jokes are largely at the expense of the Appalachians. Yet the reverberations of outsiders' representations for those of Appalachians themselves suggest again that the delineation of ethnic distinctions is a suc-cession of contradictions or meaningful disparities. By labeling non-Appalachians "outsiders," Appalachians mean, among other things, that they are "out of it," antisocial, and altogether strange. Outsiders are just "tourists" or "Floridians"—rather pejorative terms for many Ashe County people—or just plain "outlandish," a term historically used to designate people from foreign coun-tries. Stereotypes can and usually do function as put-downs. As

rhetorical devices, they substitute exogenous cultural constructions for indigenous ones. They transform Appalachians' own
concepts of identity into caricatures, thereby displacing and di-
minishing them.

The formal processes proper to stereotyping are generalization,
foregrounding, and insulation. The generalizing aspect entails reformulating the identity of the other in uniform, even universalistic, terms: All hillbillies look the same, act the same, have the
same habits and the same attributes. Variability within the stereotyped group is denied and, in consequence, the meaning of their
identity is impoverished. As a rhetorical device, the stereotype reduces multiple meanings and constrains semantic complexity and
productivity. Stereotypes are also generalizing in that they are
overwhelmingly nonspecific and truistic, blanket summarizations
often detached from any particular social context and therefore not
readily amenable to disconfirmation. The disjunction of levels between the stereotype and the particularized articulation and presentation of self enables outsiders to maintain the ascendancy of
the stereotype even while recognizing that particular persons do
not bear it out. Appalachians routinely present a fully elaborated
social self in specific social settings under specific social circumstances. Their culturally constructed conception of personal and
ethnic identity is not easily reconciled with the politicized, antago-
nistic discourse in which the stereotype plays an important role.

In its generalizing aspect, the hillbilly stereotype situates the relation between Appalachians as an "ethnic minority" and the encompassing institutional context of American society. Specifically,
this stereotype premises a structure of domination: *hillbilly* con-
descendingly denotes an ethnic minority and encourages non-
Appalachians to think of hillbillies as metaphorical minors rather
than as adults (Billy is usually a boy's name rather than a man's).
Like children, hillbillies need not be taken seriously or viewed as
equals.

All stereotypes systematically factor out and then foreground a
limited selection of characteristics from a larger array that a social
group attributes to itself. One characteristic or aspect is substi-
tuted for the totalized meaning of an identity-orienting symbol;
one characteristic or aspect is appropriated to represent the whole
(Lefebvre 1971; Foster 1973). For this reason stereotypes seem to
have a grain of immediate veracity and yet to miss the mark and

lack descriptive precision; as partial, fragmented "truths," they end up not being true at all.

Foregrounding is thus another means of reducing, simplifying, or impoverishing the symbolic universe that is both the environment and the experiential substance of an ethnic group or a culturally distinct population such as that of Ashe County. Like a framed photograph, the stereotype freezes movement, evolution, and change. It also flattens and distorts spatial dimensions, banishing depth and aspect and misrepresenting volume and roundness as a shadowed surface. And the selection and choice of meaningful details are made for the observer by the photographer, the interloper. Thus the resulting representations are subjective expressions of the outsider's own observational style, point of view, and social preoccupations.

Finally, stereotypes are used by outsiders to insulate themselves from the typed group. Through foregrounding, Appalachians may be made part of the background or scenery for social action rather than protagonists or even bit players, so to speak, in their own theater. This process of deconstruction allows outsiders to protect themselves from having to deal directly with Appalachians, who are in turn to some extent excluded from interacting with outsiders. The hillbilly becomes an object of outsiders' pity and humor, the yokel or the buffoon who is thought to inhabit a different social world. Residing on the far side of this conceptual frontier, Appalachians become something less than a threat to non-Appalachians' own chances in a competitive social arena.

Tourists may come into Ashe County to look about or to spend the summer, but many believe themselves to be in a strange and curious land, populated by metaphoric nonpersons. It is not surprising, then, that local residents are ambivalent about the arrival of tourists. The residents extend to their visitors the hospitality for which they are justly known, yet find themselves somehow diminished (except perhaps financially) and exploited, though they may be at a loss to say just how. Perhaps the source of their discomfort lies in their treating tourists according to standard social formulas and in line with economic self-interest, without entirely surmounting their conception of them as strangers who do not allow themselves to be placed within the social universe of the Blue Ridge except as foreign objects.

*Chapter Two*

# Meat and Potatoes

Sugar Run is a representative rural community in Ashe County. In 1975–1976 Sugar Run's one hundred twenty residents lived in forty-four households (family groups under one roof).[1] The thirty-one farms on Sugar Run have an average size of thirty-seven acres; much of this acreage is uncultivated. Houses are scattered at irregular intervals along a road that stretches for about four miles beside the watercourse of a small creek. Along either side of the road are houses, barns, fields, and meadows. Woods once covered most of the area, but many trees were cleared for farming and by loggers. The woods now cling to the upper portion of the hills that enclose the community, forming ramparts on either side of the road and limiting the size of the farms.

A narrow bridge crosses the south fork of the New River and then the paved road enters the Sugar Run community. On all sides are views of fields and mountains well suited for picture postcards. The road continues through the community with few curves or turns until the pavement breaks off, and a gravel road continues up over the ridge into the neighboring community of Deer Creek.

Many of the newer homes on Sugar Run are built largely of brick and are situated on scenic rises. Other recently established households live in mobile homes. Sometimes the households are clustered together; when the son or daughter of long-term residents marries, the newlyweds are given or purchase a lot on their parents' land and build their own house or bring in a mobile home. Although a newly married couple may live with parents or in-laws temporarily while making arrangements for a residence of their own, rarely do separate generations of adults live in the same household. For married couples, a home of their own not only asserts their social and economic independence but also symbolizes the definitive establishment of a distinct social unit. While the newly independent household may enlist the advice and financial aid of their parents or in-laws, they usually decide for themselves about major purchases such as a truck or a house. When more than one generation of adults do live under one roof, a separate apartment or area is set aside whenever possible. One household included a middle-aged couple, who owned the house, and the husband's mother, who had her own entry and apartment in the rear of the house.

Five households on Sugar Run occupied mobile homes. In one case, the old two-story family home was left standing on the property and used as a barn. A number of other abandoned houses on Sugar Run serve as utility buildings for storing wood and hay, or for curing tobacco in the autumn. Some of the older houses still used as family dwellings represent fine examples of indigenous domestic architecture (Figure 1). The main architectural features include wide, pillared porches that may surround the house on two or three sides, a succession of ornately articulated gables at the second-story level, and dormers. Houses constructed before the advent of indoor plumbing feature a small bathroom wing added along one side.

The houses strung out along the road constitute Sugar Run as a loose association of family groupings in symbiosis with the land, with neighbors (some of whom are kin), and with the encompassing social milieu of Ashe County. One of the most visibly dramatic activities on Sugar Run in the autumn is putting in the tobacco, which, like other activities, has both a material and a meaningful dimension. Putting in the tobacco is not the back-breaking work that cutting and spudding is, but when it is completed the field is empty, the barns are brimming, and everyone is exhausted.

Spudding involves cutting down the tobacco plants and splitting the central stalk, using a pointed copper device placed atop a stake. The tobacco stalk is pushed down the stake so that it is propped diagonally on the ground at one end and on the stake at

Figure 1. Ashe County Domestic Architecture.

the other. Four or five stalks are pushed down on a single stake, each stalk ranged above the next and spaced at an even interval. A few weeks later the staked stalks are taken into the barns and hung horizontally, so the stalks fall vertically and the tobacco cures in the air under the eaves. After six weeks or more of curing, the to-bacco is graded, tied into bales, and taken to auction.

In preparation for spudding, the stakes are sharpened at one end with a hatchet, an afternoon's work in itself. Walter Huntington, his brother Dan, and I took turns, each working until our arms were tired, while the others tied the finished stakes into bundles and carried them into the field. Two weeks later, the tobacco had been cut and spudded, and the time had come to take the tobacco into the barns. When I arrived at ten o'clock on a bright Saturday morning, Walter and Dan were already in the barn, hanging stakes from the rafters and tying stray tobacco stalks back onto the stakes before hanging them. During the day, much was said about the careless way the tobacco had been spudded and how much longer our workday would be as a consequence.

Just before noon, Walter and Dan began talking about dinner, the midday meal. Walter's wife, Jane, appeared to tell us that she would have to go to the grocery store before we ate. She suggested to her three-year-old son that perhaps he could help with the work. She talked about the tobacco crop. According to her calculations, working on the tobacco paid them about two dollars an hour. They expected to earn six hundred to one thousand dollars (in 1975 dollars) for the entire crop—pocket money for the year.

The tractor, with a flatbed trailer attached, was taken into the field. Frank Grimes, Walter and Dan's grandfather, drove the tractor slowly down the rows. Walter or Dan stood on the trailer and took the stakes and tobacco as they were pulled from the ground and handed up. The crop was stacked neatly until a large mound grew up behind the tractor, which then slowly transported the tobacco and workers back to the barn. There, one person stood in the loft and the others handed up the stakes one by one. The stakes were hung eight or ten inches apart between the cross-beams, and the barn slowly began to fill up with the pungent vegetation.

After dinner, work began again and continued throughout the afternoon. Talk ranged over many topics, the crops of the previous years, how Frank enjoys ordering around the young men, and how many hours of work still remained to be done. The field looked almost untouched after an entire morning of work. When the fan belt broke on Frank's tractor, another was borrowed from a neighbor, and the work continued.

Just as the work was beginning to exhaust the workers, John and William arrived to help finish the job. William is Dan's father-in-law, who lives over on Deer Creek. John and Dan are married to sisters. (Figure 2 indicates the genealogical connections among those present during the tobacco work.) Frank began reorganizing the expanded group, telling each worker what task to handle. A chain was formed to hand tobacco from the tractor into the barn and then to hang it on the cross-beams. Work progressed more swiftly with more hands, and everyone's spirits improved noticeably. The field gradually took on a picked-over look as the stakes were removed. Once the field was cleared, it would be sown in rye, the winter crop.

When the first barn was filled, work continued in the "tobacco barn." The logistics of filling the space required a good deal of planning, lest one "paint oneself into a corner." Here the tobacco was hung in three tiers, so that at first people were situated at each level, each taking from the person below and handing to the per-

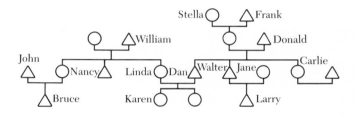

Figure 2.  Genealogy of Typical Extended Family.

son above. William talked at length about his life as a trucker driving between North Carolina and California. John quipped about
the curious people he met as a bank loan officer. As work came to
a halt, the conversation came around to a fishing trip down the
North Carolina coast that the two were planning for the following
weekend. As John and William departed, Walter made a point of
promising them a dinner at some future time. Dan returned the
tractor to its owner, and the rest of us retired to the porch of Jane
and Walter's house. Frank went home to get ready for the evening
church meeting at the Sugar Run Methodist Church.

Jane and Walter, Dan and his wife, Linda, and I drank beer and
discussed the changes in the vegetation that indicated the progress
of autumn. Someone reminded us that Frank would not be pleased
to find everyone drinking, for he considered drinking improper.
Walter's father sometimes had trouble with drinking, and although
Frank had done some drinking of his own in the past, in recent
years he has taken to a more temperate kind of life. Walter suspected that Frank knows they drink but also knows better than to
refer to the topic overtly. Jane noted that they had once had a conversation about drinking; her point in the discussion had been that
each person must come to his or her own conclusion about how to
deal with alcohol.

Walter and Dan began to talk of their grandfather and the hostile
feelings they have toward him. Referring to how Frank acted
while the work was going on, Dan said, "I could have hit him for
being so bull-headed!" Linda talked about how little she likes
Carlie, Walter and Dan's older sister. Linda said that her daughter
Karen idolizes her Aunt Carlie and constantly talks about her
aunt's wonderful cooking and everything else she does. Linda said
that she sometimes just wants Karen to shut up about it. Walter
countered that he just loves his sister to death. Linda replied that

of course she loves Carlie as kin but insisted that there was no reason for Carlie to be a snob. Linda said that she would not pretend to have any personal liking for her and stated that Carlie did not have to act superior because of her education (she holds a bachelor's degree). Moreover, there was no reason for Carlie to be defensive about not having children. She does not, in Linda's view, have any reason to feel bad about it as it is probably her husband's fault as much as her own. Linda said, "Kids don't matter that much anyway."

Linda noted that her sister Nancy and John will have no more children, though it is conceivable that they will adopt. John has had a vasectomy, because their son Bruce has a genetic defect that has left him paralyzed. (Nancy had a therapeutic abortion after Bruce's problem was diagnosed, but most of the family, including her parents and sister, do not know about the abortion.) John grew up as an orphan, so his genetic background remains unknown. It is not expected that Bruce, who is a precocious and intelligent child, will live beyond the age of twenty-five or thirty.

Dan and Linda talked about their aspirations for the future. Linda emphasized her desire to move away from Ashe County. She and Dan live in Beaver Creek but come to Sugar Run frequently to visit Frank as well as Walter and Jane. Linda said that she would move anywhere at all as long as it was far away. Dan had been an electrician in the armed forces and had served in Vietnam. They had enjoyed living in Florida during Dan's basic training, so perhaps they would go to live near the coast in North Carolina or Florida. Dan pointed out that Linda had always been something of a wanderer, but he did not disagree with her preference.

Dan hoped to find something better to do than to be a school principal for the remainder of his days. Both Dan and Walter are oriented toward full-time professional careers, unlike the men of previous generations, who usually worked in the fields and supplemented the family income with various kinds of temporary or seasonal employment. Linda and Jane are similarly oriented toward careers for themselves and for their husbands. For them, living on the land does not mean gaining a livelihood from it nearly as much as it does for Frank and others of his generation. Dan and Walter often talk about building homes for their families on the land that Frank has given them on Sugar Run, but neither of them seems to take very seriously the notion of making any appreciable part of their living from farming. They do the work, no doubt with an eye to optimizing the likelihood of future land ownership. Carlie and her husband have recently begun to build a home on Sugar Run just across the road from Frank's house. They have been living in West Jefferson for a number of years and have no long-term commitment to farming. Having secured a homesite, perhaps they feel less pressured to participate in cooperative work groups. They did not appear that day to help with the tobacco nor would they share in the money realized from these efforts.

The intermittent farming activities that Jane, Walter, Dan, and Linda undertake, their incomplete farming expertise, their career orientation, their rhetorical self-identification as farmers, and their ambivalence toward living in a rural community and toward traditional patterns of land utilization—all indicate a corresponding ambivalence about traditionalistic life-styles, an undercurrent of dissatisfaction with the social milieu (including felt obligations to kin), and an uncertainty about choosing a social and cultural identity.

Tobacco grading commenced later in the season and again provided a setting for articulating social and economic self-placement as well as for expressing alienation from such placement. The day was humid enough for grading—the tobacco must be "in case," moist rather than brittle and flaky so it can be handled without disintegrating. The previous night had been foggy and warm, so the tobacco had become pliable, almost rubbery. If the weather continued to be sunny and windy, the tobacco would "go out of case" and grading would have to be resumed another day.

Tobacco is graded into three classes: lug, bright, and tips. A tobacco stalk is grasped at the lower end and the leaves stripped off with a rapid movement beginning at the bottom of the stalk. The leaves lowest on the stalk are lugs. The brights take up most of the central portion of the stalk and bring the highest price. Tips begin up near the top. As leaves are stripped, they are stacked in appropriate piles and then tied into a bundle. One leaf is used to wrap the end of the leaves into a compact sheaf. These sheaves are bundled into large bales and taken to auction.

As the morning wore on, work slowed to almost a standstill. Dan was lying back on a basket piled high with bundled tobacco,

Walter was grading, and Linda was waiting for the coffee water to boil. The women worked right along with the men in grading, although they had not helped with putting in the tobacco. They also did some cutting of tobacco stalks in the field.

Dan and Linda's three-year-old daughter played in the sun with a ball, as Dan drank his coffee and complained about catching a cold. Walter complained that grading is boring, tiring work, requiring little imagination and hours of standing on one's feet. "It's peasants' work," he said. They had whiled away the previous evening, grading and drinking. Linda had gone to bed early, but Jane, Dan, and Walter stayed in the barn until about 2 A.M. The slow morning was explained by the drinking of the night before. By noon, Dan rounded up his family and went home; for him work was over for the day.

A few weeks later was the slaughter. There were two beef cattle to be slaughtered, one belonging to Jane and Walter, the other to Walter's father, Donald. Donald, who lives in West Jefferson, was not present at the slaughter, but he had gone with Walter to the livestock market a few months before to purchase the animals. Despite the anthropologist's associations of slaughter with sacrificial altars and the reading of entrails, Ashe County people generally regard the slaughter as distinctly unpleasant hard work that yields an appreciable economic return. By slaughtering their own cattle, these families would have freezers full of meat for about fifty cents a pound.

Willie Clayton did most of the bloodier tasks, assisted by her burly nephew Perry, who works at the Ashe County Pontiac agency. Willie is a hefty middle-aged woman with a kind face and small features. She talked amiably throughout the procedure and smoked a large cigar. She had worked in a slaughterhouse for thirteen years and had been one of the first women to be hired at the Phoenix plant in West Jefferson. Willie had not had a marriage of any stability or duration, so she had had to work steadily to raise her child. On this particular day, she worked hard and quickly. She had an appointment for another slaughter elsewhere in the county and therefore turned down Walter's mother's invitation for dinner.

Willie closed the barn door and shot the animal in the head while we remained outside. Then she opened the door, and she and Perry began cutting up the carcass. The head was removed first, and the animal was bled. They hung it from the roof of the barn by the hind legs, and the animal was skinned with very long, very sharp knives. The belly was slit and the entrails came out in one neat sac. Green liquid ran out of a tube when this was done— partially digested grass. Next the heart and tongue were removed, and a large saw was used to cut the animal lengthwise along the backbone. This last stage of the job takes skill and strength, like cutting down a tree.

The aimless banter among the "audience" pertained to the animals, their anatomy, and which parts are best cooked and how. On this matter, as well as in regard to the fine points of the slaughter, Willie took the lead, acting as the authority she is. Someone noted that some people prepare the testicles and consider them a delicacy. Jane was horrified, Dan thought it humorous, and Willie explained that "field oysters" if properly cooked are tender and white like breast of chicken. The conversation turned to local gossip. Someone had been married four months ago, and her husband had already left her. Willie stopped working to show everyone pictures of her young nephew, color photographs that she carries in her wallet. Then Perry began recounting the events in the county on the recent Halloween. In addition to the regular revelry, someone's car had been covered with a mixture of eggs and flour, one end of someone's trailer was "blown up," and a girl was killed in an automobile accident. Walter remarked that the weather was quite warm; cool weather is preferable for slaughtering so the meat stays fresh. By this time, the work was nearly completed.

After the first animal was quartered, it was loaded into a pickup truck, covered with a large piece of cardboard, and taken to the packing house, where it would be refrigerated. It would be butchered only after having had a few days to firm up. Then the Huntingtons would go down and cut it as they wanted and wrap it for freezing. The entrails were taken up the creek and left for animals and birds to consume. Willie took the hides and would accept no more than ten dollars in payment for her services.

## Kinship

Although Sugar Run is a distinct geographical entity, its status as a community in any strict sense must be qualified in terms of present social patterns and the meanings through which residents define community, kinship, and geography itself. Kinship is a major idiom of relatedness within and without the community and a major aspect of social ideology. Community identity is often expressed through the collective representation of common ancestry, shared experience, kin relations, and what Beaver (1976, iv) calls rootedness to place. Many of the defining features of Sugar Run as a social entity are situated by local versions of history. The present social scene is talked about in terms of its history, and *community* refers more to what Sugar Run once was than to what it is today. Notions of "how things were and who we were" are juxtaposed with notions of "how things are and who we are" as people talk about the past and their sense of the present. Such themes are articulated through an idiom of kinship and genealogical relatedness.

Mary Lou Rawlins, a fifty-five-year-old resident of Sugar Run, lives with her husband, Eugene, and her eighty-nine-year-old mother-in-law. Her youngest daughter is nineteen and has recently moved to Wilkesboro (in the county east of Ashe), where she is attending a community college. Mary Lou and Eugene also have two grown sons; both are married and have taken up residence outside Sugar Run. Mary Lou is proud of her two young grandsons. Although her daughter returns each weekend, Mary Lou says, "When the last child leaves the nest, it is hard not to feel regret. Once you have spent such a long time bringing up your children, you never really stop being a parent. You know, people don't change much really. And human nature doesn't change much either."[2]

According to Mary Lou, in the "old days" one could not travel very far, or one did not do so very often. "The roads were bad," she says. "My great-grandfather, James Shepard, had a store on Sugar Run and hauled goods from Bristol, Tennessee (a distance of sixty miles). It was easier to go to Bristol than to Wilkesboro or Winston-Salem in those days, because that way one didn't have to cross the mountains. You only took that trip when you had to." She suggests that the changing character of Sugar Run has much to do with the increasing ease of transportation. There is no longer a store in the community.

She says that kinship and family matters have changed a good deal since she grew up. "When I was a child, cousins who were so far back you couldn't really count were considered real close, maybe because I grew up in a place that was easy for them all to get to. And they did come, often." In contrast, she says that when her son, Kenneth, came home with a wife whose grandfather is a Shepard, "it just shocked the tar out of me. I thought, they just can't do that. The closest connection is James Shepard. That's the closest common relative, which isn't really very close, but I think of the connection as being close because these people had been around, had lived close by. Now people go away more.

"But every summer, they all come back. They don't call before coming, and they stay sometimes for weeks. You just put up a lot of food, and when they leave, you tell them 'come back,' even if you don't always mean it. When someone dies, the family will bring the corpse back, and you have to be ready for the whole crew. Even now, a lot of people are distantly related, but you still think of them as family. That's the sort of feeling you have when they live close by. You have the same sort of family feeling about neighbors as you do towards your own kin. Eugene's brother who lives in Oregon is not really so much part of the family anymore. He lives so far away, and they don't see each other at all."

Mary Lou recognizes various social "classes" in Sugar Run but points out that these are not precisely economic categories.[3] In the rural communities and in the county, class is often submerged, only indirectly affecting interaction or calibrating influence, life-style, network status, and community respect. On Sugar Run, at least, there is limited variability among the residents' socioeconomic status. Class dynamics are situated within and qualified by the scope of kin and personal networks, by life-style particulars, as well as by political and religious affiliations. Most writing on Appalachia uses class as an analytic device (e.g., Stephenson 1968) rather than treating it as an indigenous concept (Schwarzweller, Brown, and Mangalam 1971, 45–70, is an exception). In local social ideology, the realities of class are to some extent obscured by the dominant values of egalitarianism and hospitality. Yet the existence and meaning of class categories, however vague and underdefined, also constrain the intertwining of kin networks. Certain families are more "respectable" than others. There are certain young men whom Mary Lou would be unhappy to have her daughter marry. Nevertheless, she says (however rhetorically) that in Ashe County, "You welcome anyone into your home, even people who are mentally retarded or strange. They just come down the road, and you welcome them into your house—everyone did. You were brought up to treat them with respect. If you didn't want them around, you didn't let it show." She told the story of a beggar, who was notorious in the area, named Pete Black. Pete was known always to eat large quantities of meat when he was a guest at dinner. Mary Lou recalls one of her brothers exclaiming at the table, in Pete's presence, "Watch Pete eat meat!" She said, "He got whipped for that one. It was simply not good manners. One welcomed anyone and everyone."

Robert Griffin is a large, raw-boned man in his mid-twenties who has recently been divorced. When he talks about family life or the lack thereof, it is clear how closely he associates family with meaningful social existence in a general sense. Robert is employed at the Phoenix plant in West Jefferson, working the 3 P.M. to midnight shift. He grew up in a rural community much like Sugar Run, but left at age twenty-one, when he married his sixteen-year-old wife. Now their son is three years old. Robert has taken up residence at Edna Price James's house, which he strongly prefers to living alone.

After Robert and I discussed one of the other people living in the house, who was asked to leave after repeated drinking "sprees," I noted that this man's marriage had also ended in failure. Robert replied that it was easy to see why people turn to drink after their home life falls apart. I mentioned an unmarried young man residing in the house who had become very involved in his church, devoting many evenings to beginning a career as a lay preacher. Robert said that when a man misses his family, it is far better to turn to religion than to alcohol; the church can provide support and guidance, and he had found it to be a great help. He noted how many men who are alone just drink until they are dead, and he felt it was far better to live with other people, as at Edna's house, than to live in places where people are drunk and rowdy all the time. He clearly wanted to approximate a familial atmosphere of solidarity while living apart from his kin or affines.

The problem between him and his wife, Robert explained, revolved around the presence of his in-laws, an ironic situation, given his recognition of the importance of being surrounded by family, and one indicative of the ambivalence that at times is an unhappy concomitant of an ideology and social ecology that emphasize the indispensability of kin relations. Robert and his wife were living in the southern part of Ashe County, with his wife's parents as their closest neighbors. Robert says, "They would come around giving advice, they wouldn't mean any harm, but they would say 'you ought' this and 'you ought' that." Robert resented the social pressure, feeling that his in-laws were too intrusive and he did not have enough autonomy. Robert also complained about how complicated divorce is these days and expressed considerable bitterness about his past. He said marriage "isn't exactly a rose garden on one side or the other."

For this young man, in other words, the ideal and ideological centrality of family and kin is qualified by the historical particulars of his family experience. His story bespeaks the tension between the integration of the conjugal household into a larger family unit and the desire that the married couple and nuclear family be autonomous. Localization of the extended family is a historically derived and embedded norm of sharing and mutuality among the individuals and subgroupings that make up the larger kinship milieu. Yet these patterns are qualified by a contradictory value of independent self-sufficiency. Robert faced the additional problem of balancing the prevailing lines of authority in the larger kin unit with those thought rightfully to apply within the nuclear household. Like other Ashe County people, Robert articulates these experiences in terms of the putative reality of a history of concrete events, rather than couching them in abstract principles or metaphors. Or, perhaps history is the dominant metaphor. Robert's message seems to be that one has to adapt to the limitations and potentialities of one's family milieu, as an aspect of adapting to the exigencies of everyday life. One's kin can be a comfort and an aid to adaptation; but at times one may have to set aside kin relations, often regretfully, when they impede self-sufficiency. Such "ecologic" conditions, their tacit acknowledgment in social ideology as well as their changing material constraints, fundamentally structure kin relationships in Ashe County.

The life histories of Mary Lou Rawlins and Robert Griffin seem to corroborate the point made repeatedly in the plentiful writing on the social life of the people of Appalachia: kinship and family organization are a dominant element in their style of life. Yet both informants indicate the problematic aspects of that pervasiveness and suggest many situations in which family affairs touch upon other social domains or in which other social issues come to dominate kinship. These considerations, however, are rarely emphasized in studies of community life in Appalachia; as a result, such studies impoverish the richness of Appalachian life.[4] The best known of these works are Marion Pearsall's *Little Smoky Ridge* (1959), Jack Weller's *Yesterday's People* (1965), and John Fetterman's *Stinking Creek* (1967).

Similarly, most studies of Appalachian social life largely ignore local social ideology. A fuller appreciation of social ideology, as opposed to actual patterns of interaction, would provide a corrective for the inadequate treatment in the literature of politics and religion as they relate to family life and to social organization as a whole (see Dumont 1970). As Batteau (1982b, 447) notes, kinship relations in Appalachia must be studied in the context of community and political affairs. He also rightly suggests that informants' versions of kinship patterns should not be taken as direct descriptions of the kinship system, and wonders how representative particular ethnographic reports may be for the Appalachian region as a whole.

Indicating the direction to be taken to correct these problems, Stack (1974) and Beaver (1976) describe the interplay of social practices and cultural meaning. Batteau (1982a) incisively outlines the connection of kinship with the domains of politics and religion: at the level of social action and discourse, nonkinship matters such as politics and religion often have a kinshiplike flavor, and kinship often has political and religious overtones. In this spirit, and with an eye toward examining those aspects of kinship and social ideology relevant to the political dispute presented in Chapter Three, I focus my interpretation of kinship on four themes: genealogy as culturally formulated, the family history as an indigenous literary genre, upbringing as a major aspect of kinship experience and as symbol of identity, and adoption as an aspect of kinship that promotes social inclusiveness. Throughout this discussion, history will emerge as a major cultural form, integrating

aspects of the culture of kinship with people's more general understanding of identity and society. (For a more comprehensive treatment of kinship per se in Appalachia, see Batteau 1982b.)

Discussions of the cultural meaning of American kinship relations fall into two camps. Scheffler (1976) insists upon genealogy
as a framework for exhaustive kinship analysis and tends to merge
this framework with indigenous genealogical constructions. In
contrast, Schneider (1967, 1968a) insists that descent and filiation
are cultural constructs rather than universal principles of kinship,
which in America (and in Appalachia) are articulated through a
behavioral code of "diffuse, enduring solidarity"—love. Further,
Schneider (1972, 50) argues that kinship defined exclusively in
terms of genealogical relatedness "does not correspond to any
category known to man." In Ashe County, genealogy is an essential but by no means exhaustive symbol in kinship and an element
of social ideology.[5]

Schneider (1968a, 23) phrases Americans' notions of genealogy
in terms of "blood"—shared, biogenetic substance. An outsider
might get the impression that Ashe County people are obsessed
with genealogy in this sense. But local residents also seriously
qualify the meaning of genealogical relatedness in implementing
their kinship ideology. In the Blue Ridge, genealogies are culturally constructed, as shown by the willingness of people to form,
reform, revise, and elaborate genealogies (and genealogical links
among living persons) as rhetorical figures in a wide range of social contexts.

Without regard for the distinction between "fact" and fiction,
which are merged into an integrated image of history, people in
Ashe County manipulate their genealogies in order to create continuities between the disparate elements of the past and the specifics of the present social scene. Conversely, they codify a unified
sense of the present social situation by using genealogy as a social
idiom. Existing relationships derive from or are rationalized by
what Batteau (1982b, 451) calls cumulative filiation rather than by
a consistently applied principle of descent. But actors do not acknowledge that these "blood" ties are reworked situationally. A
major feature of such ties, from which much of their meaning derives, is thought to be their fixity. Genealogical connections are

seen as external givens rooted in the past, and the task of local historians and genealogists is to document them.

A woman well known in Ashe County for her expertise in local history and genealogy, Eleanor Reeves, said that she had so many requests from residents of the county to do paid genealogical research for them that were she to take on all these commissions, she could work for the rest of her life and never be finished. This statement may be accurate, although the hyperbole is an unmistakable testament to the importance of genealogy for people in Ashe County. Both the Ashe County Public Library and the homes of many county residents are full of written genealogies and family histories. As Mrs. Reeves said, "We're all kin. If you get into one family, you get into them all."

The way that one informant introduced the relatives present at a funeral of one of his ancestors many years before shows how people associate relatives as persons with their genealogical attributes and also suggests the interweaving of genealogical placement with genealogical history:

There was Washington and his wife Linda Woodie, with Nora, Sally, Velin, Floyd, Lester, Don, and Alice. Eli was a preacher and was married twice. He wrote his mother, Polly, concerning his second one. "She is a nice obedient wife." Matthew married Miss Mary Miller and their children were George, John, and Dottie. George married a Miss Goodman and they had nine children. The mother died and the children were scattered. Some were sent to Barium Springs orphanage. One of these was the little boy Rufus Long, who later became a very successful banker in Charlotte. William was a captain in the Home Guard during the Civil War and helped hang a bunch of bushwhackers. After which he went West in a hurry. His wife Kathy Taylor shared with him a very exciting life in Kansas. Felix was killed in the war. Bill Billings, Blanche and Evelyn's grandfather, was marching into battle and saw Felix lying wounded under a tree. He gave him his canteen.

The commonsense tone of these identifications and of the descriptive details underlines the status of blood ties and of the person as relative in Ashe County social ideology. As Schneider (1968a, 24–25) suggests, relationships based on genealogical connections are viewed as "objective facts of nature." A tie by blood or birth is actual, "real," and given; it cannot be severed, it can only be ignored. The implications of these blood ties are far-reaching, and relationships based on them are thought to have profound ramifications and potential consequences for one's life situation.

Kinship ideology in America generally and in Ashe County specifically has appropriated some of its notions from the science of genetics, or at least there is a broad concordance between genetics and ideology. In this ideology, shared substance pertains between two genealogically linked persons to the degree that they have a common ancestor. The amount of shared heredity between ancestors and descendants can be gauged quite precisely, calculated and measured on the basis of generational and lateral distance. The identity held by a family or group of relatives, the attributes that are "all in the family," are seen as a correlate of shared heredity and are indicated by personal characteristics that are viewed as rooted in a person's biological constitution.

Partly through this shared biogenetic background, children are thought to "take after" their parents or grandparents, and resemblances are in turn evidence of that shared background. Personality, interests, physical appearance, and emotional disposition are all thought to be related to genealogical connectedness, although some attributes may alternately be attributed to "upbringing." Schneider says that Americans are quite explicit about these matters, and I found this to be the case among Ashe County people as well. They use genealogy to talk about blood relatedness and to define the scope of family identity by fabricating, researching, or otherwise gaining a sense of their genealogy as a whole, as an objective social "fact." They differentiate individual identity in part by specifying a particular person's unique position in a genealogical grid. In addition, they use genealogy to specify origin, thus situating both individual and family identity within history. As a symbolic form, genealogy is but one particular aspect of history (an encompassing symbolic form) that brings present family members and ancestors together under a comprehensive conceptual umbrella.

Genealogies cannot, however, provide a chart of extant networks of kinship relationships in part because, typically, many of the key figures in a genealogy are deceased. In Ashe County, the kinship network is simply a social network in which symbols of genealogical origin and filiation play a part. When I first arrived, I met a family who pointed out that it was quite possible that I was related to a local family having the same surname. The possibility was almost sufficient to give me some sort of tentative social placement and status. This kind of discourse is endemic in this part of the Blue Ridge, and it illustrates one of the major characteristics of kinship in this locality. Kinship is not a discrete system in any strict sense, neither from the standpoint of its differentiation from other social domains nor from the standpoint of rules for social exclusion or exclusivity. Instead, kinship is simply one of the main focuses of social experience, one highly charged with meaning for Ashe County people; kinship structure or patterning is to some extent ad hoc, derivative of individual negotiations and innovations within the broad parameters of social ideology.

More specifically, for the residents of Ashe County genealogies are not a means of creating boundaries or social barriers, but mainly an expressive form for defining relatedness. Genealogical connectedness, whether putative or situationally self-evident, establishes a ground for relationships without making them inevitable or obligatory. As one informant observed in a discussion of family history with one of her children, "I want you to know you come from pretty good stock. Try to live up to the best of it and be nice to everybody you meet, for most likely they are your folk."

The exuberance and ubiquity of genealogy do not go unqualified. Actual patterns of social interaction emerge as an intersection of genealogical relatedness and coresidence in a given community or locality (see Pearsall 1959, 97; Batteau 1982b, 449). The residence of a person in a given locale is necessarily a fundamental aspect of that person's participation and inclusion in a family network. Genealogical relatedness does not always ensure the continuity of social relationships once a family member moves to another locality.

On Sugar Run, genealogies proliferate (or can be elaborated) and spread out to encompass people in almost every household in the community. One family name will spill into another as genealogies intermesh and run rampant, creating a countywide social network that may extend into distant states.[6] A resident of Sugar Run who had extensive genealogical knowledge typically traced connections to a certain point and then exclaimed, "Well, Sam married Virgie who was a Shatley." This led on to another set of genealogies, which, she told me, could be obtained "by talking with old Leroy over in Shatley Springs." Or she would tell me that Ernie was related to Wayne Huntington, but "I don't know just how." And so it went, not only in interview situations but also in informal gossip sessions.

Tracing genealogies is in theory an unlimited process that at times may be only tenuously connected to existing social ties. For some people, it is also a pastime. My informants noted that the prevalence of genealogical connections in local organization is less thoroughgoing than it once was, when fewer outsiders lived in the county and mobility was more arduous. But local residents find ways to include outsiders, either through intermarriage, fictive genealogical constructions, or by reference to residence in the area. The extent of genealogical connections and the depth of genealogies vary considerably. Many informants can trace connections within their immediate family group, refer to ancestors three or four generations back, and remark upon a limited number of interfamily links. The specific genealogical knowledge held by a given resident who is not a self-designated expert is usually far from complete. Apart from providing a very serious hobby for amateur and professional genealogists (a phenomenon significant in itself), genealogical information is called forth strategically to rationalize and to model particular groupings and relationships.

Genealogical knowledge is regarded largely as social "fact," as consensual, as common sense, and under certain conditions it can be translated into social power. Ashe County people generally feel that genealogical relatedness needs to be made explicit, particularly when one's affairs run up against specific problems. For instance, although the Huntingtons discussed disagreements and disillusions within the family, they scarcely need to refer to genealogical connections in the course of organizing the autumn agricultural work. These ties are so basic, so self-evident, and so well known that they do not need to be mentioned. But when necessary, genealogies provide an important means of talking about the kinship network that allows people to map the shape, composition, and internal organization of their social world, to identify themselves as participants in it, and to mobilize personnel for agricultural work and other activities. Nonetheless, these indigenous genealogies do not constitute direct descriptions of how actual groups are formed and maintained. Neighbors also participate, though to a lesser extent, in many activities, group work, reciprocal borrowing, and so forth. (The indigenous term for this form of reciprocity is "swapping out.") Because locality and land, like blood ties, serve as symbols of identity, the distinction between neighbors and kin is not always cut-and-dried. Over the generations, neighbors in many cases become kin through marriage "exchanges."[7]

Kinship ideology and genealogy in particular are clearly viewed as far more than ideology by people in Ashe County: they are in many ways the sum and substance of everyday life. However, genealogy in the broad sense is not a major factor in patterning marriages. For the people of Ashe County, marriage is not, as among Needham's Purum or Lévi-Strauss's Australians, a matter of indigenous genealogical consideration. "Close" marriages occur—"double first-cousin" marriages (an "exchange" between two sibling pairs of first cousins) are not unknown in Ashe County—but these do not approach being incestuous in the strict legal sense.

"Exotic" genealogical connections of the sort analyzed by Mathews (1965, 41) have little meaning for people in Ashe County, apart from the augmented sense of "being family" that such connections may afford. The "double bond," the connection of persons through two genealogical pathways instead of one, should not be assigned any particular symbolic or functional importance (cf. Mathews 1965, 122). Double bonds and other such genealogical curiosities are for the most part the outgrowth of ecological factors, neighborliness, and the limited demography of the county and community; such is the significance that people usually associate with them. Thus incest, far from being an institution in the Blue Ridge, is if anything a phenomenon derivative of settlement patterns and their sociological ramifications rather than a custom or preference consciously conceived. Like other Americans, Ashe County people have the usual aversion to incestuous marriages. (Recall that Mary Lou Rawlins was initially shocked when her son married a woman whose grandfather was related to Mary Lou's great-grandfather.)

While genealogy is not usually a major factor in marriage, it is certainly a factor in the construction of social identities in the gen-

eral sense. Genealogies, social networks, particular social relationships, and assumed identities are, for most purposes, regarded as
given along with the geography and the climate. Persons, whether
neighbors or kin, are in a very real sense given in and by nature.
This understanding of the integrated, continuous reality of person, kin, and community is clearly reflected in the redundancies of
the following statement made by Eleanor Reeves during one of
our conversations: "The number of families and family names in
the county is really limited. And most of them are families that
have been here ever since their forefathers arrived here. Of course,
some of them did leave, but enough people stayed to keep the family name going."

Kin are immediately recognized per se on the basis of where
they were born and to whom they were born. That recognition
suggests a potential ongoing relationship but does not necessarily
imply one. Beaver (1976, 216) suggests that "birth is the primary
means by which identity is achieved in the community." Birth—
the particularities of one's filial ties and genealogical tree—defines,
indeed, confers upon one the particularities of one's initial identity.
Consanguinity defines the very basis of who one is; life history
elaborates identity from that genealogical starting point. Just as
blood is life in local culture, one's life is constituted by the substance that has been transmitted through the generations from specific ancestors. One is both identified with one's ancestors and
identifiable by being historically differentiated from them.

Hence, a person's identity derives from and is thought literally
to emerge from the conceptual context of the genealogical net. Illegitimate children are not necessarily labeled pejoratively; pragmatism dictates that they emerge and are merged into the community like anyone else. Every person exists socially, and others cope
with him or her as best as they can, attending to the person's
needs, both differentially and deferentially. One makes an effort to
see persons in situ, initially by identifying them in genealogical
terms. An individual's identity is often discussed in terms of genealogy, by reference to the genealogical significance of the family
name, which stands for the person's historical antecedents (ancestors): "He's a Richardson" or "Her mother's a Johnson." Community interrelatedness can be understood in a similar way, as
Eleanor Reeves indicates:

I'd venture to say that most of the people of Sugar Run, the Hooks, the Scotts, the Greers, and the Huntingtons are related. I guess way back, their great-grandparents were all closely related. Of course in some cases, you'll find a different name, but then their wife, in my opinion, or maybe the generation before, just married and brought their husband there to Sugar Run.

The name of a family's founding ancestor is associated with a particular reputation derived from narratives about his accomplishments. As long as this reputation is a positive one, the family takes from it a corresponding measure of self-respect. The reputation associated with the name lends to the family an element of its social character. In a similar fashion, the reputation of rural communities such as Sugar Run may be associated with the reputation of a dominant family (Batteau 1982b, 448–49). But the members of that family group do not always maintain ongoing solidarity; their relationships may be sporadic and subject to circumstance or need, as in the formation of agricultural work groups. The operationalization of genealogical connections appears to occur bilaterally and depends on factors that include geographical proximity, personal compatibility, availability, and ad hoc or tacit and informal reciprocal agreements. These informal, highly variable, and sometimes ephemeral "clusters of kinsmen, identified with particular localities and particular ancestors" (Batteau 1982b, 445) are common throughout much of the southern Appalachian region. In eastern Kentucky the indigenous term "set" is applied to such clusters (Batteau 1982b, 445). Such familial clusters prevail in rural communities in Ashe County and, as Batteau (1982b, 450) points out, "rather than forming a group (except in the indirect sense of voting together), the *set* can be seen as a core resource for network formation." Though I did not come across *set* or a local equivalent term in Ashe County, kinship clusters are sociologically operable and understood ideologically in the particularistic genealogical terms outlined in this chapter. But, as we will see, genealogy by no means exhausts the facets of cultural meaning of kinship clusters of this sort. Genealogy in one of its guises is instead an idiom for negotiating one's more durable and diffuse social relationships.

The comprehensiveness and detail of genealogical knowledge about a person, whether kin or nonkin in strict terms, may be used as a rough measure of both the closeness and frequency of interaction. Of primary concern to many people is not the identification of a person as kin or nonkin, or as kin or neighbor, but the recognition of some kind of social identity. Genealogical knowledge is the most frequently used idiom for establishing kin and nonkin on equal footing whenever possible, as well as for distinguishing one from the other. One informant said plainly that in thinking about whom to marry, who one's neighbors are is as important as who is or is not (genealogical) kin. The individual has rights and expectations, has a social identity, and lives as a more or less autonomous entity by knowing and being known to have been born within a specifiable community, family, and household.

Genealogy also serves as a means of rhetorical presentation of social identity. In recounting a genealogy, the individual outlines an identity in part through claiming a social network in which he or she is accepted. People stress or gloss over aspects, persons, and family lines, depending on the point they are trying to make about their own or someone else's identity. The differences between the genealogies given by Frank Grimes and his grandson Walter Huntington illustrate how genealogy rationalizes and recapitulates those aspects of social identity relevant to placement in certain social groups. Those persons whom both Frank and Walter include in their respective versions of the family's genealogy appear to be those through whom presently operational relationships are traced and rationalized (see Figures 3 and 4).

Walter is not deeply interested in genealogy and his account lacks generational depth. Many of the dead are missing from Walter's genealogy, for they do not and never did have much social relevance for him; they were never part of his personal history. But some of those persons missing from Walter's genealogy have or had a very real social significance for Frank at some point in his life, and so they do appear in his version. As the differences between Frank and Walter's accounts suggest, people who are dead (and therefore outside the purview of ongoing, operative ties) are not long remembered. When a person "passes away," he or she is often laid to rest symbolically as well. Continuity over time is rather abbreviated in these genealogies; it is instead symbolized by the many small family burial plots scattered along Sugar Run.

The differences between these two genealogies may thus be situated by individualism and by the different life histories of grand-

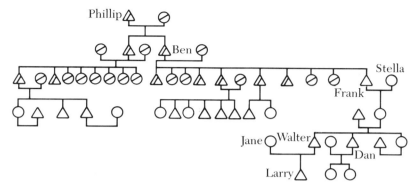

Figure 3. Genealogy Given by Frank Grimes.

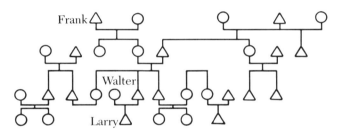

Figure 4. Genealogy Given by Walter Huntington.

father and grandson. Each version of a family genealogy is emblematic of its composer's particular place in a history and a social network. According to the composer's self-ascribed connections and interests, important ties are highlighted and negligible ties, such as those of dead kin or persons not operationally part of the composer's own social world, are forgotten or omitted.

Thus genealogies are not fortuitously different but reflect the particulars of individual social placement and identity. The differences situate and distinguish Frank and Walter in terms of their life histories and ongoing social relationships. As Walter pointed out, the genealogy specifies the particular social world of whoever "recalls" it. Genealogy as representation can be viewed as a "content" of history in its particularized, biographical manifestation. It records the passage of individuals through and out of the social time and social experience of particular persons. In addition, people in

Ashe County may explain a personal idiosyncrasy, attribute, or malady, or perhaps a case of insanity by referring to others in a person's genealogy or to the life history of an ancestor. An old woman who was thought of as "pretty" when she was young referred to her partial Cherokee ancestry to explain her physiognomy. These appearances of genealogical terms in social discourse indicate how genealogy helps people attend to their particular circumstances, "particular" sometimes to the point of meticulousness. But this particularizing use of genealogy is underwritten by a quite general, even universalist, set of meanings. Through genealogy, the individual is given in nature (biologically); one is born, and birth is irrefutably recorded through genealogical placement. From the moment a person comes into being, his or her existence is thus securely taken into account. Death is equally irrefutable; the dead exist in large measure only to give depth and stature to the genealogy and family history of their descendants, thereby legitimizing the latter's identity.

A contrasting use of genealogical knowledge is pointed up by genealogical explanations of collective rather than individual identity: "We're all kin." Genealogy as an idiom may be used to construct a global as well as a particular identity; it universalizes as well as differentiates. The unit thus constituted may be a community, a county, or even the entire Appalachian region. For example, one of my informants thought of the county's population as a whole as having common ancestry: "When we think of a county as old as Ashe, we think in Revolutionary [War] terms, and we should think of the men who served in that conflict, many of whom are our ancestors and we are descended from any number of them." Here once again history and blood are used in concert to emphasize commonality.

Cultural identity is similarly understood as a confluence of shared history and common blood; as another informant told me,

People living in one region have a common background, more or less. The reason for this more than anything else is the Scotch-Irish ancestry of these people. This does not mean that a specific community will have a higher percentage of Scotch-Irish than English blood in the people who live there. It means that wherever the Scotch-Irish lived they exerted their influence. The local culture thus reflects more than anything else the culture brought to the county by the Scotch-Irish in colonial days.

A third informant, taking a less metaphorical tack, claimed to be able to identify a distinctive Ashe County "physical type" and to explain its prevalence in reference to shared genetic makeup. From her experiences as a welfare caseworker, she felt that she could delineate an Ashe County "look" as including sharp, fine features, small lips, and thin faces. She also contended that people from particular communities within the county could be identified and categorized by their appearance and by their moral qualities. She explained this phenomenon by referring to the typically large families of past generations; the connections among these families through intermarriages over time resulted in "common blood" being widely shared. In other words, regional and local identity were for her situated in genealogical continuities.

As these opinions—a far cry from Walter Huntington's approach to his genealogy—illustrate, people in Ashe County exhibit considerable diversity and flexibility in the ways they use genealogies and genealogical "thinking," in the subjects they associate with genealogy, and in their interest in such matters. One young woman suggested that older people sometimes have less interest in genealogy than younger people because older people are more often more securely situated socially and genealogically, whereas some younger people see their communities as having been eroded by "civilization." In her view, younger people perceive some threatening discontinuities between past and present, and they see the understanding of family genealogies as a way to recapture their heritage and repair this rift. To address the problem of who they are, some of these younger people are making concerted efforts to assemble whatever genealogical knowledge they can obtain from their parents and grandparents. In recovering a genealogy, she claimed, they sense that they may be able to rectify discontinuities and recover part of their historic identity. She thus seems to understand genealogy in its function as cultural rhetoric and as a source of ethnic revival in the county and region.

As I have suggested, many Ashe County people, young and old, cultivate a lively interest in genealogy and local history, often interviewing relatives and consulting local histories and historians in order to obtain a picture of their past. Eleanor Reeves is known in Ashe County as a practitioner of this intricate art, regularly consulting people throughout the county and beyond in researching

genealogical connections, dates of birth and death, and verifying
past owners of farms and other tracts of land. As a young woman
she taught school for a few years in Ashe County before her husband made her stop working. Now widowed, she resides in a
comfortable home in the center of West Jefferson, where she pur-
sues research projects in county history as well as in genealogy,
and documents the changes in county families from generation to
generation.

For many years, Eleanor Reeves lived on the farm that had been
owned by her parents. Part of the farm had been inherited from
Captain John Cox; another part was purchased from Colonel Jesse
Ray. Both these men figured prominently in the early history of
the county (Fletcher 1960; Reeves 1986), and Mrs. Reeves claims
both as her ancestors. She has sought to legitimize her role as historian and genealogist partly on the basis of the noteworthy status
of her own ancestors. She had first become interested in her family
history through her mother and paternal grandfather:

My grandfather lived to be ninety-one. My father was the youngest, so
he lived on the farm when my grandfather finally died. He was a remarkable person, my grandfather. He had fought in the Confederate Army.
Our people were slave owners. He was intensely interested in families.
My mother had grown up in Jefferson. She was the daughter of a lawyer,
George Bower, and he, too, was a Confederate soldier. She was a bril-
liant woman, well educated, could read four languages. She went to Flora
MacDonald College, back in the days when not many mountain girls
went to college. By having a grandfather on one side of the family, and
my mother on the other, both interested in family history, and since our
people were instrumental in establishing the county, they made a good
team in teaching me the love for it. As time passed, I just became more
interested. The word got out.

People within and without the county came to her for advice or to
ask what records to consult or whom to interview in order to obtain information on a certain family or supposed genealogical connection. She makes regular field trips to neighboring counties to
track down a bit of crucial information, to look at county and
church records, or to ask where other records may be found. The
research process is made more challenging by changes in county
boundaries, with records pertinent to a certain family or plot of
land being located in Wilkes, Burke, Alexander, or Ashe counties,
depending on the span of years involved.

The mode of discourse into which Eleanor Reeves casts historical and genealogical knowledge is characteristic of the cultural
style by which Ashe County people construct a notion of "being
a person." It is ideographic and particularistic, focusing on historical contingencies and oriented toward situating the person within
a ramified matrix of putative social facts, ultimately generating
an impression of the inevitability of the identity so constructed.
Eleanor Reeves noted that her "boyfriends had to be thoroughly,
genealogically researched" in order to be established as legitimate
others. This investigatory process begins whenever a new person
appears on the social horizon. The search not only ties the newcomer into a genealogical network of other known persons but
also situates the newcomer on the land. According to Mrs. Reeves,
"North Carolina was one of the thirteen original colonies. People
came here and bought land, back then, in my grandfather's day. If
you didn't have land, you didn't make it. I remember so well, he
told me any number of times, 'Don't ever leave here unless you
know you're going to a better place.'" Identity and land prove to
be closely associated for Ashe County people, perhaps in recognition of how land and land ownership allow continuity of place, a
continuity intrinsic to a secure identity.

Farming epitomizes the giving of meaning to persons in terms
of land. A father, according to Eleanor Reeves, would make a
point of settling each son with land, while the youngest son inherited the old home; the continuity of the agricultural system was
ensured through a continuity of genealogical relatedness. She told
of going to a convention honoring persons whose families have
held the same land for "at least a century," noting that in her case,
the century was actually about 175 years. "It's not just in Ashe
County," she said, "but all over North Carolina. If you're born
into that family with that idea, it's natural that you'd want to hold
onto it too." She also accounted for patterns of migration out of
the county by reference to land. Not all children of a family could
always be given land, so they sometimes had to seek their fortunes
by leaving the county. Migrants, particularly those who moved
out of state, might be dropped from the genealogy or otherwise
forgotten; with this loss of land and continuity, their social identity within the county often became uncertain (see McCoy and
Watkins 1981).

But for those who maintained kin ties, social identity can be seen as overdetermined by the sheer density of genealogical and historical knowledge accumulated about them and their kin. Taking Captain John Cox as prototype and example, Eleanor Reeves recounts that

he was in the American Revolution, but before that he and his brother, David, and some other brothers and a sister, two of them were captured one time during the French and Indian War, and I think that they got away and came lower down to Montgomery County, Virginia. Grayson County [just north of Ashe] was taken off of Montgomery County later. David was a lieutenant in the Revolution and John was captain. We have the Sons of the American Revolution now in Independence, Virginia. Most of Lieutenant David's people lived over in Virginia. Captain John lived in Grayson County, Virginia, until after the Revolution. But soon after, he came to Ashe and just got worlds of property and owned a lot of Rutherford County, Tennessee. He had daughters who married Bakers, and another one went to Tennessee. He also had a daughter who married a Gambill and another who married Thomas McGimpsye, one of the early lawyers here.

Contemporaries are talked about in a similar way, in an idiom that marshals historical details to construct a link between past and present. Thus, speaking of family names common in Ashe County, such as Blevins and Greer, Mrs. Reeves remarked that

most of them are from families that have been here ever since their forefathers came. Of course, some of them left, but enough people stayed to keep the family name going. My great-uncle, John Baker, was elected sheriff on the Democratic ticket, about one of the first after the Civil War, which was hard to do, you know, after the war. The way he did it, we had an intermarriage with the Blevins family, and all the Blevinses supported him. That's what I've always been told.

In this type of discourse, speakers move from the initial point of entry—a question or an item pertinent to a given person—directly into a dense recounting of historical antecedents. These recitations permit a sense of continuity to be generated through the arrangement of details in a chronological framework. Genealogical and historical particulars are legitimized by means of their chronological continuity and geographical contiguity, while that arrangement is made concrete through those particulars.

As I have presented it here, genealogy is a flexible idiom for articulating individual placement and "producing" the histories of families. Genealogy provides the framework for a "knowledge of persons." It is the armature of history, a dominant representation for Ashe County people in the domain of family affairs. In particular, the genealogy is the backbone of the family history, which elaborates genealogy by adding details, episodes, and characterizations. The family history also traces the history of marriages, through which the genealogy grows as new generations of family members are produced. Thus there is a complementary, reciprocal relation between genealogy and the family history as a more elaborate cultural form. While the family history elaborates the genealogical framework, the genealogy is in turn accounted for by the details of the family history as recorded in the memories of family members or as sometimes written out by an ambitious researcher. The family member who turns researcher is in a good position to obtain information and can often rely on family interest and assistance in constructing the family history.

The family history is an indigenous literary genre of particular importance to Ashe County people. Like genealogy, family history serves as a rhetorical means of presenting, validating, and making real the identity of family members and other kin. Common ancestry is reconstructed, redefined, insisted upon as objective truth and constantly reiterated; it thereby mediates between past and present. Despite the preeminence often assigned to it, a knowledge of common ancestry in itself says little indeed about personal identity and social placement in the family context; it serves only as a general framework, which the family history attempts to fill in. Using the global comprehensiveness of the family's genealogy as a foundation, family history proceeds to supply the details.

Kinship, history, and locality are closely interwoven, as is evident in an old woman's account of the relatives who are to be present at a family reunion: "Well, I ought to know them. They are all my kin folk—everybody in Ashe County has the same grandmother, or great-grandfather, or something, whether it is a Gambill, Reeves, Cox, Taylor, Long, McMillan, Bowens, Ray, Colvard, or anything. We are all kin. Really, the history of Ashe County is our family history."

From such an assumption of common ancestry, the family history attempts to document that commonality in detail and to supplement the schematic poverty of the genealogy with a wealth of anecdotal material. Far more than a genealogical time line, the family history gives substance and character to present family members by rendering the present as an accumulation of historical antecedents and narratives. As one local resident observed, "Time meant only that which was accomplished." The family history is a record of what was accomplished, and what was accomplished is viewed as what constitutes "the family" in the present. In this sense, the family history mediates between past and present, the living and the dead, by drawing them together and by portraying the progressive unfolding of the extant social world of family life.

As an example of the form, I have selected a recent family history written by Mildred Taylor (n.d.) primarily for family members. It is at every point grounded in the specific "facts" of history. As its author states at the outset:

This book was written for my children and grandchildren—all descendants of Martin and Nancy Gambill. . . . Every character in a story has to have a NAME; and as far as I know, the names and the stories are true. I am just an IN-LAW, and not one to question or to doubt. (p. ii)

She then lists the following sources of information for her research:

Many history books, census reports from the first printed in 1790, court records (especially those preserved in Wilkes and Ashe counties), national archives, original land grants [many of which are photocopied and appear in the text] and surveys, old newspapers in the Charlotte, North Carolina, library, family Bible records, pictures and letters.

Such references, together with documentation based on oral histories collected from specified family members, lend legitimacy, substance, and reality to a history that is actually the author's creative production. In the body of her text, the author offers the particular and the concrete as a self-evident means of assuring accuracy—as natural pathways to what is real and true about the family.

The history begins with a visit to the family cemetery on the banks of the New River. There, the grave of the family's "founding ancestor" is located. Of course, the founder of the family had parents and ancestors, but beginning the family history with him indicates that, in a general way, the origin of the family itself is regarded as autochthonous. For most purposes, the origin of a family coincides with the arrival of its members in Ashe County.

Martin Gambill is said to have come to the south fork of the New River in about 1777, after migrating southward from his native Virginia. The genealogy of the family thus begins with Martin Gambill's parents and is reproduced in full as an appendix to the manuscript.

The family history includes a recitation of the names of family members, thumbnail biographies, sequential recounting of events in a fine-grain microscopic fashion, references to external political events of historic import in which members of the family participated, and repeated descriptions of the changing scenery of the land season by season and year by year. Throughout the history, Mrs. Taylor attends closely to the cycles of birth and death, the nostalgia, even pathos, of recollecting the past, and gives assurance that the accomplishments of one generation have not left an impoverished homeland for those who follow.

The key themes are the continuity of the generations and the land that supports them, the integrity and solidarity of the family over time, and the importance of respecting the contributions of each individual who has lived and died. The whole of the family history is clearly in the service of its presently living membership. The family reunion is a social drama, recorded in one chapter, that summarizes and recapitulates, at the level of concrete social interaction, the meaning of the family history as a document:

The last thing that Thomas Wolfe wrote was that there is really no such thing as returning to the places and people you remember from your youth. You realize that on this old earth with its endless changing processes we are all transient visitors and begin to count our score. This is probably less true with the Gambill family than many others because they are all "clannish" and have held annual reunions for sixty years. It is a time for greeting family and friends, to mourn the passing of an old one, to welcome the arrival of a new crop of Gambills. A time for Sunday dresses and shoes, for lunch baskets filled to the brim with the best food on earth. A time for new in-laws to learn about their family, for on the way to the reunion, the family is reviewed from grandparents and great-aunts and uncles, their children and children's children! It is truly unforgiveable not to know everybody and his brother! (p. 83)

All of the old ones are in the cemetery up on the hill. There are Papa and Mamma and my little brother Bower. There are Jim and Lucy, Nancy and Martin. There are some of the great-aunts and uncles, and some unmarked graves of infants and slaves.

Mamma (Betty Colvard) was from a large family too. I do hope some of them will be at the reunion today, but so many of them went West seeking better opportunities than they could find here in the mountains. But at one time we were all young and together. There was Aunt Neelie and Uncle John Koontz with nine children, Aunt Jane and Uncle Dock Vannoy with five children, Aunt Rose and Uncle Gordon Reeves with nine children. Uncle Feeland was married three times and had three children, Mamma (Betty) and Papa (Preston) had eight children. (p. 88)

Later chapters of the family history follow up the stories of the family members encountered at the reunion and of their forebears, recount the success stories of many family members (there are an astonishing number of doctors and dentists among them), and map out the marriages and growing branches of the family's genealogy.

Other chapters describe the educational system as the parents and grandparents of the present generation experienced it. Another chapter discusses religion and morals. The church

was the meeting place for neighbors far and wide, the good and the bad, a place to tell or hear news, to judge or be judged, a picnic, a circus, a trysting place. We were all there as the circuit rider expounded or denounced at the top of his voice until late afternoon or as long as the spirit lasted or he had good wind to keep it up. (p. 141)

In the old days, slaves were often considered part of the family, and a chapter is devoted to "Negroes" both during slavery and after the close of the Civil War. These people are spoken of with great fondness: "I remember Aunt Nan, who was Mamma's age, and whom Mamma loved like a sister" (p. 130). And, "When one of my babies would awake and cry in the night, Martha would soothe it, and put it in bed with her" (p. 132). When some of the Gambills attended Martha's funeral, they were asked if they weren't worried about being "turned out" of their own church for going to a "nigger funeral." The answer: "No [we're not worried], Martha was one of our family" (p. 133).

The family history is a compendium and codification of information on family identity, articulated in terms of solidarity and continuity. These values not only situate persons within a network but also are appropriated and exported across strictly genealogical boundaries to encompass the identity of persons not strictly related by blood, the family's slaves, for example. The point of kinship symbolism here is not to define group boundaries. Instead, a premium is placed upon inclusion and the metaphorical ramifications of kinship in forming broadly based social networks. In a broad range of contexts, exclusivity and blood relatedness are de-emphasized, while genealogical relatedness is given free reign in the construction of personal identity and personal networks.

The "family" that is the subject of a written family history includes not only a core household but usually a far-flung diversity of collaterals and ancestors, among whom are notorious black sheep as well as pride-and-joys, thieves as well as doctors and lawyers. Having "something to be proud of," such as a run of successful offspring or an oldster who has earned community respect, may be motivation for family members with leisure and background to undertake research and writing. Thus the existence of a written family history may be broadly indicative of the status and life-style of one segment of the family, but there is no direct correlation between status or "class" and the likelihood of a family's having a written family history. Obviously, the authors must be functionally literate (a criterion more relevant a few generations ago, before an effective public education program prevailed in the county). Most likely, the authors are also able to anticipate an interested audience among family members. Finally, they must have access to essential genealogies, documents, and photographs.

For people in Ashe County, the family history and genealogical modes of articulating kin relationships both exemplify and manifest the fundamental significance of history as culturally constituted, of history as a way to represent current social realities. Their style of thinking and talking about social and familial experience is suffused by such historical concepts. As a symbolic system, history allows people to order details of identity and relatedness in terms of a global understanding of time and causation, spanning the generations as well as reaching beyond the parochialisms of any one household or rural community. As a symbolic form, history is used to create an integrated image of social life. As Eleanor Reeves (1986, 4) says, "History is defined as being a complete story." Applied to shorter time scales, history acts as a symbol that harmonizes the individual life course with the experience of socialization within the family.

Like genealogy, "upbringing" (an indigenous term, referring to the socialization of children in the household setting) is a major element of local ideology, a recurrent theme in social discourse, and a decisive social experience. Whereas genealogy schematizes history, or at least family history, encompassing individual identity and situating it in time and space, upbringing delineates chronologically the person's developing internal structure, personality, or particular character. For people in Ashe County, upbringing symbolizes and summarizes the formative stages of the life history; the particulars of how one was "raised up" come to explain as much about a person as the inheritance of attributes through the biogenetic substance of one's parents and ancestors.

Because neither blood nor upbringing provide complete explanations or definitions of identity, people simply switch from one set of symbols to the other in articulating and presenting others' identities as well as their own. Upbringing, or "growing up with it" or "raising up" (indigenous terms), refers to how one was raised, how parents treated their "younguns," and the sort of experiences, activities, and attitudes present in the family setting that were incorporated into the person. A particular attribute may be ascribed to upbringing, to genealogy, or to both. Social characteristics are more often explained by reference to upbringing, physical characteristics more frequently by parentage, but there is no clear-cut distinction in this regard.

With upbringing, as with genealogy, the importance of history as a means of identity construction becomes manifest and is focused on the individual. The events of the past, recorded in the personal life history, thus become meaningful components or symbolizers of personal identity. When the Worleys talk about their children being musical, they refer not so much to inherited talent as to their children's having had music around them when they were growing up. When someone "goes bad," the wayward behavior is in part attributed to the treatment the person received from his or her parents. Upbringing is also of primary importance in discussions of political affiliations: one "inherits" membership in a political party, depending on how one was brought up. Similarly, religious affiliations are a matter of upbringing: "I was brought up a Methodist [or a Baptist]." In these domains, upbringing complements genealogy in the construction of identity in historical terms.

For most Ashe County people upbringing and genealogical relatedness correspond or overlap, since children are usually raised by their genealogical kin. In cases of adoption, however, this correspondence does not hold; such cases illustrate how kinship ideology—the meaning of blood or shared genealogical substance—encompasses nongenealogically related persons and incorporates them into that system of relationship. To understand how kinship ideology applies to adoption and nonkin relationships, we must consider the code of conduct entailed by kinship.

In Ashe County kinship ideology posits a code for conduct that Schneider (1968a, 52) defines as diffuse and enduring solidarity. However, such solidarity does not act to differentiate kinship from other types of relationships or to distinguish kin from other categories of persons. The major thrust of what might be called kinship pragmatics seems to be inclusiveness rather than exclusion. The interplay of substance (blood) and the code for conduct (diffuse, enduring solidarity) is not entirely free-form but is governed by the canons of a cultural style. Substance and code represent the qualities of persons and the meaning of relationships; they are thought to reside within as well as to be shared among persons. Substance is transmitted sexually and is shared among those who recognize one another as "blood kin." The code for conduct is transmitted through the process of upbringing and may be shared among persons who come to see their relationship as having many of the qualities of those pertaining among kin. Thus Ashe County people sometimes set aside strict genealogical boundaries and reformulate nonkin relationships by insisting on a code for conduct comparable to that associated with genealogical kinship.

During the Depression Frank Grimes took into his household a man who was not kin, Tom Miles. Tom had no family and had fallen on hard times. Tom's "adoption" into Frank's household was thus contingent on Tom's own life history and on recent national history (the Depression affected everyone). Frank asked Tom to . work from time to time, but otherwise regarded him as a family member and tacitly assumed a shared sense of diffuse, enduring solidarity between them. But one election day, as they were leaving the polling place, Tom announced, "Well, Frank, I just voted against you." Frank interpreted this statement as disloyalty, as an insult to the hospitality and familial solidarity he had extended. For Frank, shared political affiliation was a nonnegotiable given of family membership. To this day, when he tells this story, Frank says, "I just see red." Soon after this incident, Tom moved to another house.

Another case of "adoption" involved Stephen Cross and his wife. The Crosses felt lonely after their only child, a daughter, married and moved into a house farther down Sugar Run. Stephen heard from one of his nieces that a man had run out on his wife, leaving her with eight small children and that she was looking for homes for them. Ellen was seven years old when Stephen brought her home. She was homesick "for a few days" but soon became "one of the family." She remained with the Crosses until she married at the age of twenty-four. Now living with her husband and children in another county, she comes to Sugar Run frequently to visit her "parents."

Although "there was no blood between them," Ellen and the Crosses' daughter accepted each other as sisters. According to Stephen, his daughter never exchanged a single angry word with Ellen and "just thinks the world of her." Ellen feels the same way toward her "sister" and never sees her "natural" siblings, who were taken in by other families and two of whom still live in Ashe County. (This disinterest is not uncommon; as Batteau [1982b, 454] notes, "Being 'raised up' establishes both an identification with place and a filial relationship with whoever reared one; orphans and adopted children indicate a closer relationship to those who 'raised them up' than to their natural parents.") The Crosses never legally adopted Ellen, because Stephen felt that doing so would be unfair to his own daughter. (Ellen does not appear on Stephen's genealogy.) He felt that giving Ellen a good home and education was enough. He states that the only difference between Ellen and his own daughter is that Ellen will not inherit property from him when he dies.

In the cases of both Tom and Ellen, then, the code of diffuse, enduring solidarity is appropriately assumed between adoptee and adopter (cf. Carroll 1970). Adoption into a family is not merely a metaphorical exercise in kinship, for local culture stresses pragmatism. So, operationally, the kinship status of these metaphorical kin is reified to a considerable extent. In these relationships blood is not as important as ties culturally constituted through a concept such as code for conduct. Adoptees do not become equivalent to kin in the strict genealogical sense, yet the genealogical meaning of kinship is qualified or set aside, and diffuse, enduring solidarity takes precedence over blood. In the case of adoption, blood takes a "recessive" position and the code for conduct becomes the dominant meaning. Adoptive relationships are not distinguished from other familial relationships in everyday interactions, and the absence of shared blood does not substantially alter the social equivalence of blood kin and metaphorical kin. In most contexts, to suggest that the adoptee is not "one of us" is taken as an affront and quickly denied. Informants claim that the lack of blood ties has limited relevance and little meaning, even though the assimilation of adoptees as kin does not always involve the extension of inheritance rights.

Metaphorical kin are not related by blood, yet they *are* kin in terms of the code for conduct. There are symbolic means for mediating this problem. As Dolgin (1977, 128) suggests, "The merely comparable becomes the identical and yet remains the basis of comparison. . . . The relationship between structured elements in different domains becomes so powerful ('ideologically' compelling) that the domains themselves begin to merge." The diffuse, enduring solidarity associated with blood relatedness becomes comparable to the code for conduct relevant to certain nonkin relationships. One's identity as metaphorical kin ceases to be merely metaphorical. Kinship and kinshiplike relationships are not only comparable but come to be treated in the same symbolic terms.

In the process of adoption, the adoptee is initially defined as outsider (nonkin) but is eventually redefined as "one of us" by means of the sort of conceptual operations Dolgin suggests. Inclusiveness is here a controlling context, motivating the dialectical construction of identity and the consonant elaboration of social relations. An equivalent process of symbolic modification premises the drawing together of cultural domains that remain distinct only in the abstract. Thus the process of adoption or of becoming kin is the prototype for coming to an understanding of how domains such as kinship, politics, and religion can operate as conceptual forms for one another.

Ashe County people are not formalists when it comes to how they understand and organize social life. Their culture is not highly schematized. Just as the boundary between genealogical kin and persons who are brought within the family network in the absence of a genealogical connection may become indistinct and irrelevant, so the lines between kinship, politics, and religion may become unimportant or subject to systematic denial. What from the analyst's perspective may be seen as distinct domains may disintegrate or dissolve as symbols are rearranged in social discourse, as integrated definitions of persons are constituted, and as various facets of social experience are orchestrated into a coherent social representation.

Maintaining discrete categories of social activity is less meaningful to local residents than comprehending persons as units within the flow of everyday life. This premise may be situated in terms of the emphasis placed on individualism in social ideology. Priorities are established, and certain symbols and meanings are given ascendancy over others. Ashe County people are not concerned with the internal structuring of their social system except in relation to the construction of the person and the wholeness of individual social experience. Their social networks are built of cultural units motivated by the primacy of personal identity and personal relationships. The internal structuring of their social system is in this regard a means and not an end. Domains are not strictly bounded but become comparable, being situated in and by history, a shared code for conduct and the person as key meanings. The distinctions between the domains of kinship, politics, and religion are thus not thoroughgoing, since they all incorporate the same key social representations.

It is not only the anthropologist who wrestles with the interordering of domains—Ashe County residents also wrestle with that problem. In the case of kinship, they rearrange the meaning of shared attributes, restructure personal identity, and rephrase aspects of life histories in order to reassess the applicability of diffuse, enduring solidarity. This fluidity largely precludes any highly differentiated autonomous kinship *system* in Ashe County (cf. Geertz and Geertz 1975). As Schneider suggests, kinship, nationality, and religion in America may not be distinct domains in terms of a code for conduct. Schneider (1969, 124) further contends that these domains are "defined and structured in identical terms, namely in terms of the dual aspects of relationship as natural substance and relationship as code for conduct, and that most if not all the major diacritical marks which are found in kinship are also found in nationality and religion." While broadly applicable to Ashe County, this formulation glosses over the distinct focus of each domain in regard to everyday social practices.

Erickson (1968, 19) defines a sense of identity as "an invigorating sameness and continuity." Ashe County ideology stipulates the individual as the ground of social organization and as a primary locus of value (individualism). Kinship, politics, and religion are not rigid categories but spheres of meaning through which a concept of the person is articulated. The importance of these domains does not reside in their ordering within the "cultural system" but in their role in constructing the person as an anecdotal, immediate, and elementary unit from which society in the larger sense is built.

## Politics

In Ashe County, an understanding of a person's social identity is enhanced by knowledge of the person's political affiliation, which fills out what is coded about the person in terms of kinship. At first, it seems surprising that party affiliation—distinguishing between Democrats and Republicans—is so fundamental to identity when identity so readily emerges from the symbolism of kinship. But political affiliations, alliances, and categorizations augment residents' opportunities for ramifying countywide social networks. The distinction between Democrats and Republicans—the only two categories in Ashe County politics—allows people to be identified as "one of us" or "one of them." As noted in Chapter One, one informant divided the political world of the county courthouse into two camps, Republicans on one side of the main hall, Democrats on the other.[8]

One of the implications of the residential proximity of kin in communities such as Sugar Run appears to be the effective influence of senior members of the kinship network on members of the younger generation, not only in maintaining the family's morality and reputation, but particularly in encouraging, even enforcing "correct" voting at election time. One is expected to vote for the candidates of the party dictated by family tradition. Voting "against" one's kin is viewed as a gesture of disloyalty to the fam-

ily and defiance of family expectations and authority. (As Frank
Grimes's jettisoning of Tom Miles shows, these expectations extend to metaphorical kin.)

Loyalty and solidarity—"I'll scratch your back, you scratch
mine"—are the hallmarks of shared political identity. According
to the shared code for conduct, political affiliations are an enactment of the diffuse, enduring solidarity within the family. Membership in a family and in a political party are equivalent in that
diffuse loyalty, solidarity, and mutual support are the norm in both
domains. Similarly, to make one's way in local politics, one must
use and manipulate available kinship networks and the reciprocal
allegiances that derive from them. The depth of one's knowledge
of such networks is a fair measure of one's political acumen and
support.

An anecdote told by one informant clearly indicates that politics
is one element in determining who a person is:

It was bad enough for politics to get into the cemetery, but it also got into
the church. One Sunday a man wanted to join the Primitive Baptist
Church at Senter. As was the custom, the preacher said to the congregation, "Are there any questions to be asked of this man?"

Uncle Andy McMillan was there. He stood and said, "Yes, there are
several things I would like to know. Does he tell the truth?"

"Yes."

"Does he pay his debts?"

"Yes."

"Is he good to his wife?"

"Yes."

"Is he a Democrat?"

"Yes."

"I move we accept him."

Expecting political loyalties from kin (or from the members of
one's church), growing up with a particular political affiliation, or
being asked one's party membership when one seeks membership
in a church or applies for a job is a "testing out" of one's loyalties
and the cohesiveness of one's identity (integrity). It is also an exercise in social placement. Political categorizations separate the arena
of legitimate manipulation from that in which mutual trust, accord, and reciprocal support are expected to prevail. (This distinction is also relevant to the construction of ethnicity, as will become
clear in Chapter Four.)

Kinship and politics, then, are both pertinent to the cultural construction of the person, but each in a different way. This difference can be illustrated by considering two sets of contrastive terms: kin/nonkin and Democrat/Republican. Each opposition represents the inclusion or exclusion of individuals in a discrete set of existing social networks, but this process works differently in each domain. Distinctions between kin and nonkin delimit a social field and the possibility of participating in it; kinship, an idiom of inclusiveness, strategically facilitates incorporation. But the distinctions between Democrat and Republican premise political solidarity within and provide the basis for opposition and competition by determining the limits of noblesse oblige.

Because kinship, direct or metaphorical, is a primary means of constructing social identity, the kin/nonkin distinction in many instances differentiates persons having an identity from those not having one (nonpersons).[9] The porous, variable, and absorbing character of social networks—their permeability—derives largely from the tendency of Ashe County people to articulate identity by first simulating kin terms for an individual, asking questions about genealogy, or testing out the sharing of diffuse, enduring solidarity. Persons whose identity cannot be so symbolized, are, in the limiting case, nonpersons. (Examples of nonpersons include back-to-the-landers, hippies, and, often, Floridians.)

Political categorizations are not concerned with the recognition of persons per se, but with the definition of the particular *sorts* of persons they turn out to be. They are "for us or against us," "one of us or one of them," friendly or hostile. Democrats (who outnumber Republicans in Ashe County) stereotype Republicans as lacking interest in the general welfare, as money-hungry, snobby, and selfish. Republicans think of Democrats as lower class, "blue collar," and possibly socialistic in the pejorative sense. Political distinctions, like those based on kinship, may become the basis for dissension or conflict. Appalachian kinship has often been described as an idiom for family feuding and thus of political conflict as well. But kinship is not so much an idiom of conflict as of the recognition of the identity of persons who may be involved in conflict. Kinship does not premise feuding per se, though it does predicate persons who as kin to one another may become embroiled in feuds (MacClintock 1901). In the Blue Ridge both politics and kinship provide ways of mediating conflict as well as fueling it, just as shared commitments as well as disagreements are centrally relevant to social relations.

## Religion

Kinship and family affairs are also addressed in religious terms, and religion may be approached in terms of the family. Religion is overwhelmingly the idiom of moral prescription for many Appalachians, and religious forms readily become means of articulating relationships within the family. The domains of religion and kinship are drawn together and interpenetrate: meanings are borrowed from one domain to the other as religious concepts inform, serve as models for, and premise aspects of family life. Kinship metaphors and family imagery are enacted in the delineation of church as community. As Batteau (1982a, 27–28) suggests, "Church membership is recruited along kinship lines; even where it is not, one can observe that the symbols of kinship and the symbols of church membership are in many ways isomorphic."

Marshall Blevins lives with his wife and three of his daughters in a rural community northeast of Jefferson. His oldest daughter has been married for five years, is the mother of a small son, and lives with her husband near his kin elsewhere in the county. Marshall is a disabled veteran of World War II and ran a real estate firm for many years before selling the business for a large sum and retiring. He has taken an increasingly active part in the Methodist church in the last few years. He has recently made public the "calling" that he has received to become a preacher. He exhibits considerable social confidence and personal warmth. Religious concerns obviously dominate his life, and he does not hesitate to discuss religious matters at every opportunity.

Marshall asked me about my family and genealogy, and soon began discussing his own genealogy in detail. Without transition, he began to talk about kinship in the Bible. In the case of Adam and Eve, he said, "things were different than they are today." Incest was unavoidable since no other partners were available. According to Marshall, Cain must have married either his sister or his niece, since there were no other women. After the Flood, Noah's sons and their wives had children, who had no choice but to marry one another. King Solomon had many wives, and when he came into Egypt, he claimed that his wife was his sister. She might actually have been his sister in a classificatory sense—as Marshall pointed out, "It was a small world then." Moses made this same claim in order to protect his wife from being made the concubine of an Egyptian official. In each of these cases, Marshall had concluded, circumstances were such that the rules had to be different than they are at present. Marshall then noted that when Billy Graham was asked about these matters, he could not give a straight answer. Nevertheless, says Marshall, "That is how things were before the coming of Christ, before there was grace." In this older historical era, kinship and marriage patterns had yet to take their present (morally correct) form. But these transgressions were forgiven and made part of the past when the period of lawlessness was brought to an end by divine intervention, with the coming of Christ marking the discontinuity in history.

Marshall continued to explain the advent of the new era: "In the beginning was the Word and the Word was made flesh in the body of Christ. The Word became accessible through Christ. Mankind could, if it chose, become one with God through faith." Before the New Testament, he claimed, this avenue of access was not yet opened. But after the coming of Christ, sin and salvation were differentiated, marriage and incest rules were instituted, morality within the family and elsewhere was established, and loving kindness was particularized within the family setting. That is, for Marshall, the "normalization" of kinship could be delimited by a religious interpretation of history that situates the present moral regime. In the Holy Family—Joseph, Mary, and the Christ child—Marshall would have his congregation find the model of and for the nuclear kinship unit: the mother, a chaste, loving nurturer; the father, a wise, worldly guardian; and the child, a vulnerable, passive being who awaits the future, nourished by his parents' assurances. Marshall's version of this mythic history thus records the establishment of a moral system that specifies and rationalizes how kinship relations (among other things) are to be ordered. They are to be governed not by the exigencies of blind necessity, as before the coming of Christ, but conducted according to a code of loving kindness (diffuse, enduring solidarity).

Religion is also approached in terms of kinship. The nuclear family usually participates in religious activities as a unit, and kinship symbolism is readily inserted into and reinforced by an understanding of the church as community. Contrary to stereotypes of Appalachian people, not everyone in Ashe County is Baptist. Many are Methodist, a substantial number are Presbyterian, a few are Catholic—although both Catholics and Jews are underrepresented in comparison to their prevalence in urban populations—and there is a scattering of other religious affiliations. One Ashe County resident tried to start a Lutheran congregation but did not receive a favorable response. The Mennonites sponsor a mission in the county. St. Mary's Episcopal Church is also designated as a mission, under the administration of the Bishop of the North Carolina diocese. St. Francis of Assisi Catholic Church stands across the street from the county courthouse in Jefferson.[10]

There is a correlative diversity in styles of religious expression. A holiness revival sponsored by a small black church in Ashe County continued for three days. Along the road leading up to the church were automobiles with license plates from West Virginia, South Carolina, Georgia, Virginia, the District of Columbia, and Tennessee as well as North Carolina. In Ashe County, which has few black residents, the revival was noteworthy in being attended almost exclusively by black people, who came in for the event. Outside the church, carefully groomed people gathered in knots and exchanged greetings and compliments on satin hats, fancy dresses, and tailored suits. The atmosphere was festive. Some groups opened picnic baskets and relaxed on the grassy slopes surrounding the church. Inside the church, singing and preaching continued, and a number of participants slipped into trance. Collections were taken, testimonials were declared, and devotions fervently exclaimed. People moved into and out of the chapel as the session wound down.

Some months later a weeklong Methodist revival was held in a large church in the center of West Jefferson. A series of sermons was offered by guest preachers, and instructional gatherings were interspersed with inspirational invocations, possibly intended to compensate in part for the slackening social rhythms of the cold November nights. Many hymns were sung. The sermons were bland and formulaic, densely perfused with familiar scriptural quotations and delivered in uninspired, awkward attempts at exhortation. One preacher told his listeners that he found many people to be embarrassed or afraid of the Holy Spirit when they associated the Spirit with a Pentecostal style of worship that might involve "rolling about in the aisles." Although this was not a style of worship that he would find suitable, he said it could not be ruled out as illegitimate. The major point of his sermon was that the Holy Ghost works with Christ through God, the Father, to "see us through" with loving kindness; "nor should we turn away from that which is so freely given."

He ended his sermon by calling for everyone who wished to come forward to be recognized in prayer. As the organist softly played a hymn, a few members of the congregation drifted up to the altar rail to seek a blessing. Compared with the holiness revival, this one seemed subdued and aimless. The sanctuary was a plain, cavernous, brightly lit room. The stately, restrained tone of the evening service was matched without being climaxed by the simplicity of the preacher's messages.

Among various Protestant churches in Ashe County, St. Mary's Episcopal Church is unique in its emphasis on issues of change. At St. Mary's traditional approaches to religion, morality, the family, social relations, ideology, and community are being articulated and reassessed.

The Episcopal church was organized in Ashe County before the turn of the century, but it was not warmly received. An early bishop reported meeting with

the most violent opposition, accompanied by bitter abuse from Methodists and Baptists, especially the latter. It was on Sunday, the 21st day of June (1896), at Beaver Creek that I was assaulted and forceably prevented from entering the building by a mob of between fifty and one hundred men which had been gotten together for the express purpose of preventing our service that day. And the reason they gave for this action was that they "did not like Mr. Jones' (the church's minister's) doctrine" and they understood that I taught the same doctrine taught by Mr. Jones. These facts require no comment. (Fletcher 1960, 180)

Nonetheless, in 1901 an Episcopal church was started at Glendale Springs: "A Church building was erected and a residence built for the minister. This church is presently a mission point, served out of North Wilkesboro. Later a church was established at the village

of Elk Cross Roads which became known as Todd with the coming of the railroad in 1914" (ibid.).

As the bishop's story and other cases of hostilities and differences among religious groups in the county indicate, religious affiliations, like political ones, are to some degree symbolic of the
differentiation of personal attributes, as well as of points of belief,
ideology, and life-style. Not infrequently, churches in the region
have divided into hostile camps or split over fine points of doctrine
or practice, or over charged social issues such as temperance and
slavery (Fletcher 1960, 152–53 and 161). This divisiveness suggests that the institutional framework of religion as well as religious affiliations and belief were and are important representations
of individualism and cultural distinctiveness.

St. Mary's Church was built in 1905 on an eighth of an acre of
land donated by an Ashe County family. The small, white building with green trim is located in Beaver Creek, just south of West
Jefferson. The wooden structure is pierced with small, peaked
windows, and the roof is elegantly gabled. The church is surrounded by large trees and a lawn; in a small flower bed to the west
stands a statuette of St. Francis of Assisi. At the east end of the
building is a tiny cemetery, occupied by four or five mossy tomb-
stones. The interior of the church is paneled with chestnut of a
honey-brown tone. Above the altar are the words "Glory to God
in the Highest," placed there sometime in the 1930s for a Christmas play and never removed.[11]

On either side of the sanctuary are true frescoes, one of the Virgin Mary great with child (Figure 5), the other of John the Baptist
in his characteristic tatters. The style of these portrayals is highly
realistic and their effect is compelling. On the side walls are other
works of art, including a hooked rug representing a number of
theological symbols, made by St. Mary's minister, Father J. Faulton
Hodge. There is a painting of a field of brightly colored flowers
by Philip Moose, who introduced Father Hodge to the fresco-
painter, Ben Long. Another painting, by Bo Bartlett, is of the
"Laughing Christ" as a joyous young man. At the rear of the sanctuary is a small wooden table covered with an embroidered white
cloth on which sits a silver bud vase containing a single flower. On
Sundays, the communion wine and water are placed on this table
in earthenware ewers along with a loaf of homemade wheat bread.

Figure 5. "The Pregnant Virgin" (1974). A life-size true fresco painted by Ben Long IV of Statesville, North Carolina, and located in St. Mary's Episcopal Church, West Jefferson, in the Parish of The Holy Communion, Glendale Springs, North Carolina.

The young men who assist Father Hodge during the mass pull a cord hanging from the narthex ceiling, ringing the bell in the steeple. A small staircase nearby leads down into the undercroft where Sunday School classes are held for the children. Orange juice, coffee, and pastries are served there after the services. Meetings for church activities not held at Father Hodge's home are also held in the undercroft. At one side hangs Father Hodge's wardrobe of vestments, many embellished with colorful patterns or embroidered with symbols.

On another wall are photographs of church events, lists of volunteers for various activities, and newspaper clippings about the frescoes. Ben Long's fresco of the Pregnant Virgin is the only known representation of Mary with child. Long, a native of North Carolina, studied art in Italy and is one of the few artists in the United States who knows how to paint Italian fresco using authentic historical techniques. He also installed and plastered a large wall behind the altar. There, he painted a large fresco of the crucifixion

Figure 6. "The Mystery of Faith" (1977). A true fresco by Ben Long IV of Statesville, North Carolina, located in St. Mary's Episcopal Church, West Jefferson, in the Parish of The Holy Communion, Glendale Springs, North Carolina.

and resurrection. Entitled "The Mystery of Faith," this work was completed in 1977 (Figure 6).

Father Hodge grew up in the Blue Ridge, a hundred miles south of Ashe County. His father was a textile worker, and his mother managed a small farm. He received degrees from two small southern colleges, studied in England as an exchange student in a program sponsored by the International 4-H Foundation, and studied at Yale and at St. George's College in Jerusalem. Despite these travels, he always insists, "I'm a hillbilly, and proud of it." He had worked for many years in the garment industry, commuting between New York and North Carolina. But he became disenchanted with what he said had become a harried, empty life. He was converted at a prayer meeting in New York and decided to attend seminary. Father Hodge came to Ashe County directly after completing his studies at the General Theological Seminary in New York City. He had been at St. Mary's for almost four years at the completion of my fieldwork in 1976, and everyone agreed that

St. Mary's had changed significantly since his arrival. Membership in the church had increased from a half-dozen to more than one hundred. Father Hodge likes to point out that St. Mary's is one of the few mission churches in the state that is financially self-sufficient.

In Ashe County at large, Father Hodge has a reputation for his demonstrative loving kindness and his dedication to his parishioners. He makes much of his Appalachian identity, often asserting that the region's people are noteworthy for their hospitality and kindness. He is also a controversial figure because of his departures from traditional theology and his elaborate and moving ritual presentations during the church services. One informant, not a member of St. Mary's, said, in response to a question about the church, "Isn't that where all those liberals are?" Others attributed the church's increased membership to numbers of widows and spinsters who joined, knowing that after the Mass, the unmarried Father Hodge embraces each parishioner as a gesture of fellowship. But once they learned that the minister was not "available," the explanation ran, they stopped attending. Some parishioners were shocked when he grew a beard, but others thought it gave him a biblical appeal. He often wears a clerical collar, a dark sports jacket, and a large iron cross. His collection of jewelry included a silver Navajo necklace and an apple core on a chain, which he said symbolizes temptation.

Father Hodge's stated policy was that the church welcomes everyone. He and the parishioners described the church as a community of people who provide support for one another, a community in which love prevails. The consensus of the congregation was that this ideal was largely fulfilled. Members' criticisms of the church were always qualified by praise for its remarkable success in creating a "true community" for its members. (A genuine *feeling* of community would be more accurate.) Father Hodge eschewed credit for creating this ambiance, claiming that his presence or absence made little difference, since the community had a strength and solidity of its own.

Father Hodge blesses any endeavor or any relationship to which the persons involved have a commitment. He defines sinfulness only as "that which destroys the personhood of one's self or another." Clearly, he is not a strict theologian. Nor is he interested in

establishing fixed rules of morality. His expressive style is heightened by an ability to cast his beliefs into artful rhetorical form and
thus to persuade parishioners of their moral substance. One informant confessed to Father Hodge a difficulty in gaining a clear
understanding of God, not being certain of His existence. Father
Hodge responded that he had uncertainties himself. In such contexts, Father Hodge chose responses that conveyed an idea he
wanted to stress, at the same time striking a responsive chord in
his listener. His parishioners recognize the persuasiveness of his
ideas and admire his rhetorical skills.

There have, of course, been some disagreements. A number of
parishioners were disgruntled when Father Hodge had a female
house guest, and they asked him if he would like to have her stay at
one of their homes. Another, more serious case involved a family
that left the church altogether. The Salisburys had come to St.
Mary's after leaving the Baptist church. But their son later told Father Hodge that his father was "gunning for him," waiting for him
to make a "mistake." Father Hodge's repeated efforts to come to
terms with the Salisburys were unfruitful, and he was saddened by
their departure, counting it as his only failure.

Father Hodge's success in transforming St. Mary's from a mori-
bund congregation into a vigorous religious community can be
understood partly through the character of the ritual experience of
the communion. The meanings made accessible through communion and the cultural definition of the congregation as a group reflect the communal ambiance that people throughout the county
try to bring out in their everyday lives. The code of diffuse, enduring solidarity is reaffirmed and replicated through religion,
through the importation of kinship symbols, and through their
application in ritual and in the "work of the church." The congregation of St. Mary's formed a familylike community that exemplifies the continuity between kinship and religion in both cultural ideology and social practice.

St. Mary's is usually crowded on Sundays. Father Hodge is an
accomplished choreographer, dramatically using the ritual pattern
of the Mass such that parishioners imbue the bread and wine with
meaning and sense something of what Christian belief regards as
their sacred efficacy. For the ritual symbolism to compel and convince, members of the congregation must take it as a representa-

tion of the real. Reenacting the motions of a prescribed ritual is insufficient; ritual must intimate or insinuate something of the definitive order of things and the moral stance to be taken given that order. Ritual must be cast into rhetorical form: its style of articulation, its every detail must be orchestrated so as to give meaning to otherwise empty forms. Only in this way can ritual evoke a sense of reverence in the congregation and achieve a persuasive force that rings of the truth (Lévi-Strauss 1963b, 193; Turner 1969).

Father Hodge's celebration of the Mass is intended to predispose the members of the congregation to orient their reflection and action toward the Christian virtues of loving kindness and brotherhood. He tries to create an ambiance that allows individuals to articulate a personal identity and to recognize their participation in a protective and supportive social milieu. Although this ideal is only sporadically and fleetingly glimpsed in everyday life, church members are encouraged to uphold this ideal in the religious domain and to seek more fully to put it into practice. In a broad sense, these values are long-standing elements of social ideology, and the communion rites model the social environment. People come to Mass seeking to be persuaded by the model it provides.

Season by season, the interior of the sanctuary at St. Mary's and the materials used in the ritual are designed to enhance the meaning of the Mass. In the fall, the sanctuary is decorated with bright autumn leaves, softened by the glow of candles, the fragrance of incense, and the murmuring of the congregation. During Advent, poinsettias are banked about the altar, and a large fir tree is decorated with tiny white lights. The children make wreaths and garlands for "the blessing of the greens," and the congregation gathers to drink hot cider and to sing carols. At Easter, a plethora of greenery, lilies and other spring flowers, and balsam boughs are brought with song from the woods. Father Hodge and his acolytes wear colorful robes during the Mass. The visual display is complemented by the music of organ, violin, and guitar, and the solo voices in counterpoint with singing from the entire congregation. A bell is struck at the moment of consecration of the bread and wine. All these elements are woven into the fabric of the familiar ritual and transform it, as is Father Hodge's intent, into a sensuous experience, redolent with meaning.

The ritual experience encourages, even compels, participants to embrace the liturgical meanings and social ideals that Father Hodge stresses. The Mass becomes a representation of community and brotherhood, ideals that are the keynote of St. Mary's message and its prime motivation. It may be passé to regard ritual simply as a symbolization of social forms and their meaning, but this is exactly what Father Hodge and his parishioners have in mind. Intention and outcome significantly overlap. The sensuous character of the ritual at St. Mary's, which in part accounts for its impact, was in striking contrast to the spare simplicity of the Methodist ritual pattern. At St. Mary's people sometimes leave the service with tears in their eyes, stating how profoundly they have been moved. The emotional intensity generated by the Mass motivates participants to modify their approach to social life and to understand it in a new light.

Father Hodge does not emphasize the sermon in the service, because he regards himself as a poor speaker. He treats the sermon as a meditation, a thought-provoking, often sober interlude in the flow of symbolic actions. Father Hodge often invites ministers from other churches to give the sermon—Baptists, Catholics, Methodists, and Presbyterians, anyone who can be persuaded to come. After the sermon, hymns are sung. Members of the congregation often give readings of the Gospel and the Epistle and bring forward the bread and wine for the communion, along with seed to feed the birds or other gifts for particular celebrations. Throughout, an effort is made to integrate members of the congregation into the ritual rather than leaving them as a passive audience.

The communion collectivizes the congregation, transforming diverse individuals into a unified body through the sharing of the body (bread) and the blood (wine) of the Mass. Surprisingly, the Mass is also an occasion for articulating personal identity. The individual is given ascendancy by being the vessel for the consecrated bread and wine. At the climax of the Mass, Father Hodge holds the bread and wine and comes before each parishioner kneeling at the altar; he intones the prescribed prayer and addresses each person by name. Individualism is also heightened by leaving matters of theological doctrine and moral judgment largely up to personal choice.

Unlike the ecstatic drawing into the self of the trancelike states sometimes experienced by participants in holiness revivals, informants at St. Mary's describe a radiant outflowing of sentiment, a refreshing exhilaration, and an assurance of support from other parishioners. Personal identity and community are bolstered dialectically through cultural forms common to their experience of kinship and religion.

The associational dimension of the ritual becomes most evident during "the passing of the peace." This portion of the service follows the offertory, during which a plate is passed to collect money for the church along with a basket to help "the hungry of the world." The passing of the peace, a regularly prescribed segment in Episcopal liturgy, is usually accomplished at St. Mary's by an embrace or even a kiss and the words, "peace be with you, brother [sister]." Father Hodge comes down from the altar to enter into the passing of the peace. All are encouraged to express their goodwill as warmly as possible. Signs of affection are expected regardless of age, sex, or social position—an enactment of Turner's (1969, 131ff.) *communitas*. General confusion prevails in the sanctuary as parishioners leave their seats to greet their friends and neighbors. The central aisle fills with people, young and old, liberal and conservative (indigenous categories), wearing all manner of clothing.

As befits Ashe County ideology, the major themes of the communion are social engagement, shared substance, and identity. Sharing bread and wine replicates the Last Supper and represents the oneness of the communal body, a shared spiritual substance. Through communion, individuals define themselves by their commitment to a collective enterprise. The meaning of togetherness for the congregation is loving kindness, diffuse, enduring solidarity pertaining to and obtained through relationships as they develop within the congregation. In this way, communal solidarity carries over into nonritual interchanges among church members, shaping them by covertly ritualizing them.

Kinship terminology is used extensively during the passing of the peace and at other times during the communion. As in many other churches, parishioners address their minister as Father, and throughout the recitations in the service they call one another sister or brother (see Batteau 1982b, 454). The kinshiplike feeling among the congregation illustrates how kinship and religious meanings enhance one another. The concordance between religion and kinship allows reification of the church community through ritual action. Parishioners see "the church" as a prototype for their behavior in other domains. For some the church becomes a community in some respects comparable to the family, with the Holy Family as a point of reference in both domains. In many formulas of the liturgy ("God the Father, God the Son"), the meaning of kinship and spirituality are brought together and elaborated in terms of one another. God is not only manifested as Father and Son, but he also nurtures and gives substance to all his children.

Father Hodge stresses the diffuseness of the religious code. He never locks the door of the church or of his home even when he goes away for several days. Anyone may enter his home, drink his liquor, watch television, or use the kitchen, and he encourages members of the church to avail themselves of his home. He maintains his "flock" by organizing groups, introducing people to one another, talking with nonmembers who show an interest in the church, counseling members, and reminding people of the solidarity they should expect from one another. He spends much time visiting people who are shut in or ill, helping them in a variety of ways. He is often on the telephone giving advice and comfort. He tries to work by example, regarding religious activity as a learning process. Rhetoric as well as solidarity and charisma are invested in this community.

When his cabin on Bluff Mountain was vandalized by teenagers, Father Hodge declined to press charges, which would have included violations of hunting regulations, possession of marijuana, and breaking and entering. The culprits were all unemployed high-school dropouts from poor families. Father Hodge met with them and asked them to pay for the broken windows, slashed sofa, and melted cooking utensils. He said he could not understand why they had caused this damage, why they did not simply make themselves at home. "Why did you have to break things?" he asked. "The door was unlocked anyway." Each young man paid fifty dollars, which covered only a small part of the damage. Father Hodge counseled them not to repeat such activities, adding that they were welcome to use his house whenever they wished. The house was to continue to be unlocked and available to all.

As expressed in Father Hodge's handling of this situation, sharing as a code for conduct is initially formulated in straightforward, concrete terms. The young men are invited to share the use of his house, having been made familiar with the ground rules of sharing and how they differ from abuse. As Leach (1961, 21) observes, the process of incorporation, endowing "the individual with membership in a 'we group' of some kind . . . [is] distinguished symbolically as [involving] relations of common substance." As with adoption, incorporation results in a kaleidoscopic suffusion or opening up of meaning, with implications for the symbolic construction of the autonomous person and for the premising of relations among persons so constituted through the representation of shared substance or code. As noted earlier, the individual, once incorporated into an encompassing social milieu, is taken as given and recognized as having certain self-evident needs. For Father Hodge, sharing situates the expectation that others will be mindful of such needs. It predicates the meaning of Ashe County people's self-ascription as customarily responsive, hospitable, and caring. In the religious domain, this collective responsibility is replicated as a moral dictum and is motivated by the concept of Christian charity.

Many parishioners were explicit in seeing Father Hodge as a charismatic figure, citing the charisma of his office as well as the personal magic he works into ritual and social encounters. *Charisma* denotes a public recognition of exceptional powers or qualities not possessed by the ordinary person (Weber 1968, 48). Through such personal qualities, the charismatic individual may exercise leadership from which comes a public acknowledgment of spiritual gifts to a special degree. Parishioners attribute much of the cohesiveness of the church to Father Hodge's exercise of such qualities. In this liminal context of charismatic leadership, metaphor assumes an aura of reality and meaning becomes compelling. Just as the liturgy becomes a vehicle of conception that motivates and energizes participants, Father Hodge, as viewed by others and by himself, is a channel through which conception and motivations are posed, exemplified, transmitted, and, whenever possible, put into action.

Weber (1968, 18) suggests that one context in which charismatic

leadership often appears is that of political, social, or religious unrest. Such conditions are present in the Blue Ridge in the form of
pervasive social and cultural change. In response to these conditions, nonroutinized, heterogeneous modes of authority (charisma)
readily occur, affording a liminal setting in which social meanings
routinized through custom may be rearranged, reassessed, or set
aside. Old symbolic forms may be revised, new conceptions of social relatedness may be tested, and their applicability to everyday
life may be determined. Extant social ideology is not jettisoned,
but elements of that ideology are reworked, and rearticulations are
viewed as harking back to a historical past. At St. Mary's this process of ideological transformation and historicizing is evidently
underway. The charisma of Father Hodge, the rhetoric he poses,
and the exemplifications he sets forth fit neatly within the larger
context of change. Charismatic authority can supersede established cultural forms and routinized meanings and can legitimize
changes in them. Through charisma, the representation of social
realities may be subtly altered or dramatically transformed.

Parishioners were uncertain of how long the remarkable social
openness could be expected to prevail. They speculated about what
would happen if Father Hodge were to leave. Intuitively, they
understood Weber's (1968, 22) point that "the existence of charismatic authority is specially unstable." Furthermore, the church
subsisted on a specifically nonrational economic calculus, largely
dependent on voluntary contributions. "Rational" economic conduct was not expected. As is frequently the case in this kind of social setting, "individual patrons provide the necessary [financial]
means for charismatic structures" (Weber 1968, 21).

Those parishioners who were disconcerted by Father Hodge's
revisions of dogma or his interpretation of morality and those who
were shocked by events at the church—the blessing of farm animals in the spring (a fertility rite?) or the feeding of birds with
bread consecrated for the Mass—were in part reacting to this charismatic frame. The Salisburys were unable to tolerate the pervasive fluidity and constant (liminal) rearrangement of religious concepts. Others welcomed just that sort of cultural transformation
and symbolic differentiation, which allowed them to reappropriate
and reintegrate components of traditional ideology under changed
conditions and to bridge discontinuities between past and present.

Many parishioners sought escape from the rigid dogmas of other churches, gravitating toward a religious setting in which dogma was malleable and meaning negotiable.

At St. Mary's, Father Hodge wholeheartedly exemplified and aggressively encouraged sharing and solidarity. Through a discourse of imperative meanings, he tapped into local people's conceptions of community and relatedness, making explicit values and intentions that for most people in Ashe County remained an implicit cultural style of inclusiveness and hospitality. His charisma and his rhetoric of overstatement reinvigorated reified meanings and motivated their pursuit through action. In particular, diffuse, enduring solidarity became a semantic environment for the exercise of charisma in which particular meanings (loving kindness, good works, community ambiance, and mutual support) were made actable: "Seek and ye shall find. Knock, and all doors will be opened unto you." Diffuseness became a cultural form that opened a space in which each parishioner could articulate individually determined meanings.

Sharing is a symbolic action that allows and encourages an acknowledgment of the identity of others. But sharing does not necessarily merge discrete individuals into an undifferentiated blur. By particularizing what is shared and differentiating shared elements from those not shared, it becomes a cultural form for clarifying the specifics of individual identity. Consuming bread and wine during the Mass is a symbolic act, postulating shared substance—the body and blood of Christ. By communion, people do not just mean a liturgical and spiritual rapport among those sharing the meal. In everyday life, sharing is enacted through the exchange of labor and goods; a family or neighbor with an apple orchard takes a bushel of apples along when visiting kin, friends, or neighbors. Sharing is similarly a basis of gossip groups, political loyalties, religious affiliations, kin ties, and cooperative work groups.

At St. Mary's, the communion is a ritualized form of the daily meal at which household members fortify their bodies and are also reminded of their membership in a social body, the church at Mass, the family at dinner. Both sorts of meals involve shared substance, the body and blood or the shared genealogical substance situated within the person. The family and church each provide a form of nourishment and nurturance. Shared substance situates the person; the material representation and coordination of metaphors and meanings from kinship, politics, and religion in this setting participate in the symbolic production of individual identity. Of course, such meanings are also embodied in events such as church and political dinners.

## Community

Generally speaking, Ashe County people do not seem to think of their social world either in terms of absolutely discrete and bounded groups or in terms of social structure as a fixed and timeless entity. Perhaps social structure is not for them a major category of social thought, social organization not being viewed as "a lattice of structural positions" (Errington 1974, 25). Instead, social relations are understood concretely as relationships between specific persons with specific attributes (individualism), and these relationships emerge, evolve, and are embedded in a community context. An overall cultural style, rather than a fixed structure, lends coherence to social life. Of course, fairly discrete groups and categories exist (for example, household units and political parties), but in many social contexts, inclusiveness is stressed over exclusion; most groups are defined by reference to those persons who are members rather than to those who are not.

What then of the concept of community, understood in Ashe County as a context of particular social experiences and involvements? Beaver (1986, 52) suggests that community must be seen in historical perspective:

If early maps are taken as a guide, "community" was a cluster of dwellings, with a church, a school, a store, and a post office forming the center. A named place then, and still named on the map, community as it was then is a cluster of memories, historical relationships, and events for the old.

Today, *community* seems to refer neither to a particular sociological system nor to definable groups, but to a means of articulating a sense of community or groupness. Beyond the particular exigencies of the nuclear family or household unit (which often correspond), the exact boundaries of groups, their internal structure, and their rules for incorporation remain situational and negotiable. Community is a concept of diffusely supportive social ambiance with an equally diffuse geographic localization, varying in shape and size depending on the particular ties in question at a particular moment.

In other words, community is not so much a social group as a potential, an environment, a context or resource conducive to the pursuit of a variety of personal goals. Community members act in concert as a group only in times of crisis (Beaver 1976, 219), and even then, it is a matter of action motivated by the particular circumstances of its members—action remains tied to persons, the group is derivative. Beaver correctly stresses an element of pragmatism: "groups emerge when groups are needed" (ibid.). In the broadest sense, a community is a locus within which understandings, experiences, ancestors, kin ties, and histories are exchanged, shared, and articulated.

Given this formulation of community and groupness, the incorporation of members into groups, social categories, or institutional localizations is not a formidable difficulty. Incorporation is readily arranged, and symbolic constructions are easily modified to take account of new persons. In this milieu it is exclusion that poses a problem. Outsiders unfamiliar with local culture who withhold themselves from sharing a sense of common identity sometimes exasperate and confuse natives of the county and may thereby alienate themselves from them.[12]

In referring to the sociological literature on Appalachia, I have pointed out that some analysts give undue attention to the community as a social unit. In so doing, they make the community more concrete and socially real than it is, at least in Ashe County, since *community* is not a sharply defined indigenous concept and, for the most part, is not emphasized culturally by local residents themselves as a social unit. Rather, *community* is currently recognized as a social issue. There is considerable variation on this matter throughout the Appalachian region. On Sugar Run and in other rural enclaves throughout the county, *community* seems to have a provisional socioecological existence. I would venture a dual notion of community as a diffusely designated geographical space in which particular familial, political, and religious forms of life are pursued and localized, and as a discursive space in which local forms of knowledge regarding family life, political life, and religious life as culturally understood are inscribed and appropriated. This characterization and contextualizing of the ethnographic "baseline" presented in this chapter will become useful in examining the politics of representation and change, to be discussed in Part II.

More concretely, the meaning and relevance of community, as a key element in how local residents approach social life and social change, has gradually become more explicit and, perhaps ironically, more problematic as Ashe County has grown less autonomous and has increasingly come into contact with social networks beyond the county line. At the level of existing social patterns, too, the sociological integrity and relative autonomy of communities like Sugar Run have been degraded and their relevance as centers of activity circumscribed by the advent of better transportation and concurrent social change. The same can be said of the county as a whole. And so, community as concept and even as an element of rhetoric has gradually come into focus in local discourse, has become an explicit cultural element, in measure as it has become a less certain and viable social entity. Community has increasingly become a rhetorical figure that Ashe County people use to express their sense of what social life should be, what it can be, and possibly what it once was without being so called.

In reference to social categories, Ashe County people differentiate and identify residents of the various social communities such as Sugar Run, residents of the town, the people of Ashe County as a whole and, beyond that, Appalachians as distinct from outsiders. As might be expected, defining these categories and hierarchically ordering them are not abstract exercises but practical matters, of interest mainly insofar as particulars must be referred to in articulating relationships among persons within them. Such articulations proceed largely along historical lines and in terms of episodic details pertaining to specific persons and relationships. Relationships are phrased primarily in terms of the histories of specific persons, families, and localities, so that further histories and relationships may be generated. The irrelevance of social structure per se and matters pertaining strictly to the structure and boundaries of groups in local ideology raise significant problems for those Ashe County people concerned with coming to terms with outsiders, as we will see in Part II.

The nuclear family mediates conceptually between groupness and individual autonomy. Thus the household group looks outward toward the extended family and beyond to larger social networks, and inward toward the enshrinement of a value of the independence and autonomy of self-sufficient individuals. Because the person, rather than the group, is the basic unit of meaning and action in local understandings of social life, relationships are seen as emerging from the particular expectations, capabilities, and attributes of individuals. History, operating as a symbolic form in local discourse, is thought to account for the distinctive attributes of persons as well as for the existence of each individual. Groups, rather than being a major locus of meaning or a major means for accounting for the particulars of social experience, are viewed as derivative of persons who come together under specific circumstances and develop a history of encounters. Ideologically, a group is not a thing in itself but an outcome of the intrinsic gregariousness of individuals.

Thus at the symbolic level, community may be regarded as located halfway between history and the individual. It cuts history down to size, narrows its meaning, personalizes it, makes it more specific, and reduces its temporal scope to manageable proportions. By bracketing the monumental dimensions of history, the notion of community delimits the space in which the individual moves, creates, and constructs a personal history; it thereby sets off history writ large from the meticulously detailed history that is more directly one's own. The community moves through a portion of this historical space, which is thus not altogether outside the compass of human intervention and action. In turn, community provides the background for articulating one's personal biography and those of one's immediate forebears.

The correlative importance of kinship and genealogy does not derive solely from their pervasiveness; nor are they thought to exhaust the scope of interaction. For residents of Ashe County, genealogy alone does not dictate patterns of interaction or the cultural construction of the person. Kinship is meaningful at least in part because it is thought to have historical precedence both collectively and for individuals. Extant kin relationships are historically situated, derived from a genealogical progression inaugurated in the past. Ashe County people might also readily agree with social theorists who see other institutions as differentiated outgrowths of

kinship, which dates back to the dawn of human history. Such is
the conviction conveyed by Marshall Blevins's interpretation of
the history of the family in the Bible and by Mildred Taylor's family history. The appropriation of the kinship symbols of sharing
and substance by other cultural domains is in a sense naturalized in
a social ideology that treats kinship as having historical priority.
Generally, the meanings associated with kinship seem to have
symbolic ascendancy and, as a result, shape and cue other meanings as social experience broadens, trails off, or is differentiated
into other domains such as politics and religion.

Thus history, as particularized in genealogies, in family and life
histories, and in upbringing, provides a context and stylistic orientation for the symbolic-interpretive activity of constituting the
person. In everyday life, both history and the individual are elaborated and made meaningful in a mutually reinforcing manner in
order to situate the individual in the real. Contrary to the view
of some analysts of Appalachian culture, however, history is by
no means the sole determinant of identity and individuality in
Ashe County ideology. For example, Weller (1965) claims that
fatalism—a perception that people are the victims of history—is
a key element in Appalachian ideology. Such may be the case
in eastern Kentucky, where many people have lived in poverty,
worked in the coal mines, or have otherwise been exploited. As
Weller (1965, 37) explains,

In the mountains . . . nature did not yield, instead the harshness of the
land overcame the man. His confidence in himself was slowly but surely
undermined. From this grew a fatalistic attitude which allowed him to
live without the guilty feeling that he himself was to blame for his lot and
assured him that this way of life was fundamentally right even when he
was discouraged by it.

But in Ashe County, as residents make clear, nature and history
have been less harsh. The meaning of history is seen as embedded
in the particular history of the locality, and history is given meaning in terms of its particulars. Ashe County people do not regard
history as overwhelming; its power is qualified by a measure of
human self-determination. Each person eventually passes away,
but not without having left a mark on the times and thus having
participated in history itself. Within one's alloted segment of time,

one participates as an active, even creative, agent who exerts some control. As mentioned earlier, one informant phrased this relationship between history and human activity by saying "time is what was accomplished." Time becomes meaningful as history, and history is the product of persons' accomplishing something in their lives, "making something of themselves," inscribing their image on their moment, and thereby achieving a sense of identity and continuity.

Barnett and Silverman (1973, 15) note that "the 'individual' is taken as primary, prior or stressed; and 'the whole' (say the 'social whole,' for simplicity) and the individual's relationship to the social whole as the thing having to be 'worked out.'" This statement applies directly to the ideology of Ashe County. History as a cultural element is both the means and the idiom for working out such relationships, while the working out is itself a further elaboration of history. The following general formulation by Dolgin and Magdoff (1977, 352) does much to elucidate how Ashe County people experience social life:

> The process by which the historic is made real in the present, and the present is grounded in the past is seen as an aspect of the cultural construction of reality. . . . Each event of history . . . is constantly redefined, through the redefinition of successive moments, of the ongoing, the unnoticed, the history of everyday life. An "event," meaningful in reflection in comparison to the past, itself becomes the object of future comparisons once it is historic.

This process of "working out" or redefinition—the transposition of the discrete individual or the discrete event into the continuous historical flow—is for people in Ashe County a matter of sustained reflection only insofar as reflection accompanies social practices or is performative. The "working out" involves acts, is constituted by acts; detached philosophizing about these matters is not a priority.

While history is a controlling context for the representation of the person, the dialectic of this symbolization process also "calls out" history. The person as symbol goes in search of context and thereby becomes a symbolic interpretive operator and active agent, creating that context, articulating and therefore constituting history. For example, in his *Ashe County, A History* (1960), Fletcher devotes many pages to naming and cataloguing the persons who have "built" the county, lived there, and given it human substance. The monumental recitation of specific persons' names, reminiscent of the roll call of warriors before battles in epic narratives, unfolds in recognition of the person as constitutive of history and as its raison d'être.

The people of Ashe County struggle to make everyday life a cohesive and harmonious experience, encompassed by community and embedded in history. Their cultural style highlights informality, hospitality, and inclusiveness. Their concept of history situates both personal identity and the identification of the person with a locality and a social network. In the next chapter, this distinctive form of local knowledge is viewed as the backdrop for a political dispute in which outsiders, in effect, sought to subordinate central features of local knowledge and ideology to external priorities. The dispute, a fine-mesh and ever-changing filigree of power, produced changes in local knowledge that residents regarded as marking a discontinuity in their history. The increasing intrusion of outsiders and the entry of unfamiliar cultural elements into local social discourse have provoked an ambivalent response among residents: social and cultural change seem both threatening and inviting. Recognizing the problems that change poses for their style of life, Ashe County people have attempted to retain their culture and identity. Their effort to resolve the dispute entailed rhetorical transformations of ideology and the creation of links between explicated elements of their tradition and external meanings.

No doubt, there are differences between how Ashe County people presented their realities to me, an outsider, and how they present them to one another. Their articulations of local forms of knowledge to an ethnographer diverged, to an unknowable extent, from the style and substance of conversations among themselves. It is but a few steps from this recognition of discrepancy to Foucault's (1980, 51) insistence on a fundamental "relation between power and knowledge, the articulation of each on the other." The difficulties I have encountered in summarizing the social life of Ashe County in part reflect the remarkable fluidity and dynamism of that way of life, but Foucault's issue of power and knowledge also plays a significant role. The problem of certifying my ethnographic "knowledge" of the county is linked closely to the question of what sort of knowledge outsiders can acquire about Ashe County's culture, given the inescapable relations of power that exist between local people and outsiders. Ashe County residents rightly claim that there are important differences between what they understand their culture to be and how outsiders understand it. The ethnographer is not exempt from this difficulty. Indeed, this margin of uncertainty opens up the discursive space in which power and knowledge were articulated through each other during the political dispute over the New River. Ashe County people attempted to certify the "local knowledge" they articulated during this dispute as the definitive description of their culture. Similarly, the problem of assessing "the truth" of my knowledge of Ashe County culture must be set in the context of the problem of understanding change and the way local knowledge has become subject to political arbitration and appropriation.

My outsider status was least pressing in discussing St. Mary's because the congregation represents a heterogeneous collection of inside outsiders or outside insiders, people working self-consciously toward new self-definitions and relational concepts. This group was comfortable testing out aspects of their social ideology with an ethnographer because they engaged in that same activity among themselves. They were also aware of my own status as "inside outsider," in my role as ethnographer and as someone incidentally brought up in the church's tradition. The cases of kinship and politics are somewhat different. Although social discourse in these domains was perhaps no less fluid, people were not nearly so overt in probing and reformulating ideology; these forms of discourse were perceived to be more historically entrenched, time-honored, and self-justifying than those forms drawn into the liminal ferment of meaning and representation at St. Mary's.

Any ethnographic "reality" or "baseline" reflects the power relations obtaining among local people, on the one hand, and between them and the ethnographer, on the other. Both the shooter and the target are always in motion. The substance and self-definition of local knowledge oscillate relative to changing networks of power that situate the broader relations of local people to outside interests, administrative constraints, and government impositions. So, too, local forms of knowledge modulate relative to the presence of an ethnographer and other outsiders—a point fundamental to the analysis posed in Part II.

What I have said about Ashe County and its people taps into

local forms of knowledge, power, and discourse, but also derives from the particular power entailments implicit in ethnographic tactics and techniques. Similarly, in Part II, the forms of power and knowledge implicit in various administrative "technologies" of corporations, federal agencies, and the law will be seen to intersect in complex and unstable ways with local forms of knowledge. The advent of a major political dispute over the New River provoked various changes—distortions, displacements, exclusions, improvisations, and transformations—in how Ashe County people present their understandings of their culture to one another and to outsiders. For this reason, I have here insisted on the uncertainties of my ethnographic "baseline," posing such uncertainties as an introduction to the theme of cultural change and negotiability.

The emerging cultural problematics that characterize change in Ashe County can, I believe, be understood in terms of the history of forms of power and knowledge within and without the county. The exact consequences of this interpretive strategy will emerge from my account of the political dispute that I lived through with Ashe County residents, and one which I take as emblematic of the more general social and cultural issues now facing such local populations.[13]

# Part II

*Chapter Three*

# Of Time and the River

The bicentennial of the American Revolution, which occurred as my research in Ashe County was in progress, became the occasion in the county for a publication that summarized local history, geography, and social institutions. *Rambling Through Ashe,* as it is titled, claims that the New River is today as it was when the first settlers crossed the Blue Ridge and entered the county:

It acquired the name of Wood's River when exploring surveyors, probing west into the wilderness from Virginia about 1740, discovered a river running north that no one had ever heard of. Major Abraham Wood headed the exploratory group that found the stream, and it was named in his honor. Later, for reasons unknown, it was renamed New River. New River is a stream of rare beauty, eye-catching and soul-satisfying in its loveliness. The rapid flow of water carries away evidence of soil erosion quickly and the water of the New sparkles again. The recent controversy over the construction of two dams in Ashe and Alleghany [counties] threatened the complete destruction of this miraculous beauty and the destruction of numerous homes, churches and rich farmlands in Ashe and Alleghany. Fortunately, the entire nation joined in a plea for the continued flow of this old and beautiful river. (Goodman et al. 1977, 45)

This text is accompanied by photographs of scenic New River vistas. Both the storied beauty of the Blue Ridge mountains and the sweep of the New River are reference points for Ashe County residents, who assert an aesthetic of their geography and associate with it an ascendant value for their way of life. These natural resources account for both the county's appeal to tourists and its attractiveness to developers. Such contending symbolic associations

and their enmeshment in a complex matrix of power led to the
emergence of a social movement in the county in response to
threatened changes regarding the disposal of county resources. For
the people of Ashe County, the New River has become a symbol
of change, representing complex meanings made explicit during
the fourteen-year-long New River dispute. The history of this
controversy deserves detailed attention because the tactics, strategies, and technologies of power and discourse employed to resolve
it situate recent change as a recurrent and formidable difficulty for
people living in places like Ashe County.[1]

The north and south forks of the New River flow northward
through a maze of hills and hollows to join in the north of Ashe
County. The river then runs through Virginia and West Virginia,
eventually discharging into the Ohio River. This geography was
not simply the backdrop for nor the content of the controversy.
Both literally and figuratively, the river became the site of the dispute and the locus for a debate in which values and concepts—
such as personal worth, independence, local autonomy, economic
survival, security, and well-being, as well as cultural identity—
whose meanings were long implicitly assumed were explicitly defined.

The politics of the New River generated a rhetoric through
which Ashe County people sought to legitimize their life-style in
opposition to the priorities of outside interests. Their efforts in this
regard were only partly successful. In the process, significant
changes were effected in the forms of local discourse, knowledge,
and social practice. As a result, the meaning of local cultural identity and many of the concepts associated with it have become uncertain, the underlying premises having been seriously questioned.

The changes in how Ashe County people define themselves and
present their self-understandings to outsiders can best be explained
in terms of the tension between historically, or internally, derived
definitions of identity and the various ways these definitions were
tactically modified during the dispute. The local residents' problem became one of negotiating cultural authenticity. The dispute
imposed constraints on local knowledge and ideology because it
compelled residents to articulate their identity in externally comprehensible terms still recognizable to themselves as their own.

As a result, the New River controversy both eroded and revitalized the local sense of identity. Like the parishioners at St. Mary's Church, Ashe County residents rearticulated and historically redefined their understandings of themselves, others, and their own desires in life. In this process, cultural symbols assumed a rhetorical function, the major vectors of which are persuasion, admonition, and exhortation. As Kenneth Burke (1950, 19) suggests, rhetoric is "par excellence the region of the Scramble, of insult and injury, bickering, squabbling . . . cloaked malice and subsidized lie."[2] It is one of the paradoxical effects of modernity that acrimonious contention and debate should also allow the creation of new, if often unsatisfying, forms of representation. During the dispute, an emerging local rhetoric drew upon traditional elements and thus elaborated orthodox social ideology, while outsiders' rhetorical maneuvers made cultural identity into an issue of power. Culture—the term itself as well as some of its particular traits— became a figure in the rhetoric. Not just the land and its resources, but the viability of local culture itself was in dispute.

The origin of the controversy over the New River may be traced to June 1962, when the Appalachian Power Company (APC), a subsidiary of American Electric Power, announced its plans for the Blue Ridge Power Project, including a dam on the New River.[3] The American Electric Power Company, headquartered in New York City, is the largest power company in the United States. At the beginning, the Blue Ridge project was of little concern to people living in North Carolina; most of the 20,000 acres to be flooded for the project were in Virginia, a state to which APC provides electric power. Six months later, in January 1963, the U.S. Department of the Interior filed a request to deny the APC application for a permit to perform feasibility studies for the Blue Ridge project. The Department of the Interior contended that a government-sponsored project further downriver, in the New River–Kanawha River Gorge, would better serve the public interest. Two months later, the Federal Power Commission (FPC) granted APC a permit despite the Interior Department's injunction.

The following year, APC asked the FPC for a license to build the project. In February 1965, after another full year of deliberation, the FPC dismissed the portion of the application that would have allowed the installation of power generators at the federal

Bluestone Dam in West Virginia. APC then had to reconsider
much of the rest of its plan. If there were to be no generators at
Bluestone, the dam on the New River would need to have a much
greater generating capacity.

Further complications arose in 1966, when the Department of
the Interior proposed its own scheme, known as "pollution dilution." They noted that the Kanawha River, into which the New
River flows, is severely polluted in the industrial region around
Charleston, West Virginia. The Department of the Interior called
on the FPC to double the size of the Blue Ridge project so that
additional water, released from the dam to produce power, would
also flush industrial wastes downstream. The potential effects of
these plans on local residents were not a major point of discussion
during this period. The new plans for the larger Blue Ridge project called for the flooding of 42,000 acres, about 14,000 of which
were in North Carolina: 8,400 acres in Ashe County (about 3 percent of the county's total land area) and 5,800 acres in neighboring
Alleghany County.

The Environmental Protection Agency eventually overruled the
"pollution dilution" scheme, and Stewart Udall, then U.S. Secretary of the Interior, subsequently stated that it was not a viable
concept. In 1968 APC concluded that increased demand for power
necessitated the construction of the larger project—with or without pollution dilution. But rural residents in Ashe County who
lived along the New River began to complain that their land and
their homes were being sacrificed to solve someone else's problems, since none of the electricity generated by the Blue Ridge
project was to be sold in their area. By May 1968 the stage was set
for a confrontation between the people living in Ashe and Alleghany counties and the "outsiders," who were regarded by the
residents as exploiters of their homeland. Meanwhile, four electric
cooperatives, including the Blue Ridge Membership Corporation,
which serves Ashe and Alleghany counties, intervened, contending
that any development on the New–Kanawha River system should
be undertaken by the federal government rather than by a private
utility.

The revised Blue Ridge project called for the construction of
two dams on the New River in Grayson County, Virginia, just
north of Ashe County. The upper dam would flood lands in North

Carolina. Water would be released by the upper dam to generate supplementary power during peak-use periods. During periods of lesser demand, water would be pumped from the lower reservoir back into the upper reservoir in readiness for the next period of high use. But the power needed to pump the water into the upper reservoir meant that the system itself would be a net consumer of power, consuming four units of power for every three it produced. Moreover, the facility was estimated to have a useful lifespan of only twenty-five to thirty years before silting would make it obsolete.

The short-term fluctuations of the levels of the lakes, the down-draws, were to exceed thirty feet on the lower reservoir and ten feet on the upper reservoir. The shoreline of the lakes would recede an average of five feet for every foot of down-draw, and down-draws would occur daily. At their lower levels, the lakes would thus be surrounded by unsightly mud flats. Although APC hired consultants in June 1968 to draft a recreational plan for the project area, it was never made clear how tourists were expected to contend with the muddy areas. The down-draws would reach their lowest point on Friday afternoons, about the time visitors would arrive for the weekend. Opponents of the project claimed that the river would be more attractive to tourists than the proposed lakes. In late 1968 the North Carolina State Wildlife Resources Commission issued a report contending that the lakes would not provide an environment conducive to fish, a detail that cast further doubt on the desirability of the lakes for tourists. On December 15, 1968, the *Winston-Salem Journal* reported the commission's findings and news of growing opposition in Ashe County to the Blue Ridge project.

APC, meanwhile, followed up its study of the recreational potential of the project by filing a report with the FPC that included a proposal to create two state parks, one in Virginia and one in North Carolina, adjacent to the lakes. APC would donate for public use the parkland and the thirty-one islands to be created along with the lakes. The power company also planned to spend more than a million dollars developing recreational facilities that it would own and operate.

The FPC had begun hearings on the revised proposal in March 1966. Although licenses for similar projects had often been issued

routinely, repeated interruptions and postponements extended the
FPC deliberations on the Blue Ridge proposal into 1970. At that
time the U.S. Senate Public Works Committee initiated its own
inquiry into the project. The following year the Watauga County
League of Women Voters came out against the project. In October
1971 Ashe and Alleghany counties requested that the FPC reopen
the hearings, contending that irreparable environmental damage
would result from the project. Hearings were held one month
later, but no conclusive actions were taken. The FPC commissioners decided to conduct an inspection of the area to be flooded
and the proposed dam sites. Even after the inspection, the FPC
continued its deliberations.

In the meantime, APC was acquiring the lands to be flooded
once the project was built. It was expected that 287 dwellings
would be flooded by the rising waters. APC's procedures for acquiring properties came under bitter attack from local residents,
who argued that they were intimidated into selling their land by
threats of impending condemnation. They then learned that the
Franklin Real Estate Company, the buyer for the project, was
owned by the American Electric Power Company, APC's parent
company. Officials at APC stated that there was nothing secret
about the activities or ownership of the Franklin Real Estate Company, which had existed for forty years for the purpose of separating company land earmarked for future use from land already in
use for power production. APC claimed that this was standard
procedure for utility companies. But local people also began asking whether all the properties being acquired were needed for the
project. Some suggested that Franklin was acquiring land that it
would resell to tourists at a large profit after the dams were on-line.

One informant, a native and long-term resident of the county,
charged that APC was mismanaging the acquired properties, rent-
ing the deteriorating dwellings to "undesirable" people. He claimed
that as a result assessment values were dropping, saving APC
property taxes that the county would otherwise have been able to
collect. In his words, "They have bought thousands of acres they
have just let go to hell." He also observed that some buildings
were being torn down in order to be taken off the tax rolls.

APC admitted that some buildings had been removed, but
stated that these buildings were "beyond economical repair" when

Figure 7. The New River (south fork).

acquired. Other purchased properties were being rented to prevent them from becoming run down, and many of the tenants were former owners who hesitated to leave their homes until the project was under construction. A company maintenance crew had also been assigned to the area to make necessary repairs. In sum, APC declared itself in compliance with all laws pertaining to the rental of substandard property. As to the charge that more property had been purchased than required for the project, APC explained that some properties had been acquired before the project plan was revised; these would be sold or traded with property owners on land within the revised project boundaries.

Despite various objections voiced at the hearings, the FPC licensed the project on June 14, 1974, effective the following January. Construction could not begin, however, until litigation brought by the State of North Carolina against the project was resolved and until Congress had studied the feasibility of designating the New River a "national wild and scenic river," thus ensuring environmental protection.

Local opposition had grown rapidly once the enlarged Blue Ridge project was proposed. During the North Carolina gubernatorial campaign in 1972, both candidates denounced the project. After his election, Governor James E. Holshouser asked the Department of the Interior to designate a portion of the New River in

North Carolina a national wild and scenic river. Under the Wild and Scenic Rivers Act, the Interior Department is authorized to promulgate such a designation once a state proposes it. The designation was thought to constitute an effective block against the Blue Ridge project, since federal law prohibits construction of dams along such rivers. On December 12, 1974, the U.S. House Rules Committee defeated a bill that would have prevented construction until the completion of studies of the New River's qualifications as a national wild and scenic river. But the State of North Carolina asked the U.S. Court of Appeals to reopen the FPC hearings even after the effective date of APC's licensing.

North Carolina argued that the FPC did not take into account the decreasing demand for energy, failed to consider the scenic-river designation, and did not adequately weigh the required environmental impact statements. An objection was also raised concerning APC's failure to compare other means of power production with the proposed project. The Interior Department delayed considering Governor Holshouser's request, unsure whether it could take action while the case was before the courts. But at the end of January 1975, the court announced that APC could not proceed until a full inquiry had been completed.

A few weeks before the court's ruling, the Committee for the New River was formed at a mass meeting in Raleigh, North Carolina, to orchestrate opposition to the project. The committee organized numerous publicity campaigns in the following months, highlighted by the Festival for the New River, which was held in Ashe County on July 26, 1975, and attended by an estimated five thousand people.

Another year passed, but neither the court nor the Interior Department had rendered a final decision. But 1976 was a presidential election year, and speculation began about whether or not President Gerald Ford would exert pressure on Interior Secretary Thomas Kleppe in an effort to win votes from Ronald Reagan in the upcoming North Carolina primary. On January 16, 1976, the Sierra Club's "National Report" called for a letter-writing campaign to protest the project. Letters from local residents, environmentalists, and sympathetic "Tar Heels" poured into the Interior Department and into the offices of congressional representatives. Geologists pointed out the importance of the river as the second-oldest river in the world (after the Nile), a history documented in *Scientific American* (Janssen 1952). Environmentalists noted that as many as twenty-three plant, animal, and insect species unique to the New River would be endangered by the dams and that many important unexcavated archeological sites (located but not reported by APC) would be flooded. Local people and their representatives in Washington, D.C., waxed eloquent on the natural beauty and historical importance of the river and the virtues of indigenous styles of life in Ashe County. Nationally syndicated columnist George F. Will quipped, "The FPC says the [power] plant's reservoirs would make dandy recreation areas. Yes, and Paris could demolish the Louvre to build a bowling alley" (January 26, 1976).

In the course of 1976, the New River dispute received considerable national attention. It was appropriated as a vote-getting issue in the presidential primaries in North Carolina, and major newspapers including the *New York Times,* the *Washington Post,* and the *Wall Street Journal* carried stories on the controversy's latest developments. The outcome still remained unclear: the New River's designation as a wild and scenic river would not necessarily prevent the construction of the dams, since the license had first been approved prior to the designation.

Indeed, in March 1976 the U.S. Court of Appeals in Washington, D.C., upheld the FPC's licensing of the project, requiring only one modification: the archeological remains were to be removed before flooding. The opposition immediately mounted an appeal to the Supreme Court. Interior Secretary Kleppe said he was uncertain that any decision by his department could interfere with a license already issued by the FPC, but on April 14 he signed a declaration including the New River in the national wild and scenic river system. Kleppe also said he would try to persuade the Justice Department to enter a friend of the court brief in support of North Carolina's appeal of the court's decision to uphold the license. Kleppe's action came on the eve of President Ford's campaign appearance in western North Carolina and included the statement that "the President is very much in support of these actions."

By May the stockholders of American Electric Power Company had been told that more than two hundred newspapers had come out against the Blue Ridge project and that presidential candidates

Jimmy Carter, Henry Jackson, Ronald Reagan, and Stewart Udall had gone on record against it. American Electric Power was threatening to sue the federal government for $500 million if Congress blocked construction of the project. The company's chairman was quoted as saying, "So help me, we're going to build it."

During the summer months, the House and Senate both considered bills to invalidate the license. Opposition to the project continued to grow. George Meany, president of the AFL-CIO, was invited to inspect the sites of the dams by the National Committee for the New River, a group organized by opponents of the project living in Ashe and Alleghany counties, and in Grayson County, Virginia. In the Blue Ridge and throughout North Carolina, bumper stickers and T-shirts featured the slogan The New River Like It Is. Although exact figures on the sentiments of Ashe County residents are unavailable, a poll taken by a regional newspaper found 233 against the project and 44 in favor—a ratio that reflects my impressions in mid 1976.

On August 11, the House of Representatives voted 311 to 73 to approve the bill introduced by Representative Stephen L. Neal (D-N.C.) designating 26.5 miles of the New River in Ashe County as a national wild and scenic river. The bill reaffirmed Secretary Kleppe's earlier designation and effectively revoked the license the FPC had issued. On August 30 the Senate approved the bill by a margin of 69 to 16. President Ford signed the bill into law two weeks later. The Securities and Exchange Commission subsequently ruled that American Electric Power had to sell all lands it had purchased to build the project. The Committee for the New River donated its archive to the Ashe County Public Library.

This sequence of events suggests, in broad outline, the sort of maneuvers undertaken by outsiders on behalf of their own interests and ostensibly those of the people living in the region. Although local residents, with the help of interest groups outside the region, defeated the dams, many changes were wrought by the fourteen-year "struggle," a word Ashe County people used to describe the dispute. To succeed, they had to "sell" their views to outsiders, to government officials, and to the media. As they sought to come to terms with outside institutions, they had to form an organizational matrix that could dovetail effectively with allies outside the county. And as they sought legitimation of their own social ideology in their representation of it to outsiders, their ideology was codified and changed, as was the context in which ideology was expected to endure as a basis of indigenous styles of life. This context was reordered materially and symbolically through the split between outsiders' efforts to appropriate it for their own uses and local people's efforts to contain that appropriation.

The success of the local residents who opposed the dams was thus purchased at the expense of partial accommodation, an accommodation consisting less in the adoption of or adaptation to the outsiders' cultural traits and orientations than in the imitation of outsiders' modes of argumentation and discourse. This move was more strategic than ideological, though it resulted in a certain restructuring of forms of local knowledge as well.

For the Appalachian Power Company, the issue was one of the "rational utilization of resources." The meaning of *rational utilization* came to be a focus of debate during the dispute. APC's approach to the argument was primarily based on geographic, economic, and demographic data, surveys, and statistics concerning the current and projected needs of the energy consumers that the company served. These projections, summaries, and representations of the proposed project and its "rationality" within the socioeconomic context defined by such data informed APC's politically constituted version of reality—one that Ashe County people had to encompass and counter in their responses.

The necessity of responding to outsiders' arguments compelled Ashe County residents to take account of both the data and the forms of discourse resulting from the imposition of this complex apparatus of observation and surveillance. That APC proposed to survey the river and adjacent land through such means of data collection and analysis immediately enmeshed local residents in a veritable wilderness of facts, figures, measurements, and delineations that did much to define the idiom in which the dispute would be fought.

The maelstrom of data referred to by APC claimed to codify the "rational utilization of resources." For many Ashe County people, the network of facts, figures, and projections constituted an incitement to create a comparable discourse of their own. In engaging the battle against the project, local residents thus acceded to this incessant mode of discourse about themselves, about their territory, and about the social patterns of relatedness to and domination by outside or national interests. Residents learned to quote statistics and survey data on acreage, hydrology, power generation, and erosion. They determined the impact of the proposed project on the local economy and identified habitual and valued social practices that would be affected by the project. And they learned to express such relevant "information" in the very terms outsiders used to promote the project. Thus when I suggest that for Ashe County people culture became more explicit and more problematic, I refer to this proliferation of discourses, self-understandings, and questionings.

The buzz and murmur of these new discourses at the same time constituted an ideological position, a positive form of knowledge about local identity and styles of life, and a rhetorical instrument for articulating power. What Ashe County people said about themselves to outsiders and to themselves was a mélange of traditionally based knowledge about families and domestic affairs and newly assimilated forms of analytic and statistical argumentation. Moral custom and well-researched "facts" kept uneasy if strategically felicitous company in their modes of self-representation.

Authorities and spokespersons for the county—and against the project—became adept at utilizing statistics, polling data, and their own survey research in coming to definitive and clear-cut conclusions and moral judgments on the matter. For instance, the chair of the Ashe County Board of Commissioners stated: "The dam is just not compatible with our environment as a rural, farm county. It would disrupt our whole road system in the north part of the county and would destroy a lot of farms in the area." One informant said that the dispute "hurt this county in so many ways. It's kept farmers from doing the things they would have done because they don't know whether their land will be flooded." A long-term resident of the county, and a small-scale farmer, said, "I wish they'd make up their minds. I've got some land that won't be flooded that I could move to. But I don't know whether to start building because I don't know what will finally happen." Referring to the problem of finding a new livelihood if forced off his land, another farmer said that "when a man has to change his life, doggone it, it costs him. If you are in the fertilizer business and that's all you know, it's tough to get started in something else."

Another farmer pointed out the implications of the project for local styles of life: "There are plenty of people around here who farm a half-acre of tobacco, keep a few cattle, and grow their own food. They're not rich, but they live good on an income of less than $3,000 [1975 dollars] a year. You take them out and put them somewhere else, and they won't be able to live in a rat race."

Others were more pejorative: "Our land is being destroyed to put money in the pockets of companies in Charleston, West Virginia." One man said that his great-great-grandfather fought in the Battle of King's Mountain, October 7, 1780: "[They] took up muskets to found the nation. Now we have just about thrown it away and I think we are going to have to take up the muskets again to get it back." Another informant had his own ideas about how to organize to prevent construction of the dams: "The dams proposed for the New River cannot be built if snipers simply shoot every man who appears on the location intent on building the dams."

In the words of another local resident, "It's home. I don't know if you know what I mean by that. Always spend your old days where you spent your young days. If you've sunk down roots, that's the way you feel." The interconnections of history, land, locale, and person are evident in many of the statements Ashe County residents made about the implications of the project for their lives: "I don't know what it is, but this little valley has a strange hold on the people who have lived here." Such statements are more than simple sentimentality: "Many of the people who have to leave say that they do not merely own their land. They say that they are part of it and it is part of them."

The emotional overtones in these statements are unmistakable: "The New River was part of my growing up. The thought of it dammed, its lovely course swallowed by a lake, the mountain coves and valleys drowned forever cuts like a knife. . . . If and when the New River vanishes, a part of my life will go with it." After the project was finally stopped, an older woman said that the dams "would just be too much uprooting of people's lives. I'm glad it didn't go through. My family is eating better, sleeping better, and working harder since the President signed the bill, and I have gained about a pound a day."

But before the outcome was certain, a particularly outspoken informant put the matter this way: "Let's save the New River for

North Carolina people. Otherwise, high-handed public utility officials in New York and the bureaucrats they control in Washington will have a free hand along the New River." A similar view was expressed by another informant: "Most people just flat aren't giving up. They're just bound and determined to stick this thing out, to stay with it till we win. All this has made people realize the bureaucratic system we're up against." The *Winston-Salem Journal* (January 25, 1976) reported: "Musician David Sturgill, who owns a guitar-making company in Piney Creek, said that if the river is dammed, his land will be left on a peninsula surrounded by water. He feels that the dams will not be built. 'It's time the little people won a battle against the bureaucrats,' he said."

Drawing from statements of this kind, the National Committee for the New River summed up the situation as follows: "Surely, the time is now here to bring an end to the uncertainty that has hung over the mountain people all these years and to preserve forever a unique part of our American heritage." In expressing these views in their own terms, local residents put "in solution" symbolic materials that would appeal to potential supporters on the outside, from environmentalists to members of other minority populations who have faced similar circumstances. Congressman Neal, whose district would have been affected by the construction of the dams, codified the rhetoric in a statement he read before the House of Representatives:

There is in my district a quiet place where Nature has wrought a masterpiece. It is in the highlands of Ashe and Alleghany counties, through which the New River and its tributaries flow. In all my wanderings, I have never gazed upon a scene more tranquil than this Valley of the New; nor have I ever met a people so obviously "at home." Here civilized man has lived in harmony with nature for more than two hundred years. Even in these turbulent times essentially he is at peace with himself and with his neighbor because he had learned, while still subject to the crown, that nature yields most to him who loves nature best.

This rhetoric eloquently stresses the aesthetic value Ashe County people associate with their environment. Land also provides a sense of rootedness, an intimacy and historical depth, and a source of nurturance. Local residents presented this set of meanings in universalistic and dramatic terms, clearly designed to make them immediately comprehensible, indeed compelling to the listener, and to promote their acceptance.

Not all Ashe County people were in sympathy with these views. Some local residents "shuddered at the thought of intrusion by outsiders," said one informant. But once the project was defeated, others argued that "now our population is going to stay in its normal decline. We can look forward to no industry, and kids driving down the street with no education." A few noted the economic benefits promised by the dams. One man cautioned those who worried about the county's tax base to consider that the land to be flooded would remain on the tax records at the value assessed at the time of the flooding. Others pointed out that such a procedure favored APC, precluding any appreciation of assessed values. Arguments on both sides frequently took on a pragmatic tone:

People think meat, milk and eggs are produced at the Piggly Wiggly. We can't go on covering up our most productive land. And the company is trying to seduce county officials by telling them they will gain a million dollars a year in taxes. But hell fire, they will lose more than three million dollars a year in agricultural production.

I asked a friend of mine who owns land along the river why he favors the project. You know what he told me? He said he could sell half of it for the state park and put up hamburger stands on the other half. Those were his words. (Laycock 1975, 62)

Outside proponents of the project structured their arguments mainly in terms of particular benefits rather than global parameters or overall impact. They frequently downplayed the local problems that the project might bring and stressed the national and regional advantages. Rarely did proponents refer to local values or ideology. For instance, APC ran an advertisement in *Time* (February 2, 1976), the *New York Times,* the *Washington Post,* and the *Wall Street Journal* that pointed out such benefits as a reduced dependence on gas and oil, the capacity for emergency energy for the eastern part of the United States, flood control, and economic and recreational development for the Appalachian region. This advertisement, which became notorious among infuriated conservationists and local residents, repeatedly referred to the "needs of the Nation" and the benefits of the project "for the people." But it referred to the acreage targeted for flooding as "underdeveloped"

and "not productive." The ad said nothing about the loss of land,
homes, and agricultural production. As a number of residents
pointed out, no one at APC seemed to have asked local people
what their preferences were, perhaps because they knew the project would garner little local support.

In response to the materialist arguments for the project and
those referring to national interests, opponents of the dams noted
the great wealth of archeological and historical material that would
be lost and cited the remarkable geological history of the New
River. While these various exercises in rhetoric continued, local
support groups, most of whose members were against the project,
developed. The Ashe County Citizens' Committee, formed in
1974 to oppose government control of the river, at first received
little attention from local newspapers or residents.

For the opponents of the dam, the major elements of the rhetoric of the dispute were codified on July 16, 1975, at the New River
Festival, held on the river bank near the joining of the north and
south forks. One member of the committee that organized the
event said it was to be "a day for fun and not politicking." This
statement, itself rhetorical in its persuasive and exhortatory intent,
in a sense served to premise the festival as a rhetorical statement on
a larger scale. The newspapers in surrounding counties and nearby
cities provided advance publicity. The festival's political objectives
were lost on no one.

The festival was held on a farm in the bottom lands that had
been worked by the same family for more than two hundred years,
a site chosen to accent the import of the event. As speakers pointed
out to those in attendance, if the dams were built, this land would
be under one hundred feet of water. Estimates of the turnout for
the festival varied: "thousands" of people from as far away as California were said to have attended to listen to the music, to picnic,
and to enjoy the scenery. Many local craftspeople displayed and
sold their woodcarvings, leather goods, jewelry, quilts, and other
wares; according to all reports, they did a land-office business.
Many local people contributed food and other necessities, and
costs were covered by a donation bucket that kept overflowing.
An information booth provided materials about the New River, its
history, its geology, and the dispute itself.

Actors in authentic costumes dramatized an epic written by local historian and genealogist Eleanor Reeves (1986, 9–16) to illustrate the grand sweep of local history from colonial times to the present. The narration sketched the changes that had come to Ashe County; it was punctuated by musical interludes, dances, and tableaux appropriate to each episode.

The narrator of the epic recounts the discovery and naming of the river in the eighteenth century, early surveys of the county, and the arrival of the first settlers just before the American Revolution. The number of "pioneer families" increases, and the first churches are founded by 1800. Soon, a territory that becomes Ashe County withdraws from Wilkes County, and the narrator tells the story of the founding of Jefferson as the county seat. Episodic details from the lives of prominent county figures of the early nineteenth century emphasize the rough-and-tumble life and landscape. The Civil War years follow. The railroad comes to Ashe County in 1914, and World War I takes its toll of Ashe County citizens. Mention of the "Roaring Twenties" situates the county's history in a broader context. The Great Depression does not hit Ashe County as hard as other places, thanks to the county's "agricultural advantages." The WPA (Works Progress Administration) provides employment and improves the county's road system. World War II takes the lives of some of Ashe's "promising young men."

This history is one of progressive movement. Impediments are turned to profit and tapped for the meaning each comes to have as testimony to the resilience and durability of Ashe County people. Throughout the narrative, the New River symbolizes Ashe County as a human landscape and a historical entity. "Ashe County is the best county in the state," a county notable announces. "Ashe County is a corridor of unspoiled beauty. New River was here when the only access to the outside world was by an old turnpike that followed the streams and wound around the hills rather than over them. The New River is our heritage. We want it left to flow gently on its way."

Entertainment during the festival was presented in a natural amphitheater formed by a curve in the river. The musical performers assembled by a local musician and lyricist included musicians from North Carolina and elsewhere. Bluegrass and country music predominated, and six original songs about the New River were premiered. Speeches given by state and federal officials, including members of Congress from North Carolina and West Virginia, were excerpted for television newscasts. Many of these speakers appropriated the rhetoric long in use among opponents of the project.

The celebration came to an end at nightfall. Hamilton Horton, an attorney from Winston-Salem and president of the National Committee for the New River, who had acted as master of ceremonies for the festival, was delighted with the results: "I've never seen anything like it. I've never seen volunteers work as hard and with such enthusiasm and such imagination. Everything went exactly as planned and without a single hitch."

The success of the festival was widely reported in newspapers and by North Carolina television stations. While organizers had presented the event as nonpolitical, as, rather, an elaborate family reunion, the political implications were unmistakable. The participants had come together to reinforce their opposition to the Blue Ridge project; the presentations on stage had distinct propagandistic tones. The event provided a forum through which grassroots opposition was transmitted to a larger public.

The festival was both a revitalization of some elements of local tradition and a rite of return. It was an attempt to give form to the uncertainties of the situation and to reinforce some of the meaningful associations that the Blue Ridge project threatened to neutralize. The symbols and meanings embodied in local culture—historical continuity, social inclusiveness, the primacy of the person in association with land—were not merely expressed but made more explicit in the context of a threat. The festival was an occasion for local people to become more self-conscious about who they were and what constituted their cultural background. It was a social setting for conjoining meanings aimed at reaffirming identity and defining cultural difference.

Key meanings in Ashe County social ideology were correlated with meanings from outsiders' political ideologies. For Ashe County people as well as for sympathetic outsiders, particular meanings were amplified, enriched, and modified by harmonizing elements from one domain with those of another. In summary, the key premises were basically these: We as local people are concerned with ensuring the continuity of our way of life. Because our life-style depends essentially on our land as a source of nurturance, the flooding of lands along the New River constitutes a threat. At the festival this conjunction of premises was aligned with those advocated by environmentally minded outsiders, who also perceived the flooding of lands along the New River as a threat. Similar algorithms prevailed for those valuing self-determination, local cultural distinctiveness, and the meaning of tradition as well as for those critical of "mass culture."

Although local residents and sympathetic outsiders both opposed the dams, their initial arguments began from differing assumptions. The commingling of their views was mutually reinforcing: the meanings, associations, and exemplifications of each group augmented and elaborated the other's, giving them each a much broader social scope. This mutually elaborated and shared discourse allowed alliances and reciprocal support to develop between people from the two groups. County residents recognized in the idiom of the environmentalists an echo and an elucidation of their own sense of the beauty of the land as well as its economic value. And in the residents' arguments environmentalists were reminded of the ecological basis of particular styles of life and means of livelihood. Moreover, the residents helped the environmentalists expand their ideas of air, land, and water pollution to include the pollution of an indigenous culture.

Those attending the festival came from diverse geographical and historical backgrounds. Together, they experienced a reaffirmation of local culture through the pageant of local history, protest songs, and the premising of the event as a great family reunion. But beyond that, the interaction among participants broadened the range and depth of meanings available to them for delineating a problematic situation. The festival shifted the import of the dispute from the local to the national level; it thickened the soup–mix of a growing culture of protest that had developed once the situation was predicated as a dispute. Among the social repercussions of the festival were a multiplied density of social contacts through which political influence could be conducted, the formation of new personal alliances and the strengthening of old ones, and an increased likelihood that individuals would actively participate in protesting the project. Letter writing—the pressure of public opinion—became another major channel of protest after the publicity and "consciousness raising" afforded by the festival and through the work of the National Committee for the New River. As an exercise in rhetoric, the letter-writing campaign appropriated persuasion, admonition, and exhortation to argue the case. It codified a particular approach to handling a collective problem; as Crocker (1977, 37) suggests, "the rhetorical strategy . . . is a stereotyped 'answer' for a general class of situations, an answer which in intent, codifies social opinion."

Premising the festival as a family affair integrated Ashe County canons of inclusiveness and diffuse solidarity into the discourse of the dispute. These elements of ideology functioned rhetorically to allow both the amplification and authentication of meaning. People from diverse backgrounds were encouraged to negotiate a sense of shared substance, sympathy, and understanding. The festival had a synergistic effect. In dramatizing the increase of protest into a veritable deluge, it also reproduced that growth, providing a rhetorical model and synopsis. The festival was not so much a turning point in the dispute as a wave that emerged from a tide of political consciousness that had risen little by little over time.

Ronnie Taylor, one of the organizers of the New River Festival, is a songwriter and musician who grew up in Ashe County. His ballad about the river was performed by his musical group, Homemade Jam, on the afternoon of the festival:

### Memories of My Mind

Well, I ran into a friend of mine
A-walking down the road the other day.
He said have you seen
        the valley full of water
Down there where I used to play?
Still in my mind I see it now,
The sky so blue, the sun so far away.
But they've torn the old homeplace down,
It's goin' under twenty feet a day.

Oh, when I was a little boy, I wandered
In green fields lost in time.
Oh, the sky was blue the sunshine through
Most all of the time.
But it's a hundred feet and rising
In the memory of my mind.

Oh, when I grow old I am told
I'll understand those questions
    in my mind.
Oh, I'll sit down in an easy chair.
Those questions will be answered
    there in time.
But it's two hundred feet and rising
In the memory of my mind.

Oh, the asphalt on the highways,
And the smog upon the skyways
Brings me down.
And it's two hundred feet and rising
All down around Mouth of Wilson town.
Yes, it's two hundred feet and rising
All down around Mouth of Wilson town.


(Located on the border that separates Virginia and North Carolina, Mouth of Wilson would have been entirely flooded by the
dams.)

    The composition and performance of the ballad was a symbolic
action and a rhetorical casting into dramatic form of themes of political import: the intrinsic worth and aesthetic meaning of land
and its association in Ashe County ideology with the continuity of
a rural style of life, and the essentiality of the homeplace and the
consequences of forgetting its importance. The song treats "civilization" as a polluting agent (asphalt and smog) that interrupts the
continuity of history and of the free-flowing river. Ronnie Taylor
wrote the ballad according to his own traditionally based sense of
musical and poetic form, but he also composed it as a public statement that would inject a certain set of meanings into the political
arena and structure the attitudes of his audience. He did not intend
the song to have a particular concrete result, but to prepare the
ground for bringing about a political outcome by crystalizing a set
of symbolic elements and presenting them compellingly. Clearly,
the efficacy of the ballad resides not only in its content but also in
its strategic performance in a certain social context, though the intended audience was not limited to those attending the festival. In
its ordering of complex meanings within the discourse spiraling
about the New River dispute, the song is addressed to local residents, outsiders, and anyone else willing to listen.

Ronnie Taylor's views on the dispute stressed the destructiveness of outsiders' interests. He distrusted their motives and strongly suspected that politicians might appropriate aspects of the dispute to promote their own objectives, while maintaining only a passing interest in the local situation. The planners of the festival were similarly conservative in their estimates of the interest in the dispute taken by people outside the county. They were also modest in their assessments of their own organizational expertise. Given their individualistic style, residents within the county formed a diffuse and somewhat unstable nucleus for a wider political organization. But, significantly, they provided the texts and symbols for building a movement. Ronnie Taylor explained that the festival was originally planned on a small scale, using "real down-home methods of publicity." It was to be strictly a gathering of local people. Although informal strategies of this kind appeared futile to some people associated with the dispute, the informality was in accord with the local cultural style and became the modus operandi for the struggle.

The festival was as unprecedented as it was unlikely, given local people's customary distrust of organizations, family reunions being a notable exception. Sidney Gambill, retired attorney and prominent organizer of the National Committee for the New River, summarized the scope of the festival and specified its importance for the larger struggle against the project: "The idea of a local home-town gathering appealed to people in Ashe County in a way that a large-scale thing would not have. The festival became a great success. There were literally thousands of people present, and a good time was had by all." Six months later, in January 1976, student organizers at Appalachian State University, adopting the idea of the festival, staged New River Preservation Week. There were again presentations of local music, history, and handicrafts; speeches were given; information on the many aspects of the dispute was disseminated. That day the organizers of the event obtained 5,100 signatures on a petition against the building of the dams. They hoped to present the petition directly to President Ford.

The many Ashe County people who did not become actively involved in the dispute limited themselves to hopes that somehow the Blue Ridge project would not be built. They made eloquent statements about the value they placed on their relation to local geography. Many offered recollections of family histories and of early settlement near the river, and they repeatedly praised the astounding beauty of the river and recited the tragedies that would befall people caught in the wake of the rising waters. Ronnie Taylor pointed out that "these local people don't do anything because they don't know what they can possibly do. When the eleventh hour finally arrives, there is nothing to do but capitulate to the power company's last offer, which is lower than the replacement price." He gave the following example of what would happen if the dams were built: "There is Gerald Crouse who farms the land where four previous generations of his family were born and raised and now lie buried. His property would be partially flooded by the dams."

Some of the more active Ashe County residents understood the value of addressing the local protest to the larger institutional framework while retaining their commitment to indigenous ideology. Stella Anderson, owner and editor of the county's weekly newspaper, did much to help form a small core of local people against the dams. She ran two or three stories on the New River in each weekly issue of the newspaper along with large photographs of the surrounding landscape. Each Wednesday before going to press, she phoned Sidney Gambill to ask him for last-minute bulletins. She was also a member of the board of the National Committee for the New River. Like Sidney Gambill, Stella Anderson had particular sorts of expertise, key social positions, and contacts outside the county that allowed her to disseminate what local people were saying and feeling about the Blue Ridge project. Ray Taylor, Ronnie Taylor's father, also used his influence as chairman of the Ashe County Board of Commissioners to spread and solidify opposition to the dams. These people, and others like them, were instrumental in amplifying the protests of Ashe County residents into a full-scale political movement. In developing networks and support within the county, local residents resorted to their long-standing cultural predisposition to mobilize the community in times of crisis (see Beaver 1976, 219; 1986, 55).

As local residents gradually became more active in the dispute, they also became more explicit about drawing a boundary between themselves as Appalachians and the external agents of "civilization"—more specifically, the proponents of the Blue Ridge project—as "outsiders." While inclusiveness became the cultural reference in seeking and broadening support and protest, premising the dispute as a struggle motivated the drawing of increasingly clear boundaries between one side and the other. Inclusiveness became contingent and functioned as a rhetorical device in negotiating political loyalties. Cultural difference and commonality became ethnicized and served as a means of defining support (see Chapter Four).

The construction of difference between "us" and "them" helped to partition the social universe delimited by the questions, who are we? and, who am I? This division may seem to counter a predisposition to inclusiveness, yet it is a familiar tactic in the local political arena, given the dynamic of party divisions. How to separate insiders from outsiders was only one of the many questions generated by the uncertainty with which local people were confronted, but it was a central one. Formerly, identity had been an implicit fact, an existential given. In the discourse of the dispute, the meaning of identity shifted, becoming an explicit element. The meaning of "being an Ashe County person" was up for debate along with the fate of the river and the land. Being from Ashe County, pursuing a particular style of life, meant and still means sharing a certain history and living out one's own history in a certain geographical region and on a particular parcel of land. But identity became politicized. Being Appalachian (an ethnic identity) and being a particular local person (a personal identity) ceased to be assumed ideological givens and became rhetorical means of asserting particular claims against the claims of outsiders as well as a means of determining alliance and support.

This construction of difference did not involve an absolute, quasi-racist distinction between local resident and outsider; individuals from the Blue Ridge joined with those from elsewhere during the struggle. But discussing cultural identity became an important way of bolstering the individual and collective aspects of Ashe County identity while outsiders were calling it into question.

In their case for the construction of the dams, outsiders implied a devaluation of the distinctive attributes of being a local resident, a discrediting of local culture, and the ascendancy of urban-industrial "civilization." As identity was politicized, the meaning of the person became articulated explicitly as but one element in an array of meanings in local culture. Culture itself became another element in the discourse of the dispute.

By explicating and emphasizing the inextricable interrelatedness of personal identity, life-style, and the meaning of land, local residents were able to argue that the dams could not be treated as an isolated issue of energy or economics. The rhetorical import of identity and ethnicity as highly charged symbols rephrased the terms of the debate. Proponents of the dams could no longer argue their case on the basis of economic advantages alone; they would have to argue against the integrity of local culture as a whole, integrity itself being a rhetorical device that county residents presented as a self-evident given. Local people based their case on this premise and the hope that no counterargument to it could be sustained. From this perspective, the rhetoric against the project was designed to back proponents into a corner. Proponents would somehow have to demonstrate legitimately how local residents could be disenfranchised from such core American values as self-determination and free choice. They would have to show that Ashe County identity, life-style, and culture could justifiably be subordinated to higher (national) priorities without invalidating enshrined meanings of American democracy and independence.

Opponents of the Blue Ridge project, in turn, had to present their arguments in particulate form, addressing each situation according to its particular demands and exigencies. They negotiated the legitimacy of their opposition to the dams on what amounted to a binary choice: the legitimacy of economic priorities and the power of "outsiders" (as one informant said, of the "officials in New York and the bureaucrats they control in Washington") versus the legitimacy of individual rights, cultural integrity and diversity, and the land as a historical source of nurturance and livelihood. In asserting the primacy of the latter alternative, Ashe County people appealed to the Jeffersonian values of freedom and the inviolability of the individual. That the dams were not built suggests the institutional ascendancy of this second alternative— but the victory was not as decisive as it first appeared.

During the initial stages of the dispute, it seemed possible for local preferences to be taken into account through administrative channels. But once the arbitration of the dispute reached the courts, it had become clear that Ashe County people would have to argue their case within particular strictures and constraints. The intricacy of the legal structure and the shifting locus of decision making became an occasion for rhetoric on both sides of the dispute. Given the limited alternatives—the dams, the scenic-river designation, or violence—a legal-bureaucratic definition of the situation, rather than a locally devised one, became inescapable.

The National Committee for the New River published a position paper in November 1975 that expressed the "official" local response to this situation. Titled "The Struggle for the New River," this document is of special interest because it represents and codifies local views and presents them in a style calculated to appeal to government administrators and politicians.

The document is carefully and lucidly written according to the genre conventions of rational fact-finding and argument characteristic of government and corporate-management discourse. Neatly typed and divided into brief chapters, it astutely summarizes the history of the dispute and the environmental and social consequences of various outcomes, and it sets these concerns within terms relevant to legal and congressional consideration. In coming to an overall assessment, the paper quotes carefully selected facts and figures as well as the opinions of strategically placed spokespersons. It also analyzes the details of the proposed project in relation to the demands of the national power industry. Finally, it provides a sober overview of the legal arguments for and against the licensing of the project.

The document as a whole made excellent fare for the boardroom, the court chamber, and the public hearing. Subdued and laconic in some passages, it becomes impassioned in its final evaluation. The arguments are clear—cut and sharply defined, concluding with a forceful overview of the situation as the committee understood it at the time:

For almost 10 years, the embattled farmers of the New River Valley have been fighting the power company's scheme to take away their land and livelihood. Today they are willing to accept control on the use of their land, under the terms of the Scenic Rivers Act, to keep their way of life. . . ."

In licensing the project, the Federal Power Commission bent the law while approving a power project that would consume more energy than it generated. Since the commission's hearings, it has become clear that projects such as the Blue Ridge contribute to our power problems rather than help solve them.

The New River may be the oldest river in North America. The project that would destroy most of the ancient river would have a lifespan of only a few decades. It would be built at a net cost both to the nation's power supply and the economy. It would uproot 3,000 people [in two states] who want only to be left alone.

A writer in the Izaak Walton League publication two years ago stated the cause well: "If those virgin lands with their pure sparkling streams and waters—these people who trace their ancestors back to the first settlers of their present homeland—this only remaining portion of a pre-historic river—are of no significance to American history and culture, then we truly have no history, and this project signifies much more than the death of a river."

While written under quite specific historical circumstances to de-lineate a specific situation, a noteworthy aspect of this rhetoric is its insistence on addressing the issues by defining them relative to the absolutes of local history and culture as unassailable features of social life.

The committee published its report as the final push for the scenic-river designation was getting underway. The report's tightly integrated rhetoric provided ammunition in highly quotable form, which could easily be (and was) cited in a variety of circumstances. Some Ashe County people were uneasy about some of the report's finer points, but by then the lines had already been drawn.

Indeed, the bargaining and exhortation on both sides of the dis-pute sometimes went against the grain of local people's expecta-tions of their social experience. Their idealizations posit a world in which doors need never be locked, in which representations di-rectly reflect the realities of everyday life, where people can be trusted, and in which meaning is not constantly contested. In the course of everyday life, the rhetoric of these idealizations operates in the molding of behavior in upbringing and in moral proscrip-tions, in the ceaseless negotiation of power relations, and in the formation of cultural identity. Up to a point, manipulation and re-formulation can proceed without threatening key points of social ideology.

Within the larger political arena of the dispute, rhetoric was of more than folkloristic interest. In a tactical attempt to win the debate with APC and various federal agencies, rhetoric was used to motivate the reworking of meaning and the reshaping of ideological form to produce a specific social effect. The resulting shifts in how discourse was formed and expressed entailed a comprehensive explication and enumeration of images, concepts, themes, and representations designed to promote a specific self-definition.

To defeat the dam, local residents had to develop a discourse that had the power to describe their culture in a way that would be taken seriously by outsiders (Hamon 1981). The discourse presented as "exhibits" by local residents to outsiders often had an abstract, schematic, even hyperbolic flavor. Yet this knowledge that they claimed about themselves resonated forcefully with actual social practices. The rhetoric thus had a normative aspect in defining practices according to a scale of values about what was expected or excluded. Emotional statements and personal anecdotes were backed up by statistics, and representative individual cases were cited to describe a general pattern. Much of the appeal of these diverse rhetorical maneuvers resided in the aura of authenticity they conveyed: to be credible to outsiders, they first had to become credible to those who expressed them. Part of the power of this rhetoric derived from the close link between discourse and practice. The discourse on local custom, geography, and history was tactically deployed but also made reference to the core of local social ideology. It became incessant, meticulous, vehement, obsessive, a veritable semiotics of identity. Its rhetorical import encompassed a pedagogy directed at outsiders, but it also instructed local people about themselves.

Organizers of the movement against the dams realized that developing a rhetoric with broad public appeal was just the beginning. They had to go on to develop strategies for communicating their message to the courts, legislatures, and federal agencies and for achieving results in each of these forums. Thus a discontinuous, fragmentary, piecemeal discourse—a medley of heterogeneous voices, styles, and stances—emerged during the dispute to fit the particular contexts through which the debate was inflected. The rhetoric structured the specific way the case was presented not only to the public but to the politicians and administrators as well. These microadaptations, the many variant discourses posed in diverse contexts, did much to enhance the effectiveness of the movement.

Once it had become clear that the FPC would issue a license, opponents had to find a specific maneuver that would result in overturning the license. At this juncture, the rhetoric produced by local residents, ranging from emotionally charged appeals to legalistic and highly rationalized arguments, posed the issue as a binary choice (the dams versus the scenic-river designation) but could do nothing to broaden the alternatives. The bureaucratic or administrative slots into which the dispute was channeled had already been fixed by legal fiat. The effectiveness and intrinsic appeal of local rhetorical maneuvers influenced which alternative was chosen, but the scenic-river designation was a choice externally formulated and imposed. It was less a choice than a concession, and President Ford's signing of the bill was politically fortuitous.

Clearly, there was substantial agreement in Ashe County that the dams should not be built. But for many residents, opposition to the dams did not mean easy agreement with the scenic-river alternative. In fact, neither alternative could be made to square readily with local preferences. Many residents felt they were "between a rock and a hard place"; the situation was a double bind that made it impossible for them to have the New River "like it is." Either way, changes would come that threatened what local people regarded as a relatively secure present, making the future problematic. Many Ashe County residents responded angrily to estimates of the large number of tourists who would be attracted to the county each year by the newly designated scenic river, a response telling in itself, given the financial gains promised by tourism (cf. Bingham 1978).

One resident claimed that few people would want the New River included in the federal system if there were any other way to stop the dams: "Federal control no matter how slight is unpopular among independent mountain families." She feared that such a designation would be "a forerunner of federal domination and intervention and muddling in the affairs of Ashe County." Not knowing what would happen in the long run, many local people expressed considerable frustration and resentment at not having any "real choice" about what sort of change was to come. Their definition of the situation as an issue of local autonomy had been instrumentally co-opted, and the dispute had become an irrelevant debate over two lines of action, neither of which was altogether desirable. By indigenous standards, effective action was precluded as it had been for most of the fourteen years of the controversy.

One angry resident stated the case in a newspaper editorial:

Land taken by the Scenic River system will be taken off the tax books forever, and the loss will have to be taken care of by raising other taxes. Land owned by the power company will be taxed forever, and the tax can be raised as the company acquires more land. All the Scenic River land could be used for is recreation. There will be parking for thousands of campers, and it is easy to see why people want to send that unwanted mob up here. . . . Some of us have pledged to vote against any man who wants the park service to take over the land.

Some people feared that the scenic-river designation might also limit their control over the use of private land. "What good is it to own land if you can't do what you want with it? I'd say, if most people had to choose between the dams and the scenic river, they'd take the dams." Another editorial dramatized the bind in which many local people felt the dispute had placed them:

And there are the people . . . who take pride in owning land and making it produce for them, people who by and large want nothing so much as to be left alone with the resources they have, to do with them as they will. That perhaps is the most poignant fact in the whole complex, 14-year controversy—that the people in those three counties would simply prefer to be left alone, with no dams and no formalities of "scenic river" designation; and that, whatever happens now, is no longer possible. The publicity and the resentments and frustrations built over the past 14 years have already brought changes. Declaring the New River a Scenic River would bring more. Building the dams would bring the most of all.

Rhetorical maneuvers had stopped the dams, but a tacit understanding of the rhetoric as politically motivated, rather than as springing unalloyed from social ideology, helped to create differences among Ashe County people. Behind the rhetoric of local residents was the perception that they were being compelled to address options imposed on local affairs by the interests and institutions of outsiders, that their choices were constrained by external

laws and bureaucracies. Although local representations emphasized long-standing local values and understandings of social life,
the debate had been framed by outsiders so that Ashe County residents could not really win on their own terms.

Once local residents recognized that they faced two undesirable
alternatives, the consensus that had made possible a unified dissent
fragmented into a range of preferences for the dams, for the scenic-
river designation, and for neither. Some people referred to "getting out the muskets and the dynamite." Some argued that either
of the available alternatives would encourage unwanted "development" in Ashe County. Others had it in mind to "cash in" on the an-
ticipated invasion of tourists—or such was the accusation launched
against them by other county residents. Everyone recognized that
the long-range consequences of either alternative could not be predicted. No single delineation of the situation seemed satisfactory.
Some people oscillated, favoring one alternative and then another,
and considerable dissension developed among Ashe County people.

Activists spearheading the opposition to the project had initially
contended that they could negotiate a viable path through the
maze of government agencies and legal structures by reformulating some of the major elements of social ideology in rhetorical
terms. But these reformulations of indigenous responses were limited or constrained, if not deconstructed, by the requirement that
they address a set of options strictly defined by outside institutions. Each of the conflicting opinions held by local people regarding the possible outcomes of the dispute represented an instance of
"being right" in relation to local definitions. Because such "right"
delineations were thwarted by the undesirable alternatives mandated by outside agencies, local understandings became somewhat
irrelevant; they were co-opted or nullified by the no-win situation.

Bateson (1972, 241) describes the disorienting experience of an
individual confronted with a double bind: "Every move which he
makes is the common sense move in the situation as he correctly
sees it at the moment, but his every move is subsequently demonstrated to have been wrong by the moves which other members of
the system make in response to his 'right' move." For Ashe County
residents, the result was cognitive and political dissonance. The
sum total of their varied responses and their negated trial formula-

tions created a perpetual, perseverative sequence, an oscillating cycle of discursive "attempts" or rhetorical ploys.

Bateson (1972, 243) also notes that persons finding themselves in a double bind experience a loss of identity. It is not difficult to understand how people whose knowledge and values have been made contingent or subordinate to those of others may come to perceive that their very identity as persons is likewise besieged. In response, Ashe County people attempted in diverse, often conflicting, and sometimes strident ways to reassert the cultural identity they felt was being lost to them.[4]

A third characteristic of a double bind is an asymmetry of power or control (Bateson 1972, 237). Although the regime of outside bureaucratic representations, conceptions, and categories was not entirely foreign to local residents, their adaptation to these forms constituted a largely nonreciprocal concession to "civilization." Discourse at the local level had to be re-formed to fit legal-bureaucratic terms, while the latter did not significantly change to accommodate the terms of Ashe County people. Local residents came to view their own ideology as encompassed by "civilization." The new relations between indigenous meanings and those of the encompassing "civilization" themselves became elements in a revised understanding of history and social life. The historical meaning of the dispute was "up for grabs," with the result that history was no longer a given, but a rhetorical form that could be manipulated and remodeled. Uncertainty and rhetoric came to be embodied as meanings associated with the particular historical events of the dispute.

The establishment of new meanings occurred as an event—the dispute itself—and so these meanings entered Ashe County ideology as historical "facts," grudgingly acknowledged. The accommodations local people formulated, the political rhetoric through which they articulated their opposition to the Blue Ridge project, became one aspect of the asymmetry between residents and outsiders.

Although it was Ashe County residents who predicated the dispute as a conflict, it was never premised as a dispute between equals. For county residents, "civilization" was a force to be reckoned with. For outsiders, the opponents of the project were an obstruction to be set aside rather than a group with legitimate demands and claims. Compromise was not initially part of APC's plan. As the dispute continued, Ashe County residents increasingly came to understand the asymmetry in terms of victimization, a not unfamiliar feature of Appalachian experience.[5] They began to see "being a victim" as unfortunately consistent with how they have to live and who they are. Understandably, a pattern of ambivalent, approach–avoidance responses derives directly from these conditions.

The various arguments in favor of the Blue Ridge project made by outsiders created a veritable wilderness of disembodied meanings. Each argument, each definition of the situation, was taken to be at least potentially real by Ashe County people. But as one definition succeeded another, as a new one replaced an earlier one, county residents realized that none of the definitions (or which?) had real substance for outsiders, though they presented them as authentic. Ashe County people were being given the runaround. Any authentic negotiation was precluded by the repeated substitution of allegedly authentic representations, each of which proved to be a pose easily set aside for yet another pose.[6] The dizzying parade of outsiders' representations, each composed of complex bureaucratic minutiae, thwarted concerted local action. Confronted with an ever-taller pile of articulations, local people found it difficult to "get to the bottom" of the matter. While residents struggled to unscramble the situation, outsiders kept their attention fixed on the "bottom line."

The last act of this struggle was played out in February 1977, six months after the New River had been designated a wild and scenic river. Landowners along the river had gradually learned that the designation brought with it some unwanted ramifications. Under the Wild and Scenic River Act, the State of North Carolina could acquire properties along the river through donations, the negotiation of a scenic easement, or an order to condemn the land under eminent domain. State officials announced they would acquire land "to the horizon," which in the irregular terrain in the vicinity denotes a fairly narrow strip of land on either side of the river. No state funds had been appropriated for land acquisition, but Ashe County landowners were embittered by the sight of state surveyors walking about on their land and by the thought of what they might have to "sacrifice" to the state.[7] In a striking oscillation of opinion, some landowners circulated a petition calling upon the government to reassess the viability of the Blue Ridge project and demanding that the FPC's original decision to license the project be upheld.

The supporters of this petition were far fewer in number than the group that had supported the scenic-river designation, indicating a "dampening" of the wave of oscillating responses to the situation. Many of the petitioners had been uninvolved in the earlier protests; others had formerly supported the scenic-river designation. One consequence of these new protests was that some outsiders inferred that local people simply did not know what they wanted and that all their preferences and objections could therefore be discounted.

It is not clear what sort of effect the protestors expected their petition to have. They thought of sending it to the White House or to members of Congress. One informant said that the petition was merely a way for people to express their dissatisfaction with the arrangement and to "say we've been stepped on." APC gave no indication that it would reconsider building the dams, and most people who signed the petition doubted that APC would stir. The "powers that be," perhaps without explicit intention, made their point more insidiously by allowing the dispute to trail off. Local people were never able to determine exactly "who had the power"—yet another source of their exasperation, since they mistakenly assumed that there *was* someone in particular who had authority.

Though the dams will not be built in the foreseeable future, all agree that "civilization" has wrought seemingly irreversible changes in Ashe County and that the New River dispute represents a major discontinuity in local history. Since Ashe County ideology holds social identity to be intimately bound up with history, both individual and collective, historical discontinuity implies a major shift in the meaning of identity. The pervasive uncertainty evoked by the New River dispute has become part of the meaning of time and "future history." (It is not the first time that intrusions of "civilization" into the Blue Ridge region have proved to be a source of uncertainty.)

History is a symbolic system that local people divide into three stages: past, present, and future.[8] The past is the totality of closed cases of experience within which they situate their social and cultural identity; the sense they have of themselves flows from who their ancestors were and what they accomplished. The past is constructed along rhetorical lines, viewed not as a panorama of exploitation and discontinuity but as a landscape pervaded by nurturance and growth. The past is fixed, determined, finished. It was progressive; it encompassed an image of life progressively opening up, going on, moving forward: the land being tamed, being gradually but assuredly domesticated and providing nurturance in return. Local culture is regarded as securely rooted in this past, the legitimate heir and offspring of that past, representing the provisional endpoint of a natural, inevitable evolutionary pathway. Genealogy is the representation of this past in the family context; upbringing is its representation in the context of personal history and identity. Ashe County history is enshrined as the compendium of Ashe County cultural identity.

The present is history in the making, the sum and substance of everyday life. It lacks the definitive clarity of the past, for it is the unresolved here and now, history in process, the undertakings of particular individuals working hour by hour and day by day. The present is this process of giving the moment a working definition, situation by situation, articulated and shaped in cultural terms and acted upon or acted out.

For many Ashe County people, the future is altogether unclear in two senses: People do not know what it will contain, and they are often unwilling to speculate about it. They have no assurance that it will "happen" at all. Their one certainty is that history cannot continue as it has, the future will not continue to embody the shape of the past, as progressive and ever-advancing. The past as culturally conceived gives no clear indication as to the content of the future, apart from its essential uncertainty. The future appears clouded and largely without prospects, since the present is experienced as the sum of oscillations that always return to their point of departure.

The New River dispute has contributed significantly to this "problematization" of the future. When local delineations of the dispute came to be experienced as unactable, progress and movement were viewed as having been negated. History had come up against a conundrum; "civilization" had erupted into history and encompassed it. Local people do not know what the future will bring or how to plan for it, only that it will be profoundly different from the past. When pressed to give a prognosis, informants were rarely hopeful. They claimed not to be able to think very clearly or optimistically about the future. At best, it will be "different" and "interesting," but devoid of the "real progress" that characterized the past.

"Civilization" is an obvious euphemism. As representation, it embodies a contradictory view of time and history in which the past is discontinuous with the present and future. "Civilization" is the intervening variable, the mediator, the newly inserted category, or so local people regard it in the course of strategically denying aspects of their past. The ancestors of present-day county residents helped arrange the cultural domination of the indigenous Cherokee, just as "civilization" now comes to dominate local residents. "Civilization has its place," said an informant, but it was not difficult to read between the lines the message, "I hope it stays away from here." The implicit paradoxes and ironies of this avowal of an acceptance of civilization exemplify the ambivalent responses Ashe County people have to other situations, such as the encounter with tourism. These ironic microslices of discourse betoken people's sense of not having the knowledge (skills or expertise) to control the engines of change ("civilization") larger than themselves.

The proposal to build dams on the New River demonstrates civilization's intrusion into an arena in which localism or local identity had been strong. As a result of the dispute, localism may have become even stronger. For Ashe County people to think of themselves as culturally distinct from middle-class Americans, as an ethnic minority in which class is overturned or underplayed, is one means of attempting to resist what are regarded as majority, perhaps national, pressures compelling them to "join the club" or "jump on the bandwagon" of modernity. Locality was brought into the rhetoric of the dispute as a representation in and of local *culture*, the "countryside" being viewed by many of its residents as a totalized, autonomous social geography. "Ashe County" was more than a way of designating "where we live"; it had become an emotionally charged representation of a definable, coherent, and besieged body of local knowledge. Ashe County was the proper space in which this knowledge would be put into action. This territory is thus the locus of a social globalism—the whole world, or the whole world for these people, is *here*. Similarly, "civilization," in the indigenous view, entails urban living, where this globalism is replaced by a fragmented, discontinuous social field in which people ceaselessly struggle to put the fragments into a livable whole. Many Ashe County people recognized the attractions of urban life, but told stories of local residents who migrated to the city, lived troublesome lives there, and were at last estranged from their families "back home."

Treating history as a symbolic system, county residents have situated the New River dispute in terms of the division of history into past, present, and future, each having a distinct character. The dispute's unhappy resolution embodies county residents' concept of an unresolved present and an unresolvable future. The "history of the present" is a trap, a no-win situation arising from discontinuities that they regard as having been thrust upon them. They say, "Well, it's been going on for more than ten years now, and it will probably go on for another ten years." By "it," they mean not only the New River dispute but a whole panoply of social and cultural transformations.

I have shown how the initial enthusiasm for the scenic-river designation was soon superseded by discontent. Was it just a political maneuver? Were the local issue and the concerns of local people used by officeholders simply to gain public recognition on a national scale? Does the outcome ensure that the dams will not be built? These difficult questions and others like them suggest how problematic the history of the present has become. The uncertain, oscillating responses to these questions and to the alternative "resolutions" are symptomatic of the pervasive distrust, disenchantment, and insecurity generated by the controversy. The intervention of "civilization" was already underway once the power company became an owner of land in the county. APC's presence initiated a powerful rhetoric of control, a discourse that bedeviled the understanding Ashe County people had of their history and culture. In demanding a response in its own terms, that discourse compelled local people to revise their understandings of themselves and their circumstances.

To dam or not to dam the New River: Either outcome promised changes that local people wanted to avoid. Even without the dams, the scenic-river designation is bound to change the ecology of the county and of the symbolic system as well. The attraction of a designated scenic river will bring many more tourists and outsiders to the county, and even a modest increase in the number of tourists passing through or of Floridians buying land will transform the local cultural and economic balance. Ashe County people are caught in an unresolved present and perceive a future shaped by others. The representations through which residents envision a life for themselves and create a viable discourse among themselves and with others are likewise problematized.

The difficulties these transformations pose for Ashe County people do not derive from an inability to cope with change as such or from a rigid adherence to tradition; they have sought change from time to time in their own ways. Instead, the difficulties reside mainly in the particular nature of these changes: they are perceived as imposed without choice from the outside. The Ashe County ideology, of history as progressive and of the person as self-sufficient, leaves residents culturally unprepared to cope with changes they have not welcomed or devised. Specifically, imposed change runs counter to a definition of the person as autonomous, self-motivating and as the locus of decision making and action; imposed change counters the delineation of history as the progress achieved by actions individually advocated and individually undertaken. The dispute over the New River has therefore undermined the understanding of history as progressive, continuous, and determined by the choices made by local people to act and thereby shape the present. A lack of confidence in the "history of the present" leads to an uncertain sense of individual and cultural identity. Sartre (1963, 96) points out that society "is presented to each man *as a perspective of the future.*" For Ashe County people, an uncertain future means a larger existential uncertainty, both in oneself and in the encompassing society.

*Chapter Four*

# You Can't Go Home Again

Henry Shapiro's *Appalachia on Our Mind* (1978) is a thought-provoking study of the emergence of Appalachian "otherness" during the late nineteenth and early twentieth centuries. Shapiro traces the social construction of the concept of the region and its culture undertaken by missionaries, philanthropists, educators, and writers with diverse motivations and equally diverse ways of understanding its people. "Appalachia" was generally recognized as an impediment to the creation of a nationwide social and cultural system. This presumption resulted in a widely shared notion that the region was a problem and had problems that were to be addressed by various social programs. Only more recently has Appalachian otherness been reformulated as an acceptably distinct region and culture, rather than a deviant society subject to normalization.

One might argue that the notion of Appalachia as a distinctive and creditable variant of American culture remains a minority opinion. As a "strange land and peculiar people," Appalachia still evokes notions of an underdeveloped, backward, and poverty-stricken region. It is also recognized as a backwater of cultural holdovers, preserving and sequestering remarkable musical, folkloric, and artistic traditions—a repository of Anglo-American heritage. The connotations and associations are profoundly ambiguous; in this guise, Appalachia is a resource from which mainstream America can pick and choose, depending on strategic necessity or the politics of a given moment. Today, the region's otherness is represented as legitimate cultural distinctiveness *and* as a problem.

In Ashe County, particular selections from this repository of images have informed the creation of conflicting discourses by various groups seeking to preserve resources or to promote certain political interests and ways of life. Negative stereotypes of Appalachia and Appalachians no doubt have long figured in the background of attempts to legitimate the appropriation of local resources by outside interests. Although rarely or only indirectly referred to, these stereotypes are the cutting edge of a rhetoric of control designed to promote and legitimate the pursuit of so-called national interests in opposition to local ones. In the dispute over the New River, this rhetoric was counterbalanced by other specifically local discourses that played up Appalachian otherness as viable, appropriate, and appealing—as a distinctive culture with a vitality and historical respectability of its own.

Ashe County is thus a crossroads where these heterogeneous and discontinuous understandings of culture and society are being played out. As Shapiro's book suggests, an understanding of the interplay of external and indigenous discourses is necessary in order to grasp what social issues prevail, what social life is like, and what social change involves in places such as Ashe County. The particular ways in which the conflicting discourses of otherness, identity, and social life are untangled, counterposed, claimed, and argued over constitute a site at which the relation between local culture and "civilization" is articulated and addressed. The particular representations of culture, self, and region manifested in these contending discourses both explain and bring about the political dynamic that structures such relations. The knowledge claimed and established at a given point in time about culture, landscape, and persons situates the filigree of power and dominance that has come to prevail. In Ashe County, this power-knowledge nexus was very much in flux and subject to hot debate during the New River struggle. In Chapter Three, I discussed how this fluctuating, oscillating, and unstable condition has informed the representation and rhetoric of local culture as understood by insiders and posed to outsiders. In this chapter, I examine in greater detail the relation between local and external representations in order to suggest a critical understanding of how the relation between "local culture" and the "dominant culture" is experienced in Ashe County.

While Appalachia represents the Other for those outside the region, Ashe County natives clearly see "civilization" as an embodiment of otherness that demands comprehension because of its presence and its interventions in the county. Personifying civilization as the Other does not, as local people would hope, lead them to a clear understanding of its operations; personifying civilization does not readily allow them to identify particular persons as accountable for the interventions and thus does not offer insights that can readily be put into practice. Alternatively, to define civilization as an inhuman force only makes the situation appear hopelessly formidable. It is only through particular confrontations, such as the New River dispute, that county residents can represent and act in response to the Other.

Such events have increasingly challenged Ashe County people to reflect upon the nature of social life, what it is, and what it should be. As "civilization" becomes a more pervasive influence in the Blue Ridge, local residents have begun to seek a more coherent formulation of individual and collective identity. They have historically viewed social experience as totalized and structured by individual initiative and self-determination, but such a notion has increasingly been called into question. They have preferred to see society as a collection of discrete persons who understand their lives as moving progressively and continuously through history. In an ideology of this kind, the person is understood to be "the unit of action which articulates what seem to be different domains and characteristics" (Barnett and Silverman 1976, 33). Thus, reflection is customarily tied to concrete, individual action. The person as concept is the basis for delineating understandings of the larger social institutions, which in turn fix the character of society at large.

In both American society and in Ashe County, the paradigmatic individual "is not just any person, but is a person who dominates and who is dominated in a particular way. People who are personally dominated appear as substantially incomplete or defective, as lesser individuals" (Barnett and Silverman 1976, 2). The notion of Appalachia as a problem and the stereotype of Appalachians as hillbillies suggest how outside domination has come to redound

on outsiders' perceptions of local identity. In order to grasp the
relevance of these constructs for the county's external political relations, one must juxtapose them with the deeply seated subjective
understandings of Ashe County residents themselves. In addressing this topic, I find it useful to begin with what may appear to be
a detour: a discussion of sex roles as a domain of central relevance
to local understandings of the person. The cultural understanding
of the difference between female and male in Ashe County is
worthy of special attention as a prelude to the topic of cultural
domination because it reveals how indigenous definitions of the
person are connected with the dynamic of local identity and
societywide issues.

As elsewhere in American society, in Ashe County male-female
differences are represented by the anatomical features distinctive to
each sex. This natural difference is elaborated socially by clothing,
comportment, and ideological assumptions about male and female
modes of interaction and behavior. The specification of a range
of tasks conventionally performed by males and by females (role
expectations) is reflected in a dimorphism in personality imagery (detachment/compliance) and in supposed sexual inclination
(aggression/passivity).

Being female or male remains a basic feature of social identity in
Ashe County. It is recognized that one may not always be able to
act out every facet of one's sexual identity, but one is expected to
do so whenever possible. The assignment of different roles to men
and women (and to boys and girls) is encompassed by history as
culturally understood. Sex roles are described in reference to upbringing, to family history, and to a recollected past. The way a
given task was performed by a man or a woman "in the old days,
on the farm" is considered directly relevant to present practice.
Thus one of the controlling contexts of sex differences is the construction of a role as a concept with a history (Keesing 1970).
People assume that everyone has a job to do, or should have one.
Social identity is conceivable once a role has been established for a
person to fulfill, and sexual identification is a basic element in establishing such roles and practices.

General expectations for the behavior of men and women do
not necessarily correspond to those pertaining to specific persons—to say nothing of the divergence between expectation and

actual performance. When one's behavior falls outside a certain
range of expectation, one may be regarded as having "stepped out
of line," having done violence to nature, having made a mess of
things, or one is being difficult, eccentric, or even a bit mad. But
under most circumstances, "mucking up the works," transgress-
ing role assignments, or contaminating the purity of customary
categories does not necessarily lead to ostracism or rejection. Ashe
County people are not irrevocably antisocial to people who take
exception to standard practices. People gossip about others' "deviant" behavior, make fun of it, or relegate contaminating "evidence" to the private domain. But they also consider certain personal information to be "none of our business" and dissemble
what may be common knowledge.

In Ashe County, the male-female distinction is not carried
through without contradiction. Women sometimes perform tasks
thought to be basically male, such as working in the fields. Men
sometimes perform kitchen work or house cleaning, though such
work is generally taboo according to social ideology. These cross-
currents themselves have an ideological basis: particularly under
the constraints of recent economic or material necessity, pragmatism may supersede the customary male-female division of labor. When a job needs doing, it may be less important who does it
than that it gets done.[1]

Crossings of the male-female boundary are anomalies that elicit
reactions of confusion, anxiety, and sometimes hilarity. Such crossings may also be regarded as polluting because they threaten the
legitimacy of an individual's social identity in its sexual aspect,
though not necessarily that of the social order as a whole. People
make excuses for masculine women and for men who seem a bit
"queer."[2] For a man to do women's work is not without its risks.
One may be teased incessantly if caught in the act by people outside the immediate family. Similarly, a woman's femininity may be
compromised if she becomes outspoken, especially on political
matters (a masculine domain). Appalachian women can be highly
articulate on politics, but in mixed company men indicate when
they feel a woman is out of her depth by ignoring her comments,
acting as though she had not spoken. Or she may be told that her
opinion does not make sense. Men dominate this sphere, considering women to be lesser (or part-) persons in the political arena.[3]

In Ashe County, purity and pollution are metaphors for sex differences in the social realm, denoting a fundamental "fault line" between categories of persons. They indicate differences which (it is often claimed) are constructed in order to allow, if not create, an understanding of the social universe as a manageable environment. As Douglas (1966, 14) observes, "Some pollutions are used as analogies for expressing a general view of the social order. For example, there are beliefs that each sex is a danger to the other. . . . The two sexes can serve as a model for the collaboration and distinctiveness of social units." In Ashe County, pollution does not just describe male-female categories but also says something essential about being an individual.

Accordingly, male-female relations in Ashe County have an ambivalent, approach-avoidance aspect. Persons move toward members of the opposite sex in some contexts, toward persons of the same sex in others. In a wide range of social settings, men and women gravitate away from each other and aggregate into sexually "pure" groups. Men's and women's gossip groups and cooperative work groups are ubiquitous. In some of these contexts, the presence of members of the opposite sex may be considered "polluting," calling forth "rites of purification" or extrusion as means of rectifying the situation; alternatively, the group may simply break up.

The dominance aspect of male-female relations is not structured in entirely consistent male-over-female or female-over-male terms. Context is again important, since each sex has its own domain of operations. For farming activities or with regard to motor vehicles, the men "call the shots"; in household matters, in issues concerning food and children, women do. Dominance is thus not absolute but follows patterns that maintain the situational purity of male and female domains. This oscillating pattern of male-female dominance, the ambivalence between the sexes and the differentiation and implementation of male and female roles, is not without exception.

These forms of male-female relations point to the workings of more general forms of social representation in Ashe County. As in the relation between men and women, domination is also a major element in the relation between people and their land and territory, a theme in turn critical to their understanding of current history and their relation to "civilization."

To explicate the substance and meaning of this analogical equivalence (man:woman::person:land), I want to reexamine here aspects
of the New River dispute discussed in Chapter Three. During the
dispute it became clear that the threat to the preservation, continuing use, and control of their land struck at the heart of local
people's personal and collective identity. They viewed the proposed dams as an immediate threat not only to the land but also to
their entire style of life and cultural heritage. Identity, articulated
in terms of history, implied the precedent of a past peopled by
other people. The linkage between ancestors and "present" persons is constructed through the continuity of genealogies (blood
ties) as well as through the continuity of residence, the geographic
occupation of a delimited homeplace. Schneider's (1976, 216) general formulation of this linkage is directly applicable to Ashe
County ideology:

At first glance, place and blood do not seem to be related as symbols, yet
a moment's consideration will convince many (if not all) Americans that
what they mean by land and place is very close to what they mean by
blood. Both are substantive, both are natural, and both are symbols
which define a person's identity—as a member of a family or a member
of a nation. The symbol of birth is closely interwoven with those of
blood and place too, because whether in Gilbert and Sullivan's formulation "For he is an Englishman" or in the Naturalization and Immigration
Service, which asks for Place of Birth, land and place are linked to birth
and blood in such a way that they can be seen as variant formulations or
transformations of each other.

Local people frequently mention the idea of "roots" as a means
of expressing their ties to their ancestors *and* to their land. Having
roots means knowing where one belongs, having a real home,
being secure, and being securely rooted in and to place. As I argued in Chapter Two, "one becomes identified with a locality by
being 'raised up' in it or 'living' in it" (Batteau 1982b, 454). Such
an identification is fundamental to "being a person" in the larger
sense. One knows who one is by knowing to whom one belongs
(one's family) as well as where one belongs (one's land). Drifters
are rootless, their social identity unsure and unstable. Conversely,
persons with roots have a clearly defined social identity, a position
in both the natural and social landscapes, and a locus for their material livelihood. "To have roots" is to be grounded, to be tied to

the soil; ideologically, it is both a social fact and a fact of nature. The land nurtures, the soil brings forth sustenance. Fertility begins with the land and situates origin, and in the idiom of religion anticipates death and decay: "ashes to ashes, dust to dust."

The land brackets history, is its theater, its ground. Land situates the transit of the person within history; the person is encompassed by the history of the land and place. Pioneering ancestors came to the land and there gave birth to their descendants. Present-day descendants expect eventually to be laid to rest in the land, while hoping for history to continue to flow on through the land once their own lives are over. Thus blood and family lines are inextricably interwoven with the history of land and place. Family history is symbolized and given meaning by the genealogical "tree"; one's identity takes root there, and one's history is generated from the continuous growth of that tree. Blood flows as the life-giving material of genealogy, which is in turn rooted in the land, the family farm, the homestead, a place, a property. The roots of the genealogical tree go deep into the land, and if one is uprooted from one's land or one's family, personal identity is ripped from its primordial substratum. One then risks becoming dominated by imposed, exogenous definitions of social identity. From this perspective, identity is an autochthonous given, or at least is regarded as such when allowed to unfold progressively through history.

A person has roots struck deep into the soil, but *soil* has profoundly ambiguous connotations. Soil is a source of nurturance and fertility, but as *dirt* it is also potentially polluting: "We can recognize in our own notions of dirt that we are using a kind of omnibus compendium which includes all the rejected elements of ordered systems. . . . Our pollution behavior is the reaction which condemns any object or idea likely to confuse and contradict cherished classifications" (Douglas 1966, 48). Dirt, like disorder, "spoils pattern; it also provides the materials of pattern. . . . We do not simply condemn disorder. We recognize that it is destructive to existing patterns; also that it has potentiality. It symbolizes both danger and power" (Douglas 1966, 114). As in relations between men and women, a person's desire to become intimately associated with the land is qualified by a movement away from it. An entity perceived as dangerous, dirt-soil is to be avoided and yet approached as a source of power, nurturance, and security. The soil of the land may be "good, clean dirt"—but remains dirty all the same.

Land is also regarded as *property,* which persons as owners control. Possession of land assures self-possession: the landowner is his or her own person, has secured a definite identity, is "beholden to no one," has acquired a measure of autonomy and independence. These meanings are echoed and replicated in local notions of individualism, and for those who farm, these meanings attain a sharpness from their expression in ecologic or material terms. Rural people who work their land acquire a considerable degree of economic self-sufficiency, enough to exempt them partially from participating in a monetized, consumer economy. Even for residents who do not farm, the land and landscape are not only key components of their definition of social experience but also the fertile ground that allows social intercourse to continue. Thus material production and symbolic production can be represented through a single set of terms. The production of everyday life is understood to depend in varying proportions on both material and conceptual resources. Person-land relations, like those between men and women, are simultaneously organic and symbolic, material and sentimental. These complementarities, which remain for the most part latent and unacknowledged in customary social ideology, became more explicit and formalized through the production of a cultural rhetoric during the New River dispute.

In the course of the changes brought about by that dispute, the ambiguities and forms of domination keyed by people's thinking and acting out of male-female dynamics were magnified. Echoing the pattern of male-female relations, domination was expressed through what Kolodny calls the "pastoral paradox." In *The Lay of the Land* (1975), Kolodny argues that nineteenth-century American writers made a conscious and determined effort to formulate a meaning for the landscape, in her terms, "to mediate between the conflicting drives for individuation and maternal union" (p. 71). How to refigure this formulation has become more of an issue for Ashe County people as they have increasingly attempted to relate the dominant meanings of "civilization" to those of their own social ideology.

For Ashe County people, man-woman relations may, by turns, be characterized as domination or cooperation, viewed as salutary accommodation or as threatening to pollute and confound sexual "purity." Similarly, person-land relations oscillate from harmonious symbiosis to pollution and human domination. A poem by Billy Edd Wheeler, an Appalachian who has written country-and-western music for Glen Campbell, June Carter, and Johnny Cash, represents man-woman relations as strictly analogous to person-land relations, with identical processes of fecundation pertaining to both:

> *Mountain Fertility Rite*
> There was a farmer so superstition bound
> That every time spring planting came around
> He'd take his wife and put her on the ground
> Under full moon and fertilize his plowin'
> While his family of kids danced up and down
> At edges of field, naked and making sounds
> Like singing—rituals quaint and past profound.
> They made quare sings and led a snow white hound.
> Everyone laughed and called him Almanac Clown.
> But he always had the best crops in town.
> (Higgs and Manning 1975, 325–26)

In this poem, a delicate balance is achieved between the rude, unrefined processes of nature and the gentle cultivation promoted by culture. Person-land relations are portrayed as having a magical element.

"Civilization," in contrast, is viewed by Ashe County people as taking a shortsighted, narrowly rationalistic, and sometimes destructive approach to person-land relations. Ashe County tradition and "civilization" differ in their definitions of the ratio of domination and nurturance appropriate to such relations. In the context of the New River dispute, Ashe County people came to regard outsiders' approach as comparable to rape, while outsiders regarded local person-land relations as backward, underdeveloped, unproductive, and infertile. The problem of achieving a balance between domination and cooperation, husbandry and appropriation, and fecundation and rape is implicit in the pastoral paradox, which throws "the organic wholeness of the natural world" up against the "unattractive beginnings of settlement" (Kolodny 1975, 92).

Person-land relations can be metaphorically posed as relations between son and nurturing mother or as those between husband and fecund wife.[4] The land-as-woman metaphor encompasses both: "Implicit in the metaphor of land-as-woman was both the regressive pull of maternal containment *and* the seductive invitation to sexual assertion" (Kolodny 1975, 67). Less explicit ideologically, but just as securely grounded in the history and pastoral experience of Ashe County people, is the motif of culture taming and fecundating the land. This motif is particularized and paralleled by a specific mode of male domination—male as husband and husbandman. Douglas (1970, 70) suggests the importance of these parallels in observing that "the human body is always treated as an image of society and . . . there can be no natural way of considering the body that does not involve at the same time a social dimension."

For Ashe County people, it is not society as a whole that is viewed through body symbolism, but the total experiential field of the individual in which the continuity of history and the land is emphasized. The social dimension of the body is not society, but the land. As man and woman are cooperative partners in marriage, the individual and the land live in harmonious relation. But as either sex may pollute the other's purity, so too the land may take the form of wilderness, or revert to an undomesticated state and be "hostile like a woman." When the land is cultivated and plowed— a common euphemism for sexual intercourse—it yields its bounty. "Civilized" or "civilizing" activities are the result of masculine pursuits in relation to land, and the ambivalence and domination intrinsic to man-woman relations inhere in person-land relations as well. Both cooperative harmony and exploitative domination characterize or potentially characterize person-land relations as well as man-woman relations. The distinction between cultivation as fecundation and as aggressive exploitation, "phallic aggression with the axe" (Kolodny 1975, 85), is a fine line. The following interpretation summarizes the harmonious side of this regime that is stressed in Ashe County ideology: "The mother, after all, must be impregnated in order to be bountiful. And insofar as the husbandman aids, but does not force, her willing bounty, he at once maintains his separate masculine and consequently human identity while reaping the benefits of an acceptable and guiltless intimacy" (Kolodny 1975, 62). It is this particular sort of relation between land and person that helps maintain local identity in the face of what many people regard as civilization's aggressive attempts to rape the landscape.

The local farmer is husbandman to the land, whereas the intruder is a ruthless aggressor. The tendency to totalize experience, a keynote of Ashe County cultural style, acts as a controlling context, keeping at bay the potential for aggression and exploitative rape of the landscape and bringing to the fore the harmony of a more benevolent kind of domination. Ashe County people stylize their experience so as to reduce the ambiguity of their historical relation to the land—their own original, ruthless appropriation of an "unpopulated" landscape generations ago for their own purposes. They instead define their relation to the land as fecundating domestication. Their rhetorical construction of their history denies and displaces the aggression of their own ancestors' entry into the area and substitutes a version of history and person–land relations that legitimates today's practices. This historical self, the identity articulated in historical terms, may be regarded in this context as self-congratulatory, a view that suggests how oppressed members of an oppressive society participate in reproducing the prevailing forms of domination.

Ashe County rhetoric evinces an ideology of global integrity in the face of both exploitative intrusions by outsiders and contradictions implicit in local history and culture. The human disturbance of the pastoral scene, the domestication and reordering of nature to mesh with human presence and preferences, is viewed by Ashe County people as part of the movement of progress. But in accelerating this process one more notch, the movement of "civilization" becomes a violation of the land and simultaneously a violation of local identity and culture. As became clear during the New River dispute, "progress" has thus generated a profound discontinuity in history located at the boundary between local culture and civilization.

The aggression and domination of "civilization" is demonstrated over and over in the history of Appalachia, but aggressive domination is countermanded in local people's presentation of their own history. As with the ethnic stereotypes of Appalachians, so with history: outsiders' imposed meanings are rejected and yet internalized by local people. County people participate in their domination by outsiders insofar as they act out imposed meanings and presuppositions, yet set themselves apart from "civilization" by their objections and dissent. They construct their own history as harmonious and within it pose themselves as gentle husbandmen of the land, glossing over those aspects of their history that could be regarded as "civilization," as polluting and disruptive. County residents do their best to obscure the symmetry between the history of civilization and that of Ashe County through rhetoric that distinguishes, and thereby preserves, their way of life from "civilization." The negative aspect of the pastoral paradox is thus suppressed in local representations of Ashe County history, but it inevitably surfaces once again in people's ambivalence regarding "civilization."

Kolodny (1975, 93) observes that "insofar as the pastoral impulse is shared by the culture at large, it becomes a pattern by which a number of cultural artifacts are shaped." One of these artifacts is the struggle between rural people and outsiders over who shall use the land and for what purpose, and who may legitimately decide about the specific character of person-land relations. Distinctive features of local ideology, such as the pastoral paradox or the importance of history, are not simply abstract or static givens but are moments in an ongoing historical struggle, charged elements in the local knowledge people claim about themselves and pose and counterpose in making claims of power. These claims of power and knowledge within and without the county touch directly on the political determination of cultural legitimacy and continuity.

Ashe County people distance themselves from "civilization" through a discursive strategy that argues that the ways and values of civilization were never part of their own history but always imposed on them by outsiders. Their claim to cultural legitimacy and autonomy is thus grounded in an irony. The ancestors of today's residents assumed the inevitability of their appropriation of an "unpopulated" landscape. The Appalachian Power Company adopted a similar strategy: the company reduced the land it wanted for the Blue Ridge project to a depopulated landscape by marginalizing its inhabitants (Pratt 1985, 128). This unacknowledged symmetry in local history between past events and present problems indicates just how situational and strategic is the knowledge Ashe County people claim of their history and culture, relative to their desire to control the power dynamic in which they are enmeshed. The significant aspect of the local rhetoric and understanding of history does not reside in its truth or falsity; rather, it is that the local style of representing that understanding is intimately connected with residents' struggle to achieve a favorable position within the prevailing filigree of power.

An executive director of the Appalachian Regional Commission is on record as having declared that some areas of Appalachia should simply be depopulated and turned over to the coal companies. A comparable situation would have resulted in Ashe County from the construction of dams on the New River. Depopulation is a powerful form of appropriating and dominating small-scale social systems, since it removes all impediments to control. American Indian groups experienced this form of appropriation when European colonists seized Indian land and again when the federal government relocated Indians onto reservations. When literal depopulation proves to be impossible, symbolic depopulation may be undertaken by means of degrading or dismantling the social identity of an area's inhabitants.

Outsiders have been able to manipulate the intimate relation of land and person in Ashe County ideology in order to deconstruct the social identity of Ashe County people. Marginalizing local residents was not just a matter of attempting to get them off their land, but also a matter of applying symbolic operations to their definitions of who they are. "Colonizing" the Blue Ridge, appropriating its resources for nonindigenous social and economic objectives (the power and tourist industries), could be accomplished by moving one step beyond the acknowledged close relation of people to land to posit a thoroughgoing equivalence between them.[5] When outsiders view the landscape as unproductive or underdeveloped, and that evaluation is tacitly taken to characterize the people who occupy it as well, then colonizing the region comes under the guise of "developing" the area rather than dominating the people. Outsiders can metaphorically depopulate the region by redefining its population as fatalistic or traditionalistic creatures, as uncultured or underdeveloped barbarians, or as hill-

billies lacking in intelligence and motivation. The subtle infiltration of such stereotypes and caricatures into outsiders' discourse
causes local culture and identity to be deconstructed, precluded,
and discredited:

> The paradox of the Appalachian situation—indeed of all such situa-
> tions—is that the oppressors *deny* the identity oppressed people wish for
> themselves at the same time that they *supply* an undesirable identity—one
> which is psychologically destructive, socially demeaning, and calculated
> to serve the manipulative interests of the oppressor. (Whisnant 1973a, 130)

In this limiting case, the local resident has already been designated
as other than a full person, as an incomplete entity who can only
profit from the intervention of outside agencies.

The intertwining of material concerns, land utilization, and resource allocation in the forms of discourse generated by the politics of the New River entered into a system of representations that
could then be contested. For county residents, modes of material
production and the continuity of everyday life are both understood
through the same social representations. The purposeful alienation
of the material from the symbolic was actively promoted by outsiders, but it was at odds with local knowledge. Outsiders strived
to maintain representations that Ashe County residents stridently
contested and critiqued because they rightly perceived that their
way of life, in its material exigencies as well as in its spiritual values, was directly at stake in the fate and the power of these nonindigenous representations.

For example, in American society land has increasingly been
treated as a commodity, its value measured by a price tag rather
than by its association with persons, family, and the continuity of
social life. This shift in the meaning of land was in the interest of
outsiders desirous of appropriating Ashe County acreage, since reducing land to an object that can be bought and sold undermines
the relation of land to culture and continuity that county residents
assumed and experienced. During the New River dispute, outsiders strategically constructed and promoted this separation of
material from social and symbolic predispositions and assumptions. This separation not only bolstered their case but also re-
lieved outsiders of the responsibility for the social and cultural
transformations that would result from their redeployment of the

land. While Ashe County people became more aware of the complex organic and symbolic ramifications of person–land relations, outsiders strived to sunder them. In response, Ashe County people repeatedly reasserted their long–standing social representations: that history, identity, ecological and social relations constitute an integrated, indivisible whole, that the source of internal disharmonies lies in the discontinuities between civilization and indigenous culture.

The outsiders' efforts to dissociate person, culture, and land broach the more general problem of how symbolic elements are to be most usefully and meaningfully related in the context of pervasive change, and particularly how much control people have over such matters. As Erikson (1976, 82) suggests,

The identifying motifs of a culture are not just *core* values to which people pay homage but also the *lines* of point and counterpoint along which they diverge. That is, the term "culture" refers not only to the customary ways in which a people induce conformity in behavior and outlook but the customary ways in which they organize diversity. In this view, every human culture can be visualized, if only in part, as a kind of theatre in which certain contrary tendencies are played out.

Ashe County people found themselves forced to delineate viable responses to a number of such contrary tendencies, relating now-disparate meanings in a piecemeal fashion. Each discontinuity had to be faced anew in each action context. For instance, Ashe County cultural patterns emphasize commitment to tradition and respect for personal independence. In Erikson's (1976, 85) terms, the county resident "can be said to cherish freedom and to be wary of it, to protect the right to do as he pleases and then consult aging tradition on the prevailing attitudes of his peers to find out what he *should* do." As in the New River dispute, he seeks a balance between the dictates or "scripts" of tradition and the value of individually innovative action. An important technique in negotiating this balance, as I have shown, is the reappropriation and reuse of "tradition" in the interest of individual initiative and self-determination.

The collaboration among diverse Ashe County residents to create a cultural rhetoric that would address the New River dispute was responsive to the immediate necessities of that political nexus but also epitomized long-standing issues and problems in the region. Ashe County people put a premium on controlling their own life histories. Under a variety of circumstances, they moved decisively to protect their property, their reputation, and their livelihood. The question, What can I do? was often raised, but people's sense of the present as a discontinuity in their history yielded responses of resignation as often as determination and concerted action.[6] For Ashe County residents, ambivalence is a "rational" response to their perceptions of the vagaries of nature, the unexpected twists of history, and the intricate maneuvers of exploitative outsiders. The mix of cognitive and affective elements in local discourse reflects an effort to set forth stable symbolic-interpretive referents given uncertain social realities. Although the representations emerging from such a process may add up to a system, it is also evident that culture is being politically constituted.[7]

Although some county residents were resigned to adverse social conditions, cultural domination, or economic and resource expropriation, their attitudes did not reproduce the stolid peasant fatalism often attributed to Appalachians or to third-world rural populations (see Epilogue). Withdrawal from unfortunate circumstances has sometimes been all too evident in the region (Gaventa 1980), but the New River dispute effected an active mobilization of social resources as well as considerable resentment and indignation. Opponents of the dams recast their rage into discourse designed to meet the demands and constraints posed by outsiders' intentions and ground rules.

In the sexual domain, assertiveness and passivity—how to contextualize and how to practice them—have always been important issues, and these arose in the discursive space opened up between local people and outsiders. County residents struggled to modulate the relation between assertion and passivity, dominance and submission, and change and tradition—within the contexts of their outrage and strategic considerations of negotiation and survival. In addressing these tensions, local residents directed their rhetoric not only toward outsiders. They also struggled against and strategically appropriated a tradition that in some ways resists revision, yet had to be revised if their culture was to remain vital rather than to become a relic of the past.

In systematizing new modes of representing and articulating

their culture, the leaders of the opposition to the Blue Ridge project were caught between the domination of tradition and the domination of imposed discourses of economic necessity and economic interest. To navigate this double bind, they appealed to aspects of both tradition and immediate circumstances. They were able to modify or displace the system of dominance and dependence imposed upon them by maneuvering the outsiders into their own double bind: opponents made the argument that the project could be built only by subverting the ascendancy of dominant representations and values that had been used as the rationale for the project itself—the "right" to the assurance of a certain preferred stylization of social life. Tradition and change, dominance and dependence, and assertiveness and passivity were not transcended but resituated, to some extent held at bay, equilibrated at a new level. Opponents' meticulous, often baroque refiguring of knowledge through discourse relied on subtle modifications, rather than revolutionary transformations, of how local residents fit into a filigree of power stretching far beyond the county line.

The working and reworking of another cultural countercurrent also found poignant expression in the new local representations and discourses. In Ashe County ideology, the individual is the alpha and omega of social life, the locus of ascendant value and motivation. Yet, particularly under conditions perceived as a crisis, group allegiance sometimes dictates obligations that countermand a strong sense of personal identity. As Ashe County people organized into groups and began to see themselves as collectively in opposition to outsiders, aspects of individualism had to be held in check.

The paradoxes of group formation and group process in Ashe County are effectively obscured by their characteristic flexibility and variability in local ideology. Yet whatever the vehemence with which individual autonomy is asserted, Ashe County individuals achieve that rhetorical autonomy at the cost of a deep-seated dependence on the group. This irony is evident in the centrality of the family even for many natives who have moved away to distant northern cities: Cut off from the group, the individual feels like an incomplete person. But to participate effectively and meaningfully in the life of a group, particularly a nonfamilial group, requires some concessions of individual autonomy: The group's objectives must be placed above more immediate personal goals. These cross-currents surfaced in the uncertainties and doubts that many leaders of the New River opposition encountered in spearheading the movement. County residents were divided and unsure of how best to face a crisis or social upheaval: Would political organizing or individual initiative and action be most effective?

The tensions and crosscurrents that arise from attempts to use social ideology to address issues of pervasive social change problematize any definitive formulation of local identity and culture. It is often difficult—and probably irrelevant in the long run—to distinguish indigenous contradictions from imposed ones. For Ashe County natives, the recognition of these problems and accompanying discontents was attended by the conviction that they originate on the side of "civilization."[8] Freud (1930, 44) could easily have been speaking for Appalachians in claiming that "civilization is itself to blame for a great part of our misery, and we should be much happier if we were to give it up and go back to primitive conditions." This sentiment, an impossible and grandiose fantasy, is more soberly recast in the words of an Ashe County resident:

In the Blue Ridge, people really are primitives in the best sense of the term. I just hate to see these Floridians moving in. The outsiders bring a lot of changes which many times are not for the best. Thank God the wholesale selling of land has slowed down in the last few years. The Florida people who live near here are real nice. You couldn't find nicer people anywhere. But it's good to be primitive, though I guess civilization has its place.

These views are a model of apologetic understatement and restraint, but the undercurrent of regret and discontent is unmistakable.

Ashe County has been spared the strip mining and widespread environmental destruction that have ravaged parts of Kentucky and West Virginia. Despite the county's relative affluence and economic viability, the subtle pattern of cultural domination—represented by the New River dispute, tourism, and land sales to outsiders—has, as throughout the Appalachian region, provoked alienation and an ethnic revival.

Since the nineteenth century the issue of cultural identity and legitimacy in Ashe County has been subject to many of the same strictures that apply elsewhere in Appalachia. Historically, Appalachian otherness has frequently been linked with an adverse judgment as to what that otherness means as well as to whether it should exist at all. Ashe County residents have become increasingly experienced with these negativities in recent years. Many have begun to realize that they "are struggling against an attempt by mainstream America and its powerful vested interests to contain, subjugate and destroy a region, its people and the few remaining fragments of its culture" (Whisnant 1973a, 125).

The concepts of purity and pollution that maintain sexually and politically pure categories and regulate person-land relations are also relevant to the relation of Ashe County people to mainstream America. Civilization is viewed as polluting local culture: "The movement for Appalachian identity has, as one of its major by-products, the strong suggestion that the mainstream is polluted" (Whisnant 1973a, 131). As noted earlier in this chapter, pollution in the sexual domain and in person-land relations "is fraught with unavoidable ambiguities which must be sorted out" (Whisnant 1973a, 136). During the New River dispute, the ambiguities implicit in local ideology were intensified; sorting them out became an increasingly formidable challenge for county residents.

The response to these adversities, which encompass immediate material concerns as well as deep-seated ideological and symbolic orientations, has been to claim an "ethnicity" for the region and its people, based on historically self-evident social and cultural characteristics (see Obermiller 1981). The turn toward ethnicity as a discursive tactic is particularly compelling since ethnicity per se claims to be self-legitimating; documenting its existence in all the richness and detail accorded by history becomes an immediate testament to its durability and viability. Appalachians' claim to a discrete ethnic identity may seem artificial to those who associate the term with clear-cut racial categories or linguistic differences. Nevertheless, Appalachians are arguing cultural legitimacy on the basis of cultural difference; "ethnicity" represents such a claim of cultural distinctiveness in this discourse.

A number of cultural attributes that I have emphasized in discussing how Ashe County people characterize their culture have become more or less standard keynotes in attempts to codify Appalachian ethnicity: "personalism, informal life-styles, relationship to land and to specific places, an essentially sacred reading of human experience" (Whisnant 1973a, 127). These themes are significant also because they readily denote values and predispositions of groups outside the county and region. In the course of the New River dispute, these shared symbols and meanings underwrote the exogenous political alliances crucial to certifying local cultural knowledge and political power.

Such alliances, and their basis in shared symbols, are reflected within Ashe County in the direct social juxtaposition of local residents and the people they call "back-to-the-landers."[9] At first, Ashe County natives were quite ambivalent about these new immigrants, just as they had been ambivalent about tourists and Floridians. But the presence of the back-to-the-landers occasioned a comparative discourse on cultural similarities and differences on the part of local residents, who became more aware of the rhetorical power of key representations. The number of back-to-the-landers in Ashe County increased noticeably during the New River dispute. Some moved into housing that became available during the Appalachian Power Company's land-acquisition program; small farms could be had for fairly low rent. Local residents were initially hostile toward these "dirty hippies" and stereotyped them as lazy people who smoked a lot of marijuana. But with increased contact, many Ashe County natives became more respectful of the "down home" genuineness of those back-to-the-landers who demonstrated their intentions to work hard, to learn about farming and husbandry, to repair broken-down barns and houses, and to create for themselves a viable alternative to urban living. Many of the newly arrived were positively predisposed to local culture and made an effort to learn more about it. County natives were particularly sympathetic and responsive to the open attitudes of the back-to-the-landers, and some local people learned to accept these immigrants as good neighbors. The subsequent interchange of ideological elements helped to engender a sense of solidarity and shared cultural commitment when local natives and back-to-the-landers alike were threatened with being flooded out.

The ethnic revival in Ashe County is expressed in diverse domains, but these expressions displace rather than resolve the con-

tradictions of the present. The construction of ethnicity within individualism poses the same problem that local culture presents to
collective action, a contradiction between person and group: How
can individual identity be articulated in the same terms as ethnicity
without submerging the individual or precluding groupness? Collective efforts in politics and rhetoric are handled through spokespersons (as were appointed, or self-appointed, in the New River
dispute), who assert and promulgate group solidarity, cultural distinctiveness, and shared values. When ethnicity is articulated by
the individual, it remains abstract, encompassing rather than constituting the person. From either perspective, ethnicity is represented in the form of the person and the group as "body," and the
individual is represented writ large at the level of ethnicity. In
other words, the individual and the collectivity are not given a
character unique to themselves; there is no general formulation
separating ethnicity from the individual. The conceptualization of
each is accomplished through rather fluid, situational representations, particulars of individual histories and attributes.

   "Instead of collective action to guarantee individuality, [ethnic]
minorities manifest deliberate differentiation to assure collective
recognition and equality" (Wagner n.d., 33). Just as ethnicity poses
problems for an ideology of individualism, it also makes it difficult to put forth a concept of society as a unified whole. In this respect, Appalachian ethnicity poses the same problem to the larger
society as did Appalachian otherness a century ago. Thus when
seeking to legitimate local culture in the eyes of outsiders, Ashe
County people try to overcome this contradiction by describing
their cultural distinctiveness in terms of representations having
societywide significance, for example, the symbolism of equality
and democracy.

   A central figure in this appeal to outsiders is the imagery of the
melting pot, which local residents appropriated as an emblem for
the accommodation of diversity and the recognition of cultural
distinctiveness. They argued for the essential priority of local identity over nationality through particularistic claims regarding the
sacredness of property, the ascendancy of self-determination, the
inevitability and necessity of regionalism, and the importance of a
nurturing person–land symbiosis. They capitalized on their perception of discontinuities in their history in order to emphasize the

importance of historical continuity in the construction of a durable sense of identity and a viable culture. Finally, they promoted their ethnicity by advertising the aesthetic appeal of particular elements of their culture.

Before discussing each of these rhetorical strategies, I want to make three quick points that apply to all of them. First, in their attempt to promote a cultural revival and by means of these rhetorical inflections of social discourse, Ashe County people in effect fetishized key representations. The irony is that at each point the distinctiveness and singularity of local identity and culture are claimed on the basis of parallels and commonalities with the dominant culture.

Second, outsiders sought to counter the arguments of local people by redefining residents' attempts to address the problems of identity, change, and culture as indicators of unrest, disaffection with unassailable values, and an activism arising from purely local concerns. Under this redefinition, deeply ideological issues could be brushed aside without serious debate, displaced by circumstantial considerations, and local activists' bid for recognition on the basis of ethnicity could be rendered irrelevant. Once ideological protest is reduced to provincial grumbling, no one local group, regardless of "cultural content," can claim an inviolable distinctiveness on the basis of its unique commitments or particular attributes. Any claims to distinctiveness and legitimacy become less convincing once ethnicity is redefined as a system of simple substitutions in which each particular element is devoid of intrinsic meaning (Lefebvre 1971; Foster 1973). In this way, local or ethnic cultures, such as that of the Appalachian region, are "normalized," reabsorbed into the dominant system.

Third, during the dispute the commitment to opposing the dams became for many county residents a passionate fervor. This was to their advantage because a rhetoric that sustains its effect strikes its audience as more than mere rhetoric: it rings of the truth, resonates with "positive knowledge," and glows with the burnished aura of believability. One's case is more likely to be persuasive if one's argument possesses a compelling authenticity.

During the New River dispute, opponents of the project demanded that their appeals to democracy, equality, and the ideal of the melting pot be substantiated in the courts and legislatures.

They contended that outsiders treated democratic notions and so-called national interests as empty yet convenient rhetorical figures rather than as core values and representations. In the land of "liberty and justice for all," county residents argued that their particular life-style deserved legitimacy; outsiders had trouble recognizing that it was even being threatened. Local people wanted their rights to be given equal weight with the interests of a seemingly monolithic technocracy; equality and democracy, they argued, demanded that a parity be established between the "big people" and the "little people" such that the "big people" could achieve their ends only if they did not jeopardize the rights, preferences, and survival of Ashe County culture.

In bargaining for their own version of reality, in seeking a specific semiotic effect, local people came to view their politicking as expedient maneuvering necessary to bring about a legitimate outcome. Their rhetoric was specifically designed to implicate the survival of their entire identity, culture, and history in the specific issue of the New River. Only by couching the particular exigencies of a particular issue in such general terms were local residents able to appeal to the dominant symbols of democracy, self-determination, and their right to survive "as they are."

Paradoxically, the imagery of the melting pot thus became a context for heightening distinctiveness rather than a mode of legitimating assimilation. Complete assimilation was exactly what county residents wanted to avoid. To alienate people from their own land and culture was posed as equivalent to disenfranchising them from America's democratic, person-oriented polity, which they claimed was a given meaning of national symbolism. In this view the melting pot does not "boil down" cultural variability, expressed as ethnicity, into cultural homogeneity, but rather serves as the vessel for peaceful coexistence.

During the New River dispute, local people also referred to the meaning of private property and ownership—one's home is one's castle. Intrusive land appropriations, despite any rationale of national interests, must be subordinated to the property rights of occupants who trace ownership back through long family histories. The usurping of private-property rights, residents argued, would disrupt the continuity of a historically validated mode of livelihood. Furthermore, they held, the concept of private property informs the expression of self-determination: owning property is the means and meaning through which self-determination may be exercised on a day-to-day basis.

By thus manipulating the meaning of property to entail self-determination, Ashe County people could argue that the Blue Ridge project posed a wholesale, illegitimate threat to their rights to make their own choices about how to live and how to cultivate or dispose of their land. Again, local people appropriated meanings—property, self-determination, equality, democracy—from the national culture to foreground local culture and place it above outside interests and imposed meanings. Their rhetoric sought to legitimate ethnicity by presenting outsiders with a delineation that outsiders could not controvert without overturning their own enshrined concepts—another double bind for outsiders. And another example of how local or ethnic groups can use "the values of the dominant society, as interpreted by them, as publicly accepted by them as sanctions against the dominant society itself" (Silverman 1970, 18).

Ashe County residents elaborated on the meaning of property and self-determination by references both to regionalism (large-scale person-land relationships) and to historical continuity (long-term person-land relationships). Indigenous definitions of survival —the historical continuity of a particular local life-style predicated on individual self-determination—were promoted and valorized. Through their rhetoric county residents sought to make accessible and acceptable their conception of history not as an end in itself, but as tantamount to the ongoing flow of social life.

Because culture and meaning are so intimately tied to action in Ashe County ideology, and because, in turn, action generates meaning, which then resides in the person, people make little distinction between forming conceptions of the person and forming conceptions of the social "body." Thus ethnicity is the locus of culture, and it is sought, demanded, and struggled for through specific activities more than through any abstract promulgation of social policy. In this way, ethnicity becomes substantialized, personalized, and made real—rather than being delivered as a set of prepackaged guidelines lacking conviction.

Another tactic used by opponents of the dams for "proving" the legitimacy of their ethnicity was to make outsiders and local people alike aware of the aesthetic value of local culture. Claims of Appalachian identity on the basis of externally perceived aesthetic values and modes of production have been resorted to in the region for at least a century. The underlying premise is that "having a culture" is certified by identifying in local practices a privileged domain through which local people partake of the higher virtues and sensibilities of Culture. In this view, nonutilitarian aesthetic standards and values through which everyday life is embellished and enriched are taken as a representation of social life: to have Culture is to have a culture.[10]

For some time, Ashe County people have made a bid to outsiders for ethnic and cultural legitimacy and autonomy by posing aspects of their productions and practices as having an aesthetic appeal and value. The individual is directly implicated in this tactic in the traditional role of musician, craftsperson, or artist. Local people assume, or lead outsiders to assume by themselves assuming, that they have a laudable artistic heritage to draw upon. The presence of craftspeople, artists, and musicians at the New River festival can be understood in just these terms.

Zell Hamby learned to make quilts from her mother, who in turn learned it from her mother. Ronnie Taylor is a musician because he has music "in his blood"; he grew up with it. Ashe County residents exercise their artistic abilities in a wide variety of endeavors, hand-crafting wooden furniture, churns, and clocks; making banjos, guitars, and dulcimers; weaving and sewing. They explain their skills in terms of their family and regional histories: their forebears had to make items for their own use and for their homes, because manufactured goods were in short supply and traders came to the county infrequently. It is a short step from necessity to art, as local craftspeople have demonstrated. And it is one short step from seeing the artistic merit of local crafts to seeing local culture in some of its manifestations as an art form. When artistic expertise is embedded in history, and when the artist as person is directly bound up with creative output, identity as artist and as indigene can both be represented and conveyed through artistic productions.

Through their contact with outsiders, particularly tourists, craftspeople have learned that their utilitarian creations can be seen as having artistic value.[11] Hence the transition from pragmatics to art. Because their creations have such immediate appeal to tourists, travelers, and seekers of exotic artifacts, the handmade objects easily become representations and envoys of local culture, acting as mediators between Ashe County culture and "civilization." The tourist vacationing along the Blue Ridge Parkway returns to Pittsburgh or Baltimore with a locally hand-sewn quilt. When he talks about how he bought his quilt, the fuller the story, the better the impression. The tourist's satisfaction with his "find" translates into a sympathy for Ashe County people and their culture.

M. C. Whirley started doing woodworking in Ashe County after he closed his sawmill a few years ago.[12] He explained, "There's a woman in Detroit who found out I was making things. She wrote and asked me if I'd make her one of those old-fashioned [butter] churns. I made two or three, and people got to see them. People started coming by, and I sold more than twenty of them. There's a fellow from West Virginia got to coming up here. He's out there one day, and I told him, 'Come here, I want to show you something.' Well, he bought a churn or two, and he's been back three times to buy more. The last time he was up here, he said, 'Now, I could have fifteen or twenty of these churns.' So I made eight, but they were all sold before he came back.

"The first banjo I made out of a cigar box. Then I got to making guitars and just kept making them. I don't know how many I've sold, and a lot of dulcimers and banjos. I've made several mandolins." He once sold a dulcimer to a woman who returned it because it had metal guitar keys to tighten the strings. She told him to replace them with wooden pegs, that it had to be all handmade. Authenticity and aesthetic value are thus invested in the object by the hands of the artist, particularly in the eyes of outside consumers. As a cultural production, such objects represent the ethnicity as well as the identity of the craftsperson:

Finding their inspiration in the work of contemporary anthropologists, ecologists and radical political theorists, young craftsmen view their work not as escapist and nostalgic, but as a variety of political activism: to reduce one's wants and thus to curtail one's consumption of the plastic products of the system is a revolutionary act since our system depends upon high rates of consumption. With an admirable logical consistency, young craftsmen also shun the synthetic materials of American industry—vinyls, for example—in favor of organic materials: wood, stone, clay, leather, natural yarns and so on. Indeed, they reserve the term "plastic" to denote anything artificial, phony or lacking in integrity and durability. (Whisnant 1973b, 230)

The local craftspeople sell their works to tourists and other outsiders. Visiting entrepreneurs buy quilts, furniture, or woven goods at low prices, reselling them in New York or Chicago specialty shops at a healthy markup. In addition, crafts workers sometimes appropriate for home use handmade objects that seem preferable to manufactured goods from "civilization." The use of such objects in their own homes helps to codify a style of life that self-consciously departs from the mainstream. This activity also suggests artistic valorization as a means of asserting ethnicity: the authenticity of handmade items is posed as an emblem of cultural authenticity. When Ashe County people put a premium on hand-made items, they reassert in new terms a continuity with their past, when only handmade items were available.

The importance of handmade items and the artistry these items represent also play a role in identity formation; Whisnant (1973b, 230) refers to "the capacity of crafts work to define and sustain identity, and its valuable, non-alienated and non-alienating character." As he points out, individuality is substantiated through material objects that can be seen to flow both from the person and the culture. A handmade object directly implies its creator and represents his or her exercise of craftsmanship (a particular cultural expertise). By endowing the handmade object with artistry, craftsmanship "allow[s] interventions of the sacred and transcendent into mundane reality, thereby enriching private experience and investing one's world with meaning" (Whisnant 1973b, 230). At the same time, craftspeople in Ashe County elaborate upon their identity by purposefully alienating themselves from the dubious and alienating mass-manufactured, synthetic products of "civilization."

In part, identity is also a function of one's sense of one's body, and craftsmanship and husbandry help to create and sustain identity by reinvigorating the body. One comes to "make sense" of the world through the reintegration of the senses in the context of the concrete activity of making things (see Erikson 1968). The crafts worker chooses organic materials "as a means of reestablishing contact with a primal reality," and this choice "is paralleled by an impulse to ground one's being in renewed sensory awareness and vitality" (Whisnant 1973b, 232).

Whisnant's treatment of the crafts worker clarifies how the formation of individual identity directly implies that of ethnicity. The meaning of land in social ideology demonstrates "the inseparability of identity and culture" by mediating between them (Whisnant 1973b, 234). Similarly, Erikson (1968, 22) regards identity formation as "a process [located] *in the core of the individual* and yet also *in the core of his communal culture,* a process which establishes, in fact, the identity of these two identities." Whisnant elaborates Erikson's formulation in arguing that craftsmanship is not merely the working of an "inner imagination" and that the product of the crafts worker's creativity is not simply an individual contribution to culture. Instead, craftsmanship demonstrates the inseparability of personal and public worlds. The practice of producing the object integrates individual and cultural identity, mediating between them by expressing a mode of participation in, work with, and exemplification of aesthetic standards and cultural values. In exercising creative abilities and capacities, the craftsperson demonstrates the coherence of skillfully manipulating physical materials and shaping personal identity. And because fashioning an identity involves the appropriation of cultural symbols and meanings, a deepening understanding of one's identity readily implies a corresponding sense of cultural identity. Crafts and craftsmanship thus become conveyances and representations of local culture and ethnicity.

In contrast, "civilization," particularly as embodied in the local styles of upbringing and education, discourages people from developing a sense of the value of craftsmanship. In primary and secondary schools, Whisnant argues, verbal and analytic skills are prized, while manual dexterity and a talent for manipulating physical material are slighted. Such separations preclude craftsmanship from serving as a major "site" of valorization, identity formation, and cultural identification. The school system's orientation to learning and the emphasis on *knowing,* as distinguished from *making* and *doing,* make it difficult for children to acquire and to value a sense of competence and craftsmanship. "Civilization" is also full of complex objects beyond the scope of craftsmanship because their construction is "hidden by the industrial designer's slickest art" (Whisnant 1973b, 231).

Thus both as a practice and as an embodiment of beliefs, craftsmanship differentiates Ashe County from mainstream America and reinforces local ethnicity: "the political and social values, models of self, and views of work and sexuality upon which crafts work is based are fundamentally opposed to most of the determinants that give American society its present shape" (Whisnant 1973b, 231). Closely associating the aesthetic value of handmade products with the integrity of local culture helps Ashe County people to set up an ethnic boundary that allows them to distance themselves from "civilization." But herein lies another paradox: Local culture is posed as having an authenticity and internal coherence that "civilization" lacks; yet county residents seek the external legitimation of their culture by asserting that it partakes of Culture as defined and understood by outsiders. Thus the claim that Ashe County culture is unique is based on claims of its legitimacy in terms of symbols and meanings comparable to those of "civilization." This simultaneous assertion of difference and similarity makes the actual "fault line" between the cultures wobble and fluctuate. But this assertion also enforces a selective emphasis on those aspects of local culture most accessible to outsiders, thereby transforming local culture in the process of effecting its revival. The representation of local culture to outsiders can never be a simple, objective description; rather, it depends in fundamental ways on the kinds of values outsiders insist upon, the sorts of priorities outsiders enact, and the kinds of markets for products, such as quilts and dulcimers, they open to local people. Craftsmanship, like political rhetoric, promotes a particular representation of local culture that is adjusted or reworked to accommodate what outsiders are likely to comprehend and value.

Julie Colvard is a young woman with a strong commitment to the Blue Ridge region and to promoting its ethnicity. She was raised in Ashe County but simultaneously exposed to outside culture through the public education system. Thus she is representative of a generation of "transitional" rural people on whom both cultures exert gravitational pulls. She is acutely aware of the pathos and ambiguities engendered by this complex and besieged milieu. She weighs the pros and cons, and finds it difficult to delineate precisely her own relation to these cultural countercurrents.

As she attempts to give shape to her convictions and to substantiate them in specific social contexts, she dismisses as disembodied rhetoric and bankrupt ideology the notions outsiders have loosed on local people in their efforts to dilute and obviate meanings in local culture. She finds herself oscillating between conviction and despair, caught sometimes in a state of suspended animation in seeking ways of instrumentally delineating local ethnicity and at the same time her own identity. She recognizes outsiders' push to bring about social change in the county as an unavoidable source of many of the formidable obstacles in her way. As her viewpoint shows, another way of making a bid for ethnicity is by setting forth a *critique* of "civilization" and deploring its consequences. This negative approach again draws a boundary between Ashe County people and outsiders and implies the intrinsic advantages of the local life-style.

Julie Colvard traces her sense of the intrusive and destructive aspects of outside culture to her early experiences in school. From the first grade, she recalls, the daily lesson on "manners" was a routinized attempt to revise children's entire way of comporting themselves. Local forms of speech were subject to routine attack ("correction") from elementary school through college. Children were made acutely conscious of being "natives" of the region and were regularly corrected for exhibiting local styles of behavior. Julie states that English teachers, in constantly correcting students' speech, did "a lot more damage than good," for in attacking speech, they attacked the "culture as a whole." Five- and six-year-olds, she believes, are particularly vulnerable: "You want to please your parents and grandparents by getting good grades. This was extremely important, because getting a good education was always stressed by the families." Teachers "have the children over a barrel," since in order to get good grades, students must alter their habits, thereby alienating themselves to an extent from their family background and familiar culture.

Julie Colvard said that many of these teachers have "gone out in the world and decided that middle-class values show the way to be. These teachers know that under their direction, the children *are* going to change," but teachers do not fully consider the consequences of the changes they enforce.[13] Teachers come from outside the Blue Ridge region and "take upon themselves as their mission in life to 'educate' the 'ignorant' mountain children. They come in with great zeal, which is like that of the missionaries." The educational system becomes an instrument for "missionizing" the students, assimilating them to the "superior" ways of the outsider. Julie Colvard noted that Appalachian State University (her alma mater) began as a local teachers' college. Today, the university continues to "grind out English teachers who go back into the mountains" to "civilize" local people. From this perspective, she suggests, the university is an "island of colonization" in the Blue Ridge.

She says that it is difficult for her not to be bitter about her educational experience: "You realize from the age of five that you must act one way at home with family and another way at school. You have to change the way you do things. I have to remember how to act in order to be accepted at home. There are two different worlds for me here in Ashe County, one at home and the other at school. School changed the way I speak, the way I eat, sing, dress, and the way I look at things. Education has always made me scared. I've had a devil of a time really getting into school work, knowing that being educated to a certain extent forces you to leave the region to get the sort of job you want or do what you've been taught to want to do." Each of these two worlds pull at once, and the resulting contradiction is not easily resolved: "The way I've tried to resolve it is to become as educated as possible about the region, to be into local culture and into learning as much as I can. I still don't know. I'm paranoid about more school. When you first go to college, your people say, 'You're getting your college education,' and they just hold that to be a nice thing, but they still put you off in a way. You can't really get back into a lot of things, and you don't always have a lot to talk about when you return home. The more I get into local history and culture, the more people at home are coming back round to accepting me for what I'm doing. But they also hold it against me. It makes them paranoid to be around somebody who's more educated; they feel they have to watch their speech. I've always told myself that if I learned as much as I could about the county and learned how to relate to people, then maybe I'd be accepted on that level. It's a study in contradictions that just goes on and on and on. The tourist is another study in contradictions."[14]

Julie makes a comparison between her experience with the educational system and the experience of Ashe County people with tourism. In her view, the educational system has done a good job in preparing the county for the entry of tourism. The schools have equated the meaning of being Appalachian with the negative connotations of ignorance. This makes it easier for the schools as well as tourists to impose their preferences. The schools also inculcate the migration motif. Julie Colvard says that she "sort of got turned around. Before that, I was so hell-bent on leaving. They tell you you're going to have to go, there are no jobs here. There aren't a lot of jobs here, but you just have to make some choices. You have to get on one side or the other. Why should county people leave the county to the tourists? I have tried short-term residence outside the county, but I always found it a strain. Why go if you don't have to? Why make yourself miserable? If living here is going to make you happy, then why should you take off?"

In thinking of the hallmarks of local culture, Julie Colvard says that "land comes to mind before people do. Land is more like culture than it is dirt. There is such a close tie between people and their land that those who have left the county often find themselves coming back. There are a lot of family ties, ties with distant kin and friends. The county doesn't change much, and so there's a lot of peace of mind to be had from knowing that. A lot of it is enjoying where you are and just being left alone rather than being harassed constantly. Just peace of mind is what it boils down to. It's very hard for people to explain the ties people have to the land—it's just there, it's always been there. The wild flowers blooming in the spring, and being a little girl and not worrying about going off into the woods by yourself."

When the developers move in, they create a separation between the people and the land: "You don't want to sell to the people from the city because that injects a foreign element. Perhaps this is narrow, but it is self-protective. One man decided to build a house on a hill and got this monstrous road going through a field, and I have a very hard time looking at that place. I always think, if he can do it, so can a lot of others. It infuriates me and a lot of other county people when people sell their land to outsiders who do this sort of thing. They sell to pay medical bills or debts, or when there is an emergency, but people are not always as selective as they could be about who they sell to." Land sales thus not only put the integrity of the land and the culture in jeopardy but also set local people against one another, which pollutes the social body and exacerbates the helplessness people feel when they lose control over their environment. Julie Colvard explains: "If you grew up on the land, knowing everyone within twenty miles of where you are, you also know where they live, you know their kin and their kids, their dogs and cats. It's a matter of being practical. It's the way things are or were. In a lot of cases, you are related to the people who own the land. But otherwise, it's a matter of not knowing what's on the other side of the fence, not knowing enough about the people. It's just there. Knowing a whole lot of very specific things adds up to a whole way of life." This global view is obscured by the arrival of tourists: "Tourists, 99 percent of them, don't care most of the time, they just don't care. They couldn't listen if you tried to explain the culture to them. This is extremely hard to put up with without getting hysterical or just going out and shooting somebody."

As the number of tourists increases, their influence extends beyond matters of land prices and land use. The itinerant tourist population alters the entire nature of the local economy. Julie Colvard explains, "The tourists always want to spend money. They want local people to provide things for them to spend money on, and that's the beginning of dependency. The spiral begins, and you begin to wait for the tourists, although you don't like them. The contradictions begin again. Catering to people is something you don't like to do, a certain amount of self-respect is lost.

"Then there are the antique shops and junk shops that come in. Outsiders come in with the tourists and try to be mountainy and quaint and cute. They associate with the tourist on the level of the middle class and upper middle class. But if they're going to live in the county, they're going to have to associate with residents on a certain level too. They realize that in the long run they aren't going to be accepted by either [the tourists or the local people]. I'm not in sympathy with them, but it must be very hard for them to make it.

"But locals are willing to leave at the drop of a hat. Maybe it's like leaving a sinking ship. To me, it's a cop-out on the part of those who do leave. I'm not talking about leaving to get an education and then coming back, or leaving for a year or so. I mean leaving for good. It's a tremendous drain on the area's resources."

Ashe County has not been as affected by tourism as the next two counties to the south. But tourism's subtle and seasonal presence has begun to effect a structure of appropriation that replicates the unfolding of the New River dispute. Local canons of hospitality and inclusiveness promulgate an initial, provisional acceptance of the tourists and other outsiders. But tourists repeatedly abrogate their hosts' hospitality by their indifference or patronizing attitudes toward local culture. Silverman (1970, 24) nicely summarizes the consequences of this contradiction: "This fact of hospitality injects an element of irony and pathos into their picture since it is a foreigner [the outsider] who is [held] largely responsible for their plight. One is being knifed in the back by the man who sat at one's table as honored guest."

County residents' pursuit of a viable ethnicity is thus more than a reaction to and recognition of the negative, polluting aspects of "civilization." It is grounded in an evaluation of "civilization" as an aggressive encroachment upon the culture and heritage of Ashe County. Julie Colvard regards the educational system and tourism as colonizing agents. In a letter to the editors of *The Appalachian*, the daily newspaper published at Appalachian State University, she extended this evaluation to the operation of ski resorts in the Blue Ridge area:

Having read your special Ski Edition (November 18, 1976), I feel the following comments are necessary. I once held some of the romantic notions concerning skiing that are evident in your edition. However, I have long since given up those notions and replaced them with the following opinions concerning skiing and other related disasters which have beset the Appalachian region in recent years.

I have come to support the idea that the Appalachian region is a colony. The same system of colonialist exploitation which is at work in the strip mines of Kentucky is at work in the land/ski/condominium debacle in the mountains of North Carolina. The system is simply couched in prettier terms.

In both instances, land is owned by outside interests and money flows out of, not into, the region. There are arguments pointing out that skiing provides employment for local mountain people. However, most of these jobs are low-wage jobs such as those of maids and nightwatchpersons on the grounds of these hallowed resorts.

I see nothing exciting in a bulldozer tearing up the land and pulling down trees to make a new ski slope. I see nothing impressive in lodges whose very presence implies much more than romantic evenings by the fire. The ski industry has brought with it many complicated problems. Answers to the problems are not to be found in the sugar-coated promotion of the industry in which your newspaper has engaged.

Julie Colvard also notes that plans are afoot to begin prospecting and possible uranium mining in the Blue Ridge area. Given these developments, county people are becoming increasingly aware that the experience they had with the New River dispute was not an isolated, regrettable encounter with outsiders, but one facet of a pervasive colonializing regime:

[Appalachia] is a captive energy colony for urban and suburban middle- and upper-class, growth-oriented America, which must have Appalachia's coal and cheap labor in order to remain comfortably on its accustomed binge of consumption and waste or to endure its energy crisis. For at least a century and a half, the region has supplied the rest of the nation cheap raw materials, water power, fossil fuels, low-wage labor, and large markets for manufactured goods. The region is—along with much of the impoverished Third World—an essential base for perpetuating our much-praised "American way of life." (Whisnant 1974, 103)

As prime instances of colonialism Whisnant mentions the proposals for damming the New River and developing adjacent recreational areas, as well as tourism, which he views as involving the appropriation of the county for "use by the leisure-hungry middle and upper class" and the exploitation of "people of the region psychologically, economically, and politically" (Whisnant 1974, 109). Others compare the federally sponsored Appalachian Regional Commission to the Bureau of Indian Affairs, using the latter as an emblem of total and pervasive domination in the guise of benevolent largess.[15]

As I have shown, some Ashe County natives couch their objections to outside domination in terms of a highly generalized critique that goes hand in hand with local attempts to revitalize local culture and to assert a viable ethnicity. County residents find they can no longer cast their experience into historical—and therefore comprehensible—form; history has become unsatisfactory as a key representation because it no longer tests out against the glaring discontinuities of the present. In a culture beset by uncertainty, discontent, and contingency, it is no wonder that some people threatened to use dynamite and guns if the bulldozers arrived to build the New River dams. Others vowed some "mountain-style" direct intervention if their land was appropriated, and one local resident planned to discourage tourists from returning by stuffing their cars' exhaust pipes with dead fish.

The construction of ethnicity in Ashe County has been only partly successful. Ethnicity has not jelled as an element of culture—it remains incipient—perhaps largely because its construction was motivated by rhetorical intent and political necessity rather than cultural authenticity. It *has* had a rhetorical impact in the political arena. But it has not been legitimated as intrinsic to social ideology; so much attention has had to be given to immediate political realities that ethnicity could not be broadly rearticulated in relation to existing cultural forms. At the same time, local ethnicity was not made—perhaps could not have been made—thoroughly convincing to outsiders, who associate the supposed Scotch-Irish background of the Blue Ridge population with the mainstream rather than with marginality. In addition, the stress on individualism and the secondary importance of concepts of communalism in local culture hindered the establishment of ethnicity as fundamental.

Finally, ethnicity, like so many other cultural elements, could not serve as the basis for delineations that could be acted on, not because of any intrinsic flaw, but because of what Bateson (1979, 48) calls the "ecological saturation of all the possibilities of differentiation." Through ever-increasing differentiation, "civilization" has come to occupy, has *saturated* the niches of the environment *and* of the symbolic system, largely precluding independent adaptations on the part of the local population.[16] Local people can create as many delineations as they care to, but none can be implemented in a social field already "colonized" by a plethora of legal, bureaucratic, and political delineations or "scripts"; everything is already delineated by the dominant social system. This saturation places marginal populations in a double bind that in turn controls, limits, and defines the actability of their definitions of themselves and their situation. Ashe County people have attempted to construct an ethnicity in order to sidestep these double binds and to locate an unoccupied niche for themselves in the dominant symbolic system; they hoped thereby to prevent the occupation of their territory by outsiders.

As historical research on the Appalachian region (e.g., Shapiro 1978; Whisnant 1983) makes clear, the problematizing of Appalachian culture has been going on for at least a century. The New River dispute is not unique, but representative. Like Appalachians in other parts of the region, Ashe County people have claimed a distinct ethnicity for themselves by emphasizing those positive characterizations that outsiders also associate with Appalachian culture. Yet in its present form, ethnicity remains problematic both as a *meaning* and as a *representation* to which particular meanings may be attached. The content of ethnicity in Ashe County and more broadly in Appalachia might best be defined as the *questions* people are asking about themselves and their situation: Have we succeeded in claiming the status of a distinct ethnicity and culture? In whose view? If so, just how can "being Appalachian," or, as some say, "being a mountaineer" be characterized? Thus far the answers to these questions have at best been partial and strategic, rather than stable and definitive.

In specifying the exact nature of change in Ashe County, one may refer to major shifts in meaning and culture but, as I have shown, the direction of such shifts is rather ambiguous; countercurrents, constraints, and contradictions abound. The assertion of ethnicity and the revival of local culture are counterposed by an erosion and refiguring of that culture through the intervention of what some social critics have viewed as a "colonial presence." Thus, Caulfield (1972, 193) suggests that the underlying form of exploitation in "internal colonies" such as Appalachia is not only that of "class over class, but rather of culture over culture." Consistent with this premise, I have interpreted the political dynamic that situates the formulation and deconstruction of meanings in social discourse; it was impossible to determine directly what constitutes "the cultural system." Change depends on this politics of culture, which in Ashe County can be understood as a change in the status of *culture* and *meaning* in social ideology, and as a change in the distribution of culture as a representation in social discourse.

In general, social ideology has changed such that culture and meaning are no longer implicit givens but explicit uncertainties.

After the New River dispute, culture and meaning for some people became explicitly formulated concepts rather than assumed forms intrinsic to how they live their lives; meaning became far more problematic than before. *Culture* became a much more common term in political rhetoric and, to some extent, rhetoric displaced the conventional symbolic system, or came to fill the void left by the fragmentation of assumed representations. As meaning and culture were cast into words, representation became increasingly alienated from social action. Life was no longer seen as harmonious with history; instead life became a form of struggle. Similarly, diffuseness as a cultural orientation to social interaction became a context that permitted outside intervention; it made Ashe County social networks vulnerable, as evidenced by the contradictions generated by the implementation of hospitality. The traditional code of diffuse, enduring solidarity allowed external intervention to gain a foothold, an example of how "diffuseness can act as an umbrella for domination, or for struggle" (Barnett and Silverman 1976, 29).

Disagreements among local people regarding the meaning of culture created an arena in which disaffection and conflict entered their own social networks. County natives could no longer take for granted a tacit cultural consensus. Julie Colvard noted that "getting an education" often meant not having "much in common" with the folks back home and that people sometimes regarded neighbors or kin with more education as "uppity" or as "putting on airs." Partly because ethnicity is an incipient phenomenon, there is considerable variation in the level of consciousness of local people—some are more politicized than others. This variation has not created explicitly opposed factions, but it has imposed an atmosphere of unarticulated divisiveness that mitigates against collective action and prompts outsiders to adopt a "divide and conquer" strategy.[17] Although county residents did take collective action during the New River dispute, the outsiders' "divide and conquer" approach succeeded: the county won a victory that was not a victory. Ostensibly local people "won" the dispute, but in the process they were further disenfranchised from culture and meaning as givens. For many people the implications of the outcome were not clear until it was too late.

The most significant change in Ashe County accompanying the

New River dispute and other encroachments is the growing willingness of many residents to verbalize concerns about events that
had previously been systematically disregarded. Conventional
usages and ideological assumptions have developed into questions
about the acceptability of imposed ideas. The dispute compelled
Ashe County people to assert their identity in relation to the
changes that threatened to engulf them. In doing so, they looked
for a point of departure to change from. Change begs a definition
of renewal as well as of continuity, but it ultimately entails a redefinition of the present, since it puts the existing state of affairs in
question.

Faced with a "colonial" presence, residents looked to history as
they sought to redefine the present. The present had to be established in terms of the past before the future could be envisioned.
Fanon's (1956) prescription for renewal—assimilation, memory,
and creation—is reflected in the paradoxes of change confronting
Ashe County people. From their contact with outsiders during the
New River dispute, they assimilated rhetorical and manipulative
skills and acquired tools through which they sought to realize their
aims and to legitimate an ethnicity. As they discovered new discursive practices, they also began to stabilize a concept of cultural
identity in terms of historical context and perspective. Finally,
based on their accumulating experience in the political arena, they
banked on their ability to reinvent a life-style and a satisfactory
pattern of accommodation *and* opposition to outsiders.

In the Blue Ridge, social change must be assessed not simply as
a perceptible difference between social formations at one point in
time and at a later point. Instead, change is a developing recognition and realization that conditions are unsatisfactory. Change and
the particular changes that people seek and desire are implicit in
the definition of those conditions. The act of defining in turn entails a questioning. In a critique of the colonial presence, there is
already change; notions that were previously assumed to be laws
of life are put into question. The transformations invoked by the
act of questioning are followed by political and collective actions,
both protest and compromise, directed toward affecting the course
of the future.[18]

In Ashe County ideology, culture and meaning were always
embedded in experience and action. But outside interventions have

muddied these concepts and the relations between them. Rather than having meaningful content, culture itself comes to be viewed as a set of problems that may be unsolvable. Although culture has been traditionally regarded as having a self-evident, self-validating status independent of outside social institutions, today it is increasingly expressed through ethnicity, the meaning of which is, in turn, contingent on the recognition of the larger society. Meaning ceases to be self-evident; authenticity has to be sought after and struggled for.

Correctly or incorrectly, Ashe County people confer the major responsibility for this state of affairs on outsiders, whose interventions displace or override indigenous discourse. But a critique of dominant social forms cannot replace cultural meaning, and so Ashe County residents transform their critiques into cultural rhetoric and pose culture as ethnicity.

This rhetoric makes possible the legitimation of alternate cultural forms. Local people attempt to locate within this rhetoric the possibility of transcendent value. The consumer appeal of selected cultural elements leads local people to seek legitimation in part through consumerism, yet they worry that their culture is being consumed. Once ethnicity enters the marketplace, its intended meaning is immediately subverted: it is no longer a representation of cultural distinctiveness and self-determination but a style for artifacts and consumer products.[19]

Craft items manufactured by local people are purchased as souvenirs, becoming artifacts of the unexpected cleverness of quaint, archaic, or primitive people. The area's musical tradition is meeting the same fate. Even local residents become consumer items, as tourists snap photographs of those they take to be "authentic hillbillies," their homes, and their homeland. Similarly, the landscape of the Blue Ridge region becomes a commodity, put to use and to profit by the recreation industry, mining interests, and hydroelectric companies. Scenic beauty is an article sold to outsiders by ski resorts, the summer-home business, and recreation areas.

Ashe County culture thus becomes a product of the "culture industry," and local ethnicity is cut off "from the possibility of differencing itself as all difference degenerates into a nuance in the monotony of supply" (Adorno 1976, 260). In a final effort to revitalize and assert local cultural representations, local people play

into the hands of outsiders by selling their culture in the marketplace from which they can reappropriate it only as a collection of
disembodied meanings.[20]

The primary locus of value is no longer within indigenous culture or in being a native. Meaning is instead calibrated in terms of
its market prospects. Ethnic distinctiveness becomes subject to
consumer demand. Particular ethnic groups, as well as the products appropriated for sale by outsiders, can be discontinued if they
lose their consumer appeal. And when the product is in demand,
the buyers literally command its purchase by offering high prices
that local residents cannot refuse. The owners of small farms suddenly find themselves alienated from their land, but land prices
become so inflated as to make repurchase impossible. As Adorno
(1976, 260) says, a semblance of freedom (to sell or not to sell)
"makes reflection upon one's own unfreedom incomparably more
difficult than formerly when such reflection stood in contradiction
to manifest unfreedom, thus strengthening dependence."

Paradoxically, the growing dependence and domination of local
people have stimulated reflection on these matters. The separation
of reflection and meaning from action has become pervasive. Artifacts are detached from their place in the Ashe County style of
life and from the flow of social discourse in order to enter the
marketplace. Consumption overtakes ethnicity, by which local
people intended to give meaning to the person and direction to
their history. Lefebvre (1971, 94) notes that in a "society of consumption, the consumer is consumed." Assimilation, a familiar
euphemism for this process, thus has the potential to perpetuate a
destructive cycle in which the cultures of minority populations are
appropriated, absorbed, and gradually dismantled. From this grim
possibility it is one simple step to a society cannibalizing itself, de-
constructing its own system of representations as it has those of
the small-scale societies that are dependent upon it.

These interpretations arose from the intersection of my research
with two major questions. The first is a thoroughly respectable
anthropological question about cultural difference: What are the
similarities and differences, if any, between the local culture of Ashe
County (or the "regional culture" of Appalachia) and the culture of
mainstream America? Behind this question was the positive value I

place on cultural difference and diversity. The more general form of this question could be stated as: Who is the Other? How is the Other different from myself? The second question is the product of the Appalachian region's history of involvement with outside interests and government and social agencies: What is the political dynamic of the relation of local people to the larger society? The first question demands an ethnographic description, but I found that ethnography cannot describe the course of such struggles simply by decoding cultural symbols, but must engage and interpret the political process through which cultural representations become unstable, contested rhetorical elements in the debate. Because the negotiations for power that Ashe County people have entered into are so closely and complexly connected with the knowledge that they claim about their culture, to describe the particular discursive practices brought about by that negotiation is at the same time to address the question of cultural difference.

The wisdom of Batteau's (1983a, 123) statement that in the case of Appalachia, "culture is politically constituted" also discloses the moral of the contorted narrative I have traced in this book: Ashe County "culture" eludes being described as a collection of traits, but instead must be represented as a process of becoming: of becoming besieged and marginalized; of becoming a political movement and possibly an "ethnic minority"; of becoming aware of the necessity of saying "who we are." "Who the Other is to us and how outsiders see us as the Other" is a major underlying theme in the discourse and the struggle of Ashe County people to establish a power base for pursuing, protecting, and defending their style of life.

Culture appears in this context as extraordinarily fluid and changeable; it operates as a placeholder, a representation that shifts, deviates, and often wobbles in an unstable and quixotic fashion, depending on the desires, options, constraints, and interventions operating at the crossroads of the present. Rhetoric, discourse, knowledge, and power interact, make bids and claims on one another, intimately inform and feed into what can be said about "the culture" of Ashe County. The "production of culture" is itself a strategic, rhetorical practice for people in Ashe County certainly, and for the anthropologist as well. For both the people and the anthropologist, a "description of the culture" is immersed in and minutely infiltrated by societywide political processes. Thus, to discuss the politics of culture in Ashe County is at the same time and through the same terms to address the problem of ethnographic description.

Under these conditions, ethnographic description has demanded that I become embroiled in and at times partisan to claims about "culture" which are and will continue to be in flux. If, as ethnographer, I hesitate to say just what Ashe County culture *is,* that is because accuracy requires me instead to talk about what the semiotics of culture have been in the county's recent history. My claim to knowledge of Ashe County's culture has been to show how meaning is fought over and attributed in diverse and contradictory ways to culture as a representation in the forms of discourse evident in the county. Throughout this book, I have been, directly or indirectly, reflecting on Foucault's trope of power/ knowledge, whereby the struggle over culture, knowledge, and representation is a determinant of power, and vice versa:

[In] thinking of the mechanisms of power, I am thinking rather of its capillary form of existence, the point where power reaches into the very grain of individuals, touches their bodies and inserts itself into their actions and attitudes, their discourses, learning processes and everyday lives. (Foucault 1980, 39)

This "take" on society—on the history of the present—and on how to interpret it has allowed me to look beyond culture, to put it in context, to recognize it as a representation in local discourse and in anthropological discourse, and at the same time to come to grips with the social and political circumstances of the people of Ashe County. Recognizing the problematic and tenuous status of identity, meaning, and culture for the county's long-term residents, I am led to the realization that the cultural system as a system in the strict sense has been obviated for them and perhaps also as an interpretive device for the anthropologist studying modern society.

In my struggle to present an ethnographic description, I have thus come to resist picturing the culture of Ashe County as a systematic whole.[21] Absolute meanings were elusive; crystalline structures did not readily emerge. I believe that in this particular case, a systems analogy would have closed off local culture into an artificially autonomous semiotic totality, misconstruing the texture of social experience of county residents and misrepresenting Ashe County people as having neither the need nor the capacity for innovation *and* as being free of the politics of culture change. A strict systems model would have suggested that the "system" itself is constricted by its own fixed ground rules. But culture in Ashe County instead represents active discourse and characterizes an emerging style of symbolization. What is a *system* is the technology of intervention, which, along with its supporting administrative apparatus, impinges on the local scene.

Once culture comes to be viewed as problematic, description also becomes a problem. A fine-grain inspection of Ashe County residents' own way of confronting the problem of describing their culture reveals a two-tiered approach. Among themselves, or outside the charged arena of immediate contention and confrontation, they view their culture as implicit and nonsystemic. Viewing meaning in terms of discourse, defining action as embodied in symbol, reflection, and conception, Ashe County people situate social experience within an ongoing discourse among persons. But in a more overtly political context, they approach description in rather different terms.

Ashe County people present their social discourse, particularly in their dialogue with outsiders, not as discourse, creativity, and ongoing innovation, but precisely as a stable "cultural system." This rhetorical maneuver is motivated by a recognition of an affinity between the system concept and the outsiders' nonrelational orientation of bureaucratic rationalism. In turn, this orientation misrepresents the tie between Ashe County people and outsiders. Outsiders define that tie not in relational terms, but in terms of technical manipulation. By posing a rationalized cultural system and thus trying to avoid being treated in technical terms, local people unwittingly play along with outsiders' definitions. That is the irony of their situation.

In the rhetorical mode of Ashe County, culture is explicit as a representation through which people formulate identity and ethnicity, differentiate themselves from and articulate their relationship with outsiders, and insist on their distinctiveness as persons. The rhetorical mode is not simply a content of their culture, a cultural style, but an outgrowth of the political dynamic that increasingly controls their modes of representation. Of course, the division between the rhetorical presentation of their culture to outsiders and its descriptive self-presentation creates additional conceptual difficulties.

American culture values pluralism in the abstract, but in practice American society has difficulty with cultural difference. Our society promotes individual self-determination, but appropriates and controls the representations through which the person is culturally constituted. For all their individualism, Ashe County people remain in many respects embedded in a communal ambiance: individuality is made possible and supported by orientations toward action that refer to and take account of social embeddedness. In contrast, the narrowly rationalistic normative matrix of American society today leads away from community, toward "freedom," utilitarian individualism, expediency, narcissistic goal attainment—the person desituated, alienated, and isolated.[22] This syndrome is accompanied by increasing social and political cynicism, privatism, and disaffection.

American society perceives pluralism, diversity, communalism, and involvement as desirable in the abstract. But how are these values to be realized? The people of Ashe County are a case in point: they have a wealth of symbolic resources, but the issue of which organizing motif is to be given primacy remains unresolved. Like other Americans, Ashe County people vehemently seek to return to the historical sources of American communalism. But perhaps communalism is a historical illusion. Change, or at least progressive change, is stalled, or perhaps impossible. Cultural difference is perceived as a threat or a curiosity rather than a valued resource. These difficult social issues throw doubt upon the fate of local communities as well as upon that of the increasingly technocratic society of which they are reluctantly a part.

# Epilogue

In August 1977, after the defeat of the Blue Ridge project on the New River, the Appalachian Power Company (APC) proposed a new project at Brumley Gap, about fifty miles northwest of Ashe County in southwestern Virginia. This new project called for a 300-foot-high dam, to retain a lake that would have been the largest pump-storage facility in the United States. APC argued that the facility was necessary to meet the region's needs for extra power during peak demand periods, the same argument it had made for damming the New River. The Brumley Gap project would have flooded 119 homesteads.[1]

The ensuing dispute over Brumley Gap and particularly the response of local residents could easily have been predicted on the "model" of the New River dispute. Forming the Brumley Gap Concerned Citizens' Committee, residents mobilized to combat the project, organizing auctions to raise funds for attorneys' fees, which were estimated to reach $100,000. As with the New River dispute, T-shirts were distributed, bearing anti-dam slogans. Archeologists turned up paleo-Indian artifacts in the hope of having the area designated a national historic site. An appeal went out to the Sierra Club Legal Defense Fund to bring the case of the local residents before the Federal Energy Regulatory Commission (FERC). The ideological basis for the opposition to this new proposal—the New River project refigured—was summed up by a Brumley Gap native: "It's hard to explain what's precious about life here. I think it's something about the earth, a sort of communion with the land when you can go out there and plow your fields and produce half of what you eat. Most people here realize they're not really college-educated types, yet within themselves they are secure" (Attinger 1979, 5).

According to Richard Austin (1984, 120–21), a local organizer, concerned citizens immediately realized that opposition should begin before a license for the project was issued. They knew that resistance would require considerable legal expertise, had to be based on the leadership of local people who had the most to lose if the project were built, and should seek support on a regional as well as a local basis. The local environmental group had just won a battle to prevent strip mining in a nearby national forest and was thus primed for a new struggle. The Sierra Club Defense Fund agreed to take the case before FERC, and local residents rapidly organized a regional coalition to analyze not only the environmental issues but also economic and energy alternatives.

When APC attempted to begin construction of access roads, preliminary drilling, and testing, residents threatened to use guns. But the American Friends Service Committee provided consultants who worked with small groups, teaching peaceful techniques of resistance. Understanding that one route to power was to acquire detailed information, the coalition raised $40,000 to pay a consulting firm to make a comparative study of the proposal and other energy-conservation options. The report concluded that APC's plan was "unnecessary, conceptually wasteful . . . and without economic merit" (Austin 1984, 122). But the county supervisors had earlier endorsed the project and were hesitant to adopt this report. Local people attended the meetings of the county supervisors, lobbied their representatives in Congress, brought in media coverage, and held prayer meetings to bolster group solidarity. FERC met in 1980 to rule on the permit requested by APC, but was compelled to delay a decision until the coalition against the project could file a report.

The permit was approved in early 1982. The Brumley Gap Concerned Citizens' Committee filed an appeal with the federal appeals court in Washington, D.C. The surprise came in October 1982, when the power company announced it was abandoning its plan for Brumley Gap as part of a cost-cutting program. The struggle was over: "On Saturday, November 20, 1982, Brumley Gap families and their friends formed a mile-long caravan of cars.

Decorated with signs, streamers, and balloons, the late-morning procession wound down a narrow road, through five miles of beauty that would have been flooded, onto the main highway, and through Abingdon, the county seat" (Austin 1984, 124).

When I returned to Ashe County in July 1987, I had considerable misgivings about what I would find. I had been told of "slums" and "shopping malls," and a totally transformed county road system; I had been led to expect the worst. But as I drove north on U.S. 221 from Deep Gap to West Jefferson, I was again struck by the extraordinary beauty of the land, a beauty that during my absence had become for me abstract, confused with the rhetorical statements I had recorded from local people. The summer weather was glorious; the mountains were clad with deep forest green; bright patches of bachelor buttons, black-eyed Susans, blue straw flowers, and purple clover dotted the mowed embankments; under the trees were a few late blossoms of mountain laurel.

As I drove into the county, I felt myself to be entering a charmed circle. I felt a rush of excitement as I passed a small sign, Entering Ashe County. Of course, nothing delimits this space but a line on a map and my invented notion of the place. By doing anthropology there, I had turned the county into a charged symbol, a complex representation that had come to stand for a land, a spirit of place, a singular gateway to an encounter with Otherness. Ashe County is a different America from that of the cities with which I am familiar. In my return, I sought completion as well as a diagnosis of current circumstances and a test of my earlier image of place, people, and their situation. If Ashe County had become a symbol in a discourse I had created, I had not elaborated it merely at my pleasure. The questions I now asked people were often painful ones: How have things changed in the county? What was to become of what it has been? I was struck by and had to think through once again the tenuous and problematic relation between the everyday lives of county residents and what I had written about them.

Edna Price James still lives in her large modern house in the center of West Jefferson. She has opened a store in the building she owns on Jefferson Avenue and sells bedding and ready-made curtains. There is a man in her life now, retired from the military.

They have been to Europe, Brazil, and Japan, experiences about which Edna loves to tell stories. When I asked her what was different about the county from ten years ago, she said, "Too many foreigners." But she went on to tell me about the country fair they had just had in town the week before, "Christmas in July." It had been a rousing success, with "people from forty-seven states attending." On the one hand, she resents the ever-increasing presence of "foreigners" in the county; on the other, local natives accommodate their presence in ways that legitimize the value of local affairs and local culture.

When I drove out to Sugar Run, I found that Frank Grimes had died a number of years ago. His father's millstones are still on either side of the walk leading up to his house. Walter and Jane Huntington have moved out of the county and live near Asheville, where he is employed in health-care administration. His sister Carlie and her husband live across the road in their still new-looking home. The community seems to have changed little since I studied it twelve years ago.

Eleanor Reeves still lives in her comfortable house on the hill above downtown West Jefferson and continues her genealogical research. She has recently published a book on county history and is working on another, about her revolutionary war ancestors. Her arthritis has slowed her down, but I told her that she seemed more jolly than I remembered her. She said that she reckoned that at that time she had still been upset about her husband's death. A former schoolteacher, she was particularly concerned about discussions in the county about consolidating many of the elementary schools and busing children outside their home communities. When I told her where I was staying, west of Creston, she immediately identified the old house and told me who built it and when. Her historical sense was as keen as ever.

A striking change had come over St. Mary's Church, and the Episcopal Church at Glendale Springs had experienced a complete renaissance. After Ben Long completed the frescoes at St. Mary's in 1977 and then at Holy Trinity Church at Glendale Springs in 1980, the extraordinary magnetism of these art works was widely publicized. The churches continued to attract new members as a consequence of Father Hodge's ministrations. When I arrived at St. Mary's, a large tourist bus was parked next to the tiny church

Figure 8. "The Lord's Supper" (1980), detail. The standing male figure is a portrait of J. Faulton Hodge. A true fresco by Ben Long IV of Statesville, North Carolina, with the help of twenty other artists, located in Holy Trinity Episcopal Church, in the Parish of The Holy Communion, Glendale Springs, North Carolina.

building. In the entryway, color postcards and large reproductions of the frescoes and the churches were available for a nominal fee. Visitors were stuffing the alms box with bills, signing the visitors' roster, and respectfully entering the sanctuary to view the frescoes and to listen to a recording of Father Hodge describing the history and meaning of the paintings.

At Glendale Springs, the parking lot was crowded with late-model cars. Again, there was a large tourist bus. Ben Long's fresco of the Last Supper is beautiful to behold, some think divinely inspired (Figure 8). The clear leaded-glass windows in the church allow maximum natural light into the interior. Here too, the offering plate overflowed with visitors' contributions. The frescoes have clearly given the churches a perpetual endowment. Across the road at the mission house, paintings of local artists cover the walls. In the undercroft a large shop sells stationery, postcards, quilts, and printed reproductions of Father Hodge's talks about the frescoes. These churches have become lively religious communities, but they are also shrines, visited by a quarter of a million pilgrims a year. Glendale Springs resembles a medieval pilgrimage center, with a commodious inn and shops where mementoes of the visit may be purchased. The church has bolstered the local economy.

Father Hodge, exhausted after fifteen years in the county, has taken a medical leave. Most people doubt that he will return. Meanwhile, a controversy has developed over a proposal that the churches be moved to a unified site in the south part of the county. Some parishioners argue that the move will allow the church to grow, while others state that it would be a "sin" to relocate the frescoes.

The New River is as it was. After finishing an interview at the mission house in Glendale Springs, I drove back toward Jefferson and turned off on a gravel road that wanders along the river bank, passing fields and farms before reaching the ranger station of the New River State Park (Figure 9). Of the area designated for park territory, only three moderately sized plots have been purchased so far by the State of North Carolina; one is accessible by road, the other two can be reached only by canoe. There is parking, a large mowed meadow sloping down to the river, and a picnic area shaded by the apple trees of an old orchard. It is a bucolic place, greenery everywhere, goldenrod blooming, and ripe blackberries hidden in the foliage along the perimeter of the meadow. I sat on the lowest step leading down to the river, letting my legs dangle in the water, and watched the gentle flow of the current, the dragonflies hovering at the surface and the tall trees on the opposite bank. There were four or five other cars in the parking lot, but none of the canoers passed along the river while I was there. The Committee for the New River still meets annually to plan lobbying activities to have funds allocated for the purchase of additional land for the state park.

Tourism has not suddenly increased in Ashe County as a result of the new park, but people come in larger numbers each year. Pamphlets available throughout the county include maps indicating access to the river, lists of motels, and directions to the Blue Ridge Parkway, the fresco churches, and Mount Jefferson State

Figure 9. Commemorative Plaque at the New River State Park.

Park. Also listed are the locations of stores carrying "mountain crafts," including the New River General Store, "a real, old-time country store" at Scottville. Whatever the ambivalences of local residents, tourism is officially promoted and continues to be developed in the county, and some tourists later become long-term county residents.

Another newly developing industry in the county is tree farming. Up and down the slopes of the mountains and in fields along many of the county roads, neat rows of fir trees are being grown as a cash crop. In fact, far more acreage is devoted to fir trees today than to tobacco, which had long been the main cash crop in the county. The trees are harvested each November and trucked to urban centers for the Christmas season. The tree farms' even rows of green cones have transformed the rural landscape. The trees are pruned and the undergrowth controlled so that the firs develop a symmetrical shape.

Fir trees seem an appealing and innocent enough way to use the land for profit. The "Christmas in July" country fair was in part motivated by efforts to promote the tree farms. Along Jefferson Avenue fir trees stand in large wooden planters, clearly labeled with the name of the tree farm where each was grown (Figure 10).

Figure 10. Downtown West Jefferson, North Carolina, 1987.

Tours were arranged of the tree farms, and the iconography of the
Christmas season was used to advertise local economic interests
and local identity as well.

Yet if the New River dispute put local culture and community
on trial in the 1970s and served as the highly politicized forum for
arguing about and negotiating change, the tree farms provide the
terms for a similar sort of argumentation and discourse in the
1980s. Again the question of change—forced change versus chosen
change—is contingent on the relation of local residents to outsiders and outside interests. The farmers depend on chemicals purchased from nonlocal companies, and the trees are sold in a market
outside the county. The money accruing to the tree farmers comes
from "civilization," from "the city"; a double dependency is implicit in this setup, and questions of land use and resource allocation are again at issue.

It is generally recognized that tree farming is a "good thing" for
the county as well as for the tree farmers, since it represents a considerable source of income. But a number of my informants questioned the long-term viability and ecological wisdom of tree farming. One was concerned about the poisonous insecticides and
herbicides used around the trees. Another informant said that the
dollars brought in by the tree farms may be at "the expense of future generations," since the chemicals used on the trees are bound

to get into the watershed and the river—she expects "man will kill himself off yet." The ecological effects of the herbicides can be seen, she said, by the visibility of the red, bare soil under the trees. She talked about seeing a dazed deer stagger out of a stream; the next day, a dead fox was found. She went on to argue that the people of the region "have always done the same sort of thing. Appalachian people have a history of letting themselves be exploited": They sold off mineral, coal, and mining rights for a pittance; now they're clear-cutting and growing fir trees for a quick dollar, never mind the long-term implications. Another informant suggested that local people are reluctant to organize and protest against tree farming because they are hesitant about preventing their neighbors from making a little money. But the underside of the situation was seen by these informants as the repetition of a destructive, even self-destructive history.[2]

These concerns are comparable to those that dominate contentions over land use and related prospects for the future elsewhere in the Appalachian region. An update in the *Washington Post* on Kentucky strip mining carried the headline "Killing Mountains for Coal."[3] A color photograph accompanying the article shows a land resembling the deserts of the American southwest; it was captioned, "Mountains turned into mesas in eastern Kentucky." While the implications of tree farming or damming rivers are subtle compared to strip mining, all these interventions problematize both ecological and cultural survival. They are also incitements to certain kinds of discourse and representation, as I will argue shortly.

On the outskirts of Jefferson and between West Jefferson and Beaver Creek, large shopping centers have sprung up. McDonald's golden arches hover below a hilltop crowned with anonymous apartment complexes. The railroad stopped coming to West Jefferson in 1977. The tracks have been taken up, and the right-of-way is grown over in grass. People's Rexall Drugstore in West Jefferson has relocated from downtown to a spot on the four-lane, where more parking is available. On Jefferson Avenue, a number of storefronts look blind and deserted; For Rent signs abound. The A&P is closed and boarded up. In this tiny, nondescript town, the mode of ecological succession closely resembles that evident in large urban centers: a gravitation toward the center from the rural periphery associated with a decentering of activity and economy

toward a suburban interstitial. In the rural hamlets scattered throughout the county, the community infrastructure has long since disappeared. No longer are offices of a doctor and an attorney, a small
post office and general store, and a few churches scattered near
people's homes. Now there is one church, perhaps the garage for
the volunteer fire department's equipment, and emptiness. The
small rural communities such as Sugar Run have become little
more than bedroom communities amid sporadic and sporadically
cultivated farms. People drive to the shopping centers; there is still
only one movie theater in the county.

As I drove through West Jefferson, I caught a glimpse of wine
bottles in the doorway of a shop. Wine and beer, but not hard liquor, are now legally sold in the county. I bought a bottle of California wine for the people with whom I was staying and took a
look at the selection of imported beers. The shopkeeper told me
that the county's dry law had been repealed a number of years ago,
although one never knew if that would change with the next election. He and his wife had moved to the county a number of
months ago from an urban center in the Piedmont. They were attracted by the excellent schools in the county and the prospects of
rural living. The county seemed to offer the possibility of "a
slower pace," and they had found "a lot of other people like us"
arriving to start a new way of life. Eleanor Reeves's description of
the county in genealogical terms was at best partial, past, or wishful thinking. The shopkeeper described a very heterogeneous
population.

Much had changed with Ronnie Taylor since I had seen him
last, but much was as I remembered. He still lives in his remarkable home off Idlewild Road, two log cabins with numerous decks
and glassed wings. He and his wife and I sat outside drinking homemade beer. He still works for his father's well-drilling business and
is still the self-possessed, quick-minded man whose rapid-fire, intense way of expressing himself gets right to the point. He is both
very much of the county and of the rest of the world as well. He
talked about how the county is changing and conveyed, as did
many other county natives, a sense of an infiltration rather than an
invasion of non-natives. He thinks many newcomers to the county
are "blue-collar types" who start with a few acres of land and
build over the years on a modest outlay until they have a summer

house or second home. They may start by camping on their land but eventually have a place where they can retire. The vast majority of these people are white and Protestant.

Ronnie describes many of these people as bringing everything they need with them into the county and often "not talking to anyone"; they are not back-to-the-landers trying to blend into the local social system. Where the native builds a set of obligations and ties of reciprocity, the "foreigner" may comport himself in a more "professional" fashion. Ronnie said that local people will have his father's company do work for them, and he may do extra favors and minor consultations free of charge, but they often take too long to pay him. Outsiders, in contrast, expect to pay for services rendered and do so in a timely manner. For better or worse, the influx of outsiders is accompanied by a stricter, more thorough-going monetization of even peripheral areas of labor and exchange; informal reciprocity and sharing are becoming increasingly rationalized. Of particular interest in Ronnie's description is his ambivalence about the sometimes isolative outsider who pays his bill *and* about the Ashe County native who still assumes a system of reciprocity and mutual aid but may twist it to his own advantage. The Floridians' attitude is a far cry from the local native who, Ronnie claimed, may use his entire vacation to drive his truck to the city to buy carpeting that is only a few dollars cheaper a yard than what is available in the county. I couldn't decide if he was maligning local people for refusing to participate in a more "legal-rational" way of living or maligning outsiders for having arrived on the scene. He seems to prefer the outsiders' "professionalism" in some ways, yet he regrets the loss of communalism. He is proud of the home that he and his wife have made for themselves, but also talks of selling it. He describes their beachside property in the Bahamas with pleasure and nostalgia. He recollected his work as a musician in San Francisco in the 1960s and gave me a copy of his record album, which his mother believed would be a good financial investment. I respected his lively but ambivalent relation to his history and his rootedness in the county. His here-and-there sense of life was perhaps inevitable, but I wondered if he overstated his "bi-worldliness" to me because I am an outsider.

When I spoke again with Edna Price James, she asked: "Don't you think that Ashe County has changed less than most places?"

Indeed, I do. But her asking this indicated that change has become a question in Ashe County, that change has opened up a space of discourse and action in which what county people say about themselves must be situated. The presence of "foreigners" is only one of many factors that affect what is possible and what happens in this space. The undercurrent of change just beneath the surface of everyday life also involves the nagging realization of how problematic are the prospects for local people deciding upon the direction that change is to take. Under what conditions is community mobilization or political action possible in relation to specific issues of change?

In the Blue Ridge, mobilization comes in response to a crisis, as locally defined. But what sort of crisis? And what preconditions make mobilization possible and likely? How does community mobilization relate to political action and resistance to unwanted change? In discussing the process of mobilization in small rural communities, Beaver (1986) refers mainly to personal crises of community members and to local situations that pose an immediate threat to survival, to shelter, or to immediate material needs. The community responds by providing help, supplies, food, shelter, or labor. Under such conditions, the particular intervention needed is obvious, a line of action is readily definable, and mobilization follows.

Erikson's (1976) study of the catastrophic Buffalo Creek flood in West Virginia in 1972 demonstrates that a similar pattern of response can be observed elsewhere in the Appalachian region. But many of the crises that have punctuated the region's history are not simply natural or personal disasters and do not have the immediacy that lends itself to a clearly defined, unambiguous response. For instance, coal mining and strip mining have been "chronic crises" in eastern Kentucky for generations. Community mobilization in this context has been unreliable, variable, and problematic in its results; to be effective, mobilization has had to occur on a scale larger than that of the local community. The history of political activism in that area has been one of long-term struggle, alliances with labor unions and other outside organizations, and has often been exhausting and enervating for local people. One can only wonder whether the reliance on allies outside the region replicates in another domain the domination and dependence to which the struggles attempt to respond. Just as the crisis has a basis in the wider interconnections between local people and outsiders, any solution must likewise take advantage of such interconnections.

This parallel was also evident in the New River dispute, a somewhat more circumscribed, long-term crisis for the people of Ashe County. In this case, political mobilization was possible because the collective threat was clearly evident, there was a substrate at the local level of intact networks and expertise, and a niche or potential in the legal structure was found through which to define resistance, to delineate the issues, and to enforce a decision. The collective threat meant that as a group, local people had much to lose. However worrisome tree farms in the county may be to some local residents today, a collective threat is not so obvious, since many local landowners and farmers have much to gain from this activity. Although the tree farms have incited an incipient discourse of resistance, which refers to ecological and historical arguments similar to those raised during the New River dispute, concerted political mobilization has not developed around this issue and is not likely to.

The identification of an event such as tree farming or damming the New River as an issue immediately opens a space of discourse and incites a questioning of the acceptability of the new undertaking in relation to local norms and expectations for social life. The resulting discourse is a comparative one, occupying the space between emerging social realities and historically situated, traditional cultural understandings. It tests the ratio of power between new and old, between what could be and what has been. A discourse of resistance represents these cultural understandings and casts itself in rhetorical form in order to gain power in relation to what is regarded as problematic. New forms of representation take on a dramatic tone and a rather abstract, global scope, addressing "all of history" or the whole of identity, because the situation is viewed as touching upon the existential core of local people's mode of being-in-the-world as well as their economic survival. Representation takes on a strident quality, perhaps rewriting tradition as utopian and its demise as tragic, total annihilation.

What begins as a narrow fissure of questioning the present can become an ever-widening, histrionic crevasse of resistance, a cascade of defiance, a conflagration of apocalyptic rage. An explosive

proliferation of discourse and representation takes place in the
struggle to find a "solution." Representation floats on the surface
of a boiling semiotics, kept in flux by both strategic and cultural
considerations and made to carry a heavy burden of affect. When
and if the discourse of those who oppose a proposed development
connects with an enforceable legal category or stricture or constitutes an effective confrontation, the "other side" backs down; the
opposition has found a way to implement its demand for power.
This space of political discourse becomes a space of political action, effective struggle. But if the opponents' attempt fails, discourse may become repetitious and compulsive, aimless, bitter or
mournful, as it may sometimes seem to be in eastern Kentucky.
How to convert the space of discourse or resistance into a space of
political action is a question facing any local population that objects to dams, tree farms, strip mining, and a wide range of other
"developments."

Appalachians have been accused of passivity and resignation in
the face of exploitation and ruthless change. But it is wrong to ele-
vate their responses to adversity to the level of a cultural attribute,
to essentialize as a cultural characteristic what is better understood
in relational terms. Appalachians' ways of dealing with change and
with outsiders have at least as much to do with the context in
which they have had to respond as to their cultural essence. Many
of the changes evident in the region, as in Ashe County, cannot
easily be defined as discrete events. Many changes have come insidiously, as infiltrations not immediately visible, or as sedimen-
tations that grain by grain seem to have only a minor effect.
The gradual incrustation by civilization of "remote" places such
as Ashe County goes by in silence; only the blatant and obvious
affronts to the ideas people have about how to live incite discourse
and representation. When I returned to Ashe County in 1987,
farmland and homesteads had not been inundated by the rising
waters of the New River dams, but areas were being engulfed
by a subtle disorder accumulating along arterials and burgeoning at unexpected intervals, the insidious disarray of metastatic
development.

From the perspective of the local native, metastatic development is an unplanned, uncontrolled, piecemeal transformation of
the county's landscape and social character. Accompanying this

process is an ongoing problematization of culture as a coherent reference point for the stylization of social life. I talked over these issues and impressions with Jeff Boyer, an anthropologist now residing in Ashe County.[4] "Local people," he said, "realize now that the Floridians are here to stay." He emphasized that the chilling notion of a "dying culture" should be juxtaposed with the understanding that something new is being created. We agreed that "the culture" certainly survives, that individualism and sharing still prevail as values, however uncertain their application. Yet today, local culture is at best strategic and circumstantial in its manifestations, fragmentary, seemingly a phantasmagoria of incoherence of the sort Taussig (1987) describes in much more virulent form for South America. In Jeff's view, Ashe County people sometimes underrate the severity of their economic problems as well as the degree of their dependency on outside industry and institutions: "The recognized, 'objective' problem is that the younger generation—especially those who go beyond high school, therefore a brain drain of sorts—are not able to stay in Ashe County and make a living." He expressed frustration about how hesitant and inconsistent local people have been in bringing their problems to the political arena. If political struggle is the cutting edge of change, then the blade now seems dull and ragged.

Jeff served in the Peace Corps and then did fieldwork in Honduras; thus he draws comparisons between Appalachians and the situation of Latin American peasants.[5] The night after he and his wife arrived in Honduras, he recalled, people began to leave heaps of food on their porch. A similar norm of hospitality, he felt, leads Ashe County natives to treat newly arrived outsiders decently. But these courtesies are usually not reciprocated by the outsiders, though they like the local people's kindness and tell their friends elsewhere about how nice people are in the county. Thus the local norm of hospitality encourages the presence of more outsiders, whose presence further strains local norms of reciprocity. This is both a demographic bind and a cultural one. Jeff told of a neighbor who "bladed" their steep driveway last winter after a snowstorm. He has not yet thanked the man, but he believes that the man knows that sooner or later Jeff will return the favor.

As we talked, I admired the spectacular view from the dining room window of the chaletlike home Jeff and his wife, Mary, have just built high in a hollow looking out over the mountains. Out of the phantasmagoria of change that characterizes modernity in Ashe County, as in many other places, arise new possibilities, some of which, perhaps, may offset the losses. One story Jeff told me, in particular, suggests the range of new possibilities for communalism and cosmopolitanism.

Jeff and Mary had a group of visitors staying at their home who were from the hinterlands of Nicaragua. Among them was Maritza, nineteen years old and vice-president of a revolutionary agricultural cooperative. As Jeff recounts, "She was *muy campesina* [peasant]—had never been to Managua before, let alone on a plane to the U.S.—and was scared to death." She did not speak English and was to stay in the county for a quick three days. Jeff and Mary hosted a covered-dish dinner during Maritza's visit. The local people all came, dressed up in their Sunday best. Maritza talked to them and they to her, with Jeff acting as interpreter. Though only one of the local guests knew where Nicaragua was, and few could distinguish a Sandinista from a Somocista, they all discussed living on the land, their lives, and the future. Maritza described the difficulties of farming without land before the overthrow of Somoza. She explained that the U.S. government's current trade restrictions meant no spare parts for the co-op's only tractor. She told them about the obstacles of drought and pests, of men who are irresponsible for the children they father in the countryside, and what the new women's organizations were doing. Jeff said that Maritza's depiction of these struggles "prompted one sympathetic neighbor to say, 'We ought to have laws like that here!' What Maritza found at our covered-dish . . . was warmth, curiosity, and the common thread of rural people who could empathize with her descriptions."

By the end of the evening, excitement was in the air. Despite the political, cultural, and linguistic barriers, Maritza was as enthusiastic about the local people she met as they were about her. During the remainder of her brief stay, she spent much of her time visiting the homes of as many of the neighbors as she could. In Jeff's words, "I think their sense of support for Maritza came from their common rural background, real solidarity expressed several times for the plight of the small farmer the world round, and as one woman put it, Maritza's spunk and sense of responsibility at such a young age."

Many Americans, and particularly amateur sociologists, talk frequently of "community," but rarely as something taken for granted. For urbanites, community is not the commonly lived social experience that they might like it to be, for it has been problematized by multiple historical exigencies. Instead, community is to be understood as a dream-image looked upon with nostalgia, as the utopian reversal of urban brutality, paranoia, and fragmentation, and as a possibility for the future, well worth struggling for and worthy of intense scrutiny in public discourse. People need such dream-images, and they may become important points of reference in devising new social forms. Community is thus a major element in the American rhetoric of history and social change. But when it is not simply a focus of wishful thinking or political propaganda, it is frequently—and cynically—relegated to an oblivion of homegrown illusions that have become devoid of meaning. This polarity—community wished-for and denied—is at the root of major debates in "official" discourse and knowledge regarding the constitution of our society and regarding possible (if doubtful) means for directing social change and local development. It has major relevance for both social description and moral inquiry.

Urban Americans cannot rediscover a sense of community simply by visiting an Appalachian town, a village in the Atlas Mountains, or a hamlet at the end of an unpaved track. But community and cosmopolitanism are increasingly contexts for each other. Maritza's presence in the Blue Ridge exemplifies a cosmopolitan project that promotes local residents' awareness of macro-dependencies and cultural diversity.[6] Thus defined, cosmopolitanism offers an alternative to fragmentation, disaffection, and the absence of community in social experience. It is a possible position from which to observe, participate in, and analyze urban alienation. From this perspective, the report, from the Blue Ridge at least, is not all bad: What has happened in "remote" places like Appalachia, and in the "exotic" societies anthropologists have traditionally studied, makes it impossible to appropriate them as projections of how social life should be, how it once was, or how it might be again if history hadn't been what it is. I observed community besieged and reasserted in disturbing, complex, and unexpected ways. Community is being refigured and reworked in ways that attempt to take into account the macro-dependencies and cultural differences that have become increasingly present in modern life. My findings readily deconstruct fantasies of community regained but do not rob us altogether of the prospect of a satisfying existence in the country or in the city, which are perhaps less different from one another than they were in the past.

In ending with the anecdote about Maritza's visit to the Blue Ridge, I do not claim a moral to the story or define a specific trajectory for historical consciousness. That consciousness is in crisis, as is the current history which is shaping it. An understanding of the ironies of nurturing tradition in order to obtain power over change was what I came to share with the people of the Blue Ridge. This understanding narrowed the gulf of otherness that otherwise yawned between us. But I was caught—also ironically—although an outsider, I could not support those outside interests that were degrading local power. I cannot capture these countercurrents in a final synthesis or in any crystalline, sharply etched representation. Instead, what echoes in my mind is the formula, so often used by people in the Blue Ridge to say goodbye: "Come back and see us!"

# Notes

## Introduction

1. My treatment of individualism and the cultural construction of the person owes much to the work of Louis Dumont and Robert N. Bellah (1975; Bellah et al. 1985). Dumont presented some of this material as the Christian Gauss Seminars in Criticism in the fall of 1973 at Princeton University (see Dumont 1965, 1970, 1977, 1986). Recent dialogue on individualism can be found in Heller, Sosna, and Wellbery (1986).

2. In this study, the term *ideology* is used as in Barnett (1977, 276):

In order to act (for an act to have meaning, to make sense), a person must situate himself in terms of some construction of the world (ideology). Or, he must be "interior" to an ideology—it must be a construction that defines the "real." And since we are talking of "reality," a person interior to a particular ideology cannot consciously manipulate its most basic points. These points are accepted; they are seen by the interior person as *outside* the ideology, as part of the putative natural (vs. constructed) world. An ideology thus grounds "reality" as well as providing the range of manipulation of that "reality." A definition of ideology should include this double distortion: that it has a "natural" ground and that its limits are "real." This definition locates the tension between ideology and history (the paradoxical replacement of ideologies which in their own terms are irreplaceable) and provides an opening for the generation of new symbolic formations.

3. On individualism as a dominant cultural construct in America, see Bellah et al. (1985).

4. The central importance of studying this relationship is emphasized by Marcus and Fischer (1986, 77): "What makes representation challenging and a focus of experimentation is the perception that the 'outside forces' in fact are an integral part of the construction and constitution of the 'inside,' the cultural unit itself, and must be so registered." This statement compactly summarizes the rationale for the approach to understanding the culture of Ashe County taken in this book.

5. Mauss (1939), Lee (1959), Hallowell (1967), Fortes (1971), Carroll (1972), Lieber (1972), Silverman (1972), Fruzzetti, Östör, and Barnett (1976), and Geertz (1983).

6. The struggles of Appalachians with the Appalachian Regional Commission regarding planning and programs for change in the region are well known.

7. Drawing on John Searle's work on speech acts theory to interpret the work of Michel Foucault, Dreyfus and Rabinow (1983) clarify the definition of "serious speech acts" relative to the entirety of an enunciative field. Speech acts "are constituted as serious by the current rules of a specific truth game in which they have a role" (Dreyfus and Rabinow 1983, 54). And "although speech acts for Foucault as well as for Searle have some sort of fixed 'information content' or 'sentence meaning,' whether or not two speech acts mean the same thing (that is, determine the same truth conditions) depends not merely upon the words that determine their information content but upon the context in which they appear" (ibid.). A given speech act may be construed as serious or as cynically opportunistic and rhetorical, depending on context and audience. How these contexts are politically determined, arranged, and constituted is analyzed in Part II.

## Chapter One

1. There are, for instance, numerous correspondences between rural life in western North Carolina and in western Massachusetts and New Hampshire, where I have also spent a good deal of time. But there are differences. People in Ashe County dislike fencing their property, regarding it as unneighborly, whereas New Englanders regard it as essential (as one character in Robert Frost's "Mending Wall" says, "good fences make good neighbors"). A characterization of some aspects of a rural community in Ashe County is given in Chapter Two.

2. Federal census reports show two nineteenth-century population booms in Ashe County, in the 1870s and 1890s, and alternating periods of increase and decline in the twentieth century:

| 1800 | 2,783 | 1890 | 15,628 |
| 1810 | 3,694 | 1900 | 19,581 |
| 1820 | 4,335 | 1910 | 19,074 |
| 1830 | 6,987 | 1920 | 21,001 |
| 1840 | 7,467 | 1930 | 21,019 |
| 1850 | 8,777 | 1940 | 22,664 |
| 1860 | 7,956 | 1950 | 21,878 |
| 1870 | 9,573 | 1960 | 19,768 |
| 1880 | 14,437 | 1970 | 19,571 |
|  |  | 1980 | 22,325 |

3. For an excellent introduction to the history, cultural geography, and social issues of the region as a whole, see Beaver (1984).

4. The U.S. Department of Agriculture determines tobacco allotments, and property owners may not exceed their allotted acreage. Sometimes the size of the allotment is a consideration for prospective buyers of property.

5. *The County and City Data Book* (1983, 409) summarizes 1980 census data for Ashe County, which show that there were 1,388 individually run or family-run farms in the county at that time. (For additional statistics on farms and farming, see Chapter Two, note 1.)

6. Batteau (1983a, 112) expresses a similar realization about how Appalachians utilize and understand "history": "The resident's description of the past is thus a statement about the present, and one can understand present cultural concerns by a careful reading of and listening to these statements."

7. According to *The County and City Data Book* (1983, 397), the mean number of persons per household in Ashe County in 1980 was 2.77.

8. Historically, moonshine became important as just about the only source of cash in an essentially nonmonetized economy. Appalachians had to pay their taxes somehow, and they did so by making and selling moonshine.

9. An essential problem in the analysis of Appalachian ethnic identity is the postulation of a separate culture, a local culture, or a subculture as a basis of Appalachian social life. Yinger (1960) indicates that these concepts have been given a bewildering variety of definitions. It is obvious that Appalachians are, in some respects, culturally American, and they would not deny it. But in other respects, they are of course distinct. It is extraordinarily difficult to establish unambiguous cultural isoglosses. For the purposes of the present study, the existence of a separate Appalachian culture is left as problematic, at least at this point. The question is not so much an analytic one as a political one, and an aspect of how Appalachians themselves construct a view of their social world and their own identity within it. Batteau (1983a, 109) comes to a similar conclusion: "if one is discussing the subculture of a collectivity that is not clearly delineated, such as the Appalachian mountain people, certain problems arise." I address some of the implications of this statement in the Epilogue.

10. "The Beverly Hillbillies" was produced by the Columbia Broadcasting System (CBS). It was aired from September 1962 through September 1971 and was then syndicated. The cast included Irene Ryan as Granny and Buddy Ebsen as Jed.

11. "Hee-Haw" was produced by CBS and aired June 1969 through July 1971, and then syndicated. The program was hosted by Buck Owens and Roy Clark.

## Chapter Two

1. By census definitions, Ashe County has no urban population. The 1970 federal census classified approximately 34 percent of the county's population as rural farm residents, the remaining 66 percent as rural nonfarm. By way of comparison: 45 percent of the North Carolina population (74 percent nationally) was classified as urban, 45 percent as rural nonfarm (21 percent nationally), and 10 percent as rural farm (5 percent nationally) (Gesler 1974, 14).

Most of the farms in the county are small, and few are worked intensively. Some farmowners live away from their farms or hold off-farm jobs as a source of supplemental income. The average size of a farm in Ashe County in 1969 was 74 acres, compared with an average of 107 acres for North Carolina and 390 acres nationwide. Of the total land area of Ashe County, 63 percent was in farms in 1969 (down from 73 percent in 1964), and this figure continued to decrease in the 1970s. Farming in Ashe County places emphasis on growing cattle feed and the use of land for cattle grazing. Little grain is grown for human consumption, and most of the vegetables grown on Ashe County farms are for home use. There are numerous apple orchards in the county, apples being grown primarily for commercial purposes.

2. All quoted passages are taken from verbatim transcripts of recorded interviews or from the author's journal entries, unless otherwise specified.

3. The unstressed meaning of class becomes distressingly clear to Appalachians who migrate to the city (see McCoy and Watkins 1981). They are confronted with being designated lower-class and backward purely because they are Appalachian. Batteau (1982b, 446) formulates the overall significance of class in the region as follows: "The 'objective' constraints and conditions of class become semantically appropriated, codified and at times (with some cultural effort) nullified, in the creation of a subjective orientation for behavior out of 'objective' facts of history."

The study of a midwestern town by Varenne (1977) offers numerous, salient points of comparison with the sociology and social ideology of class in Ashe County. According to Varenne (1977, 179), Warner (1949) saw that "the criteria for membership in all the classes were personal, individualistic, matters of likes and dislikes, perceptions and impressions." But he suggests that Warner reified informants' perceptions of these criteria and that he mistakenly interpreted them as operatives in the social system rather than seeing them as matters of social ideology.

In the case of marriage choices, *class* may be a way for informants and analysts alike to interpret the patternings of such choices. But the term is itself a cultural element; it may be inaccurate as a representation of the social processes involved. Thus Varenne points out that the issue of class-based marriage choice seems to be remarkably fluid; class may not say anything very straightforward about this fluidity, though it may structure it in the subjectivities of the actors involved. For Varenne, as in Ashe County, a concomitant of this fluidity was not so much a class *hierarchy* as a collection of "unranked segmentary cliques." Class emerges as a means of rationalizing the differentiation and boundary maintenance of such groups. In Ashe County, at least, fluidity prevails despite the loosely defined differentiations that operate dialectically with the inclusive style of Ashe County sociality.

The understated place of class in my analysis of the Ashe County social scene is no doubt related to the county's relative affluence. Too, most of my informants were middle class, and it is particularly within this class that class is ideologically understated or denied. Batteau (1982b) offers an incisive discussion of class as a major element in the politics of change in the Appalachian region; see also Schneider and Smith (1973) and Billings (1982).

4. Hartman (1957), Pearsall (1959), Weller (1965), Fetterman (1967), Stephenson (1968), Hannum (1969), Kaplan (1971), and Surface (1971).

5. I concur with the following statement by Batteau (1982b, 462), which suggests a broad similarity between the American "culture of kinship" as described by Schneider and the Appalachian case more specifically: "In its constitution, this Appalachian kinship system is little different from the American kinship system in general—the definition of who is a relative, the behavior expected toward relatives, the emphasis on the independence of the nuclear family, and the use of kinship relations for adaptation to occasional scarcity."

6. Bryant's (1983, 33) findings in the Cumberland mountains of Tennessee closely parallel my own sense of how genealogy is utilized in everyday social practice: "For the complex and intricately interwoven kinship diagrams resulting from my research revealed less the genealogical relationships among . . . families than an 'endogamous soup' from which . . . conceptually distinct family groups had been delineated through a process of selective recall and interpretation of genealogical detail."

7. I do not elaborate here the distinction between kinship and neighborliness, in the interest of stressing the parallels between them. But that is not the whole story. As Batteau (1983a, 115) observes, the relation between neighbors is based on proximity, whereas kinship is based on blood. His general formulation nicely summarizes the situation in Ashe County: "Beneath the surface of many different forms in Appalachian life—religion, neighborhood politics, residential patterns, economic transactions,

and marriage—there is a common underlying logic: the emphasis on relationships of inclusion (kinship) and reciprocity (neighborliness), ritualized in certain forms of sharing, and unified within the symbolism of a name."

8. Beaver (1986, 20) notes that there is also a geographical distribution of the county population by party membership, a pattern that dates back to the Civil War: "While Union sentiment was concentrated along portions of the North Fork [of the New River] in the western portion of the county, Confederate sentiment was stronger in the east. This configuration is reflected to this day in the predominance of Republicans on the North Fork and of Democrats in the eastern part of the county."

9. As I have indicated, kinship symbolism pertains not only to kinship per se but also to social identity more generally. This creates a difficulty in terminology, but I have not undertaken the invention of a new terminology in the present study. This same problem underlies much of Schneider's (1984) wrestlings with the concept of kinship: the clarity of the language of analysis is as much at issue as the partitioning of the phenomenal world which is its object.

Examples of metaphoric kinship can be multiplied endlessly, but the main point is that such examples are more than merely metaphoric. I quote Davis (1975, 54–55) at some length here for illustrative purposes:

A woman a few cells down gave me a fascinating description of a whole system through which the women could adopt their jail friends as relatives. I was bewildered and awed by the way in which the vast majority of the jail population had neatly organized itself into generations of families; mothers/wives, fathers/husbands, sons and daughters, even aunts, uncles, grandmothers and grandfathers. The family system served as a defense against the fact of being no more than a number. It humanized the environment and allowed an identification with others within a familiar framework.

In spite of its strong element of escapism and fantasy, the family system could solve certain immediate problems. Family duties and responsibilities were a way in which sharing was institutionalized. Parents were expected to provide for their children, particularly the young ones, if they could not afford "luxury items" from the commissary.

Like filial relationships outside, some sons and daughters had, or developed, ulterior motives. Quite a few of them joined certain families because the material benefits were greater there.

Stack (1974, 60) suggests a similar pattern for urban blacks: "Social relations are conducted in the idiom of kinship. Members of the community explain the behavior of those around them by allowing behavior to define the nature of the relationship. Friends are classified as kinsmen when they assume recognized responsibilities of kinsmen."

10. Humphrey (1984) portrays various styles of religious practice and belief in southern Appalachia in a fascinating essay that also connects religious meanings to the significance of land and locality in social ideology.

11. I am most grateful to Father J. Faulton Hodge for reading and commenting on this section and for correcting inaccuracies. He asked that I not use a pseudonym in referring to him in the text.

12. Anglin (1983) writes of how outsiders and local people are and are not able to accommodate to one another. Among the factors that make local people more likely to be receptive to outsiders are heeding the advice of neighbors, moving in as a member of a family rather than alone, becoming a landowner and working the land, and avoiding advocating changes and departures from "tradition." These factors mitigate the general situation, which she summarizes as follows:

It often seems the case that in-migrants can be accepted on an individual basis, although they may be distrusted as a group. Yet because in-migrants bring expectations and understandings with them that speak to their experience outside the area and which set them apart from the community, they are inevitably perceived *as a group* by local people. Likewise outsiders tend to group local people together because of their ties to the area. Thus, on a crude level, there is a polarizing of outsiders and local people into different camps. (Anglin 1983, 228)

13. Geertz (1973, 164–65) formulates change in its problematic guise as a growing disjunction between cultural expectations, patterns, and meanings on the one hand, and social practices on the other. Taking note of this disjunction is necessary but not sufficient for understanding the recent history of Ashe County, as I try to indicate in Part II.

## Chapter Three

1. This interpretation of the New River dispute takes its inspiration from Silverman's (1977) examination of the implications of phosphate mining on Rambi Island, Fiji. A similar analysis, which examines the politics of strip mining on the Hopi reservation in northern Arizona, can be found in Foster (1974).

2. Kenneth Burke's (1950) work on rhetoric allows an entree into this important theme. He attempts, I think rightly, to extend the range of rhetorical analysis from the realm of oratory and letters into human relations more generally and social conflict specifically. Rosaldo (1978) has also been an important source for my approach to this subject. I first presented this interpretation of the rhetoric of the New River dispute in Foster (1979).

Burke associates rhetoric directly with persuasion and then specifies its range as follows (1950, xiv): "From the bluntest quest of advantage, as in sales promotion or propaganda, through courtship, social etiquette, education, and the sermon, to a 'pure' form that delights in the process of appeal for itself alone, without ulterior purpose. . . . [It] ranges from the politicians who, addressing an audience of farmers, say 'I was a farm boy myself,' through the mysteries of social status, to the mystic's devout identification with the source of all being."

3. The descriptive and historical passages in this chapter derive from my research and from documentary sources, including newspapers, magazines, and various published and unpublished reports. As this material was widely disseminated during the dispute, much of it was "common knowledge" among participants. Because exhaustive referencing would falsify the ebb and flow of discourse as it occurred during the dispute, I have chosen not to provide detailed references in my narrative. For a historical analysis of the dispute, see Schoenbaum (1979).

4. Although psychologisms may seem to threaten the argument at this point, throughout my discussion of the dispute I repeatedly show that there is a basis on the symbolic level for local people's alienation and anxieties.

5. Batteau (1984, 100) discusses other aspects of the dynamics of "victimization" in Appalachia, although my formulation of this and related issues predates his interpretation (Foster 1977). For an excellent discussion of related issues, see Fisher (1976).

6. Cf. Lefebvre (1971, 51): 'A *system of substitutions* emerges, where every compendium of meanings—apparently independent and self-sufficient—re-echoes another in endless rotation." The importance of this observation is clarified by Barnett and Silverman (1976, 1):

The ability of the state to control struggle at the ideological level by controlling the form of substitution will be seen as basic to any understanding of contemporary symbolic structures. Marx posed the problem for praxis: how to distance the individual from an ideology that reproduces a social formation and so create the possibility of revolutionary change. That distancing, the possibility of praxis in advanced capitalism, is made more problematic by ideological substitution as new developments in productive forces are reflected in the oscillation between what is internal to the individual and what is external to that individual. Through control of the range of options, struggle, including many forms of radical struggle, are really movements within an ideology whose structure can only be seen by an examination of that range, not by initially focusing on any particular option.

In Chapter Four, the workings of this process will be evident in the cooptation and appropriation of local authenticity in the interest of obviating local assertions of cultural distinctiveness (ethnicity).

7. "Sacrifice" was another theme referred to in the rhetoric of the dispute, an indigenously acknowledged aspect of local people's experience of "civilization" in the context of the dispute. Batteau (1984, 95) talks of sacrifice as a general way of understanding the relation between local people and societywide political dynamics: "[The] 'romantic' image of Appalachia was simply a form of false consciousness intended to mask the true, predatory approach that was taken toward the region." Later in his discussion, he claims: "Like Orestes, American society, pursued by its own Furies, continually reinvents the conflict between Nature and

Culture and the political factions it engenders" (p. 103). His contention is that Appalachia, the region and its people, have been repeatedly caught up as sacrificial victims in the nation's drive to dominate Nature. These themes come up again in Chapter Four. A similar interpretation of a similar situation can be found in Foster (1974).

8. For a contrasting study of the cultural construction of historical consciousness, see Rosaldo (1980), particularly pp. 54–60.

## Chapter Four

1. Beaver (1986, 110) details the division of sex roles as follows:

Women's primary realm of responsibility can be viewed as the domestic or famil-ial realm, while that of the men, the extra-domestic or public. For the rural fam-ily in western North Carolina, the domestic sphere traditionally included primary responsibility for children and home, clothing, food purchases, storage and preparation of food, gardening, and a variety of related activities. . . . The male, extra-domestic realm included cash crops, public [salaried] work, and associa-tions with other men that may be considered the public affairs of the community. The female, domestic realm was culturally construed as subordinate to the au-thority of the male, public realm.

Beaver also notes that industrialization in the area has resulted in certain modifications in sex role distinctions. It is not clear what these opera-tional changes mean for social ideology:

Industrialization of the labor force, though unevenly felt throughout the area, seems to have contributed to greater flexibility in sex-role definition. As men in-creasingly entered the public labor market, their families absorbed their work on the family farm. Their wives and children took responsibility for running the mill, plowing the fields, harvesting and marketing produce, clearing new ground, butchering livestock, felling trees and mending fences. (Beaver 1986, 111)

2. In local vernacular, as in American slang, "queer" refers both to eccentricity and to homosexuality. Its use in this context is no doubt pur-posefully ambiguous.

3. During a gathering of Ashe County natives and their relatives who lived in various parts of the Appalachian region, a woman asked me about my work and expressed the hope that I would be able to explode some of the myths about the Blue Ridge and its people. A man—the only man present other than myself—pointed out that the region's "bad im-age" was mainly the fault of "the media." As I asked him who controlled the media and why the media projected a negative image of the region, our conversation took on a political tone, and the women withdrew from the discussion and began talking among themselves about mutual friends and family affairs. Broaching political matters had brought the man into the conversation, and perhaps the women felt excluded by my directing questions to him. But this polarization between the sexes is a fairly stan-

dard pattern in mixed groups. The political tone of male conversation is one facet of male-female role differentiation. Another facet is the segregated seating patterns seen in some public settings, men on one side, women on the other.

4. To this quite brief discussion of the alternation between husband/wife and son/mother pairings as reflecting person-land relations, let me add one point for further reflection: the Oedipal aspect of this alternation. Relations involving nurturance (son/mother) may readily be sexualized (husband/wife) and made the site of violence (rape).

5. *Colonialism* has been used recurrently to discuss the Appalachian situation, the region being designated an "internal colony." This model is summarized in Lewis (1978) and in Lewis and Knipe (1978). I independently formulated a similar approach in Foster (1977). For a critical review of this approach, see Walls (1978). The general literature on colonialism is vast. Key works for the present analysis are Fanon (1956), Mannoni (1964), and Memmi (1985).

6. This polarity of responses—resignation or concerted action—is a further indication of the oscillating reactions to the exigencies of change discussed in Chapter Three. Also see Erikson (1976, 85). For an excellent discussion of resignation ("quiescence") and action ("rebellion") in eastern Kentucky, see Gaventa (1980). Related issues are raised in the Epilogue.

7. Batteau (1983a) makes this point in an essay that covers many of the same issues I discuss here; for my earlier formulation of the politics of culture, see Foster (1977). Marcus and Fischer (1986, 85) also recognize the importance of this theme: "Not only is the cultural construction of meaning and symbols inherently a matter of political and economic interests, but the reverse also holds—the concerns of political economy are inherently about conflicts over meaning and symbols."

8. I must note here the problem raised by differentiating "civilization" as a concept to which discontents are attributed, and "civilization" as whatever reality it may have apart from that given to it by its use as a screen onto which anxieties regarding change are projected. Civilization as a representation is given its reality and begins to function as "real" through just such a projective process and through a sort of self-fulfilling prophecy. The distinctions between culture as it is variously conceived at different levels of social ideology (as value, as ontology, as analytic construct, as rhetorical device) are generated in the course of local people trying to delineate "discontents." The complexities are far greater than I have indicated in this analysis, but a psychocultural interpretation would require a different framework than the one I have set forth in this book. For an incisive beginning of such an analysis, see Batteau (1983b, 1984). One may speculate that "civilization" is a construct people reify in order

to serve as the scapegoat for local problems, but that is far too simple, since domination by outsiders is a real force in the lives of local people.

9. For a detailed, case-oriented discussion of back-to-the-landers, see Beaver (1986, 115–37).

10. Wagner (1975) makes this distinction by using the terms *opera-house Culture* and *culture;* see also Gans (1974) and Bourdieu (1984). Whisnant (1983) forcefully exemplifies this process in a detailed historical analysis.

11. Graburn (1977) and Jules-Rosette (1984, 1986a, 1986b) give many excellent examples of this process.

12. I am indebted to Sandra M. Lee of Jefferson for the material on M. C. Whirley. She interviewed him for a series of programs she prepared for broadcast on the radio station of Wake Forest University. When I returned to the county in 1987, she gave me the dulcimer that she had had Mr. Whirley make for me twelve years before.

13. Whisnant (1983) discusses the role of education and settlement schools in attempting to control the direction of change in Appalachia. His interpretation indicates clearly how middle-class values were insinuated into educational programs ostensibly designed to address the particular needs and culture of the region's people.

14. Although the case study of the New River dispute outlines the paradigm of and for cultural domination in Ashe County, tourism is another manifestation of domination in the Blue Ridge. I have not given a full analysis of tourism, since that would be another book in itself. For a thoroughly engaging account of tourism, see MacCannell (1976).

15. Another bitter Appalachian, Harry Caudill (1962 and 1971) documents the impact of civilization upon the land and people of Appalachia. In *Watches of the Night* (1976), he describes the expansion of the coal industry in the Cumberland Plateau of Kentucky during the 1960s. He examines the social programs (the War on Poverty and VISTA, for example) initiated during the same period, and the paternalism that has increasingly caught the region in a spiral of dependency. Antipoverty luminaries and groupies, do-gooders, economic forecasters, and well-intentioned Ivy Leaguers capitalized on the pervasive malaise of the area and contributed to the problems they came to "solve." My argument is that although the severity of these outside interventions are not so blatant in the Blue Ridge as in Kentucky, the overall pattern is the same throughout the Appalachian region.

16. Using ecology as a metaphor for the structure of symbolic systems is in the spirit of Bateson (1972 and 1979) in which he seeks unities and continuities among entities of different "logical types."

17. Among the Hopi of northern Arizona, this process has char-

acteristically fed on traditional forms of social organization, creating stable factions that are activated when political controversies intensify (Foster 1974).

18. The approach to change employed in this section was suggested to me by Nadia Benabid in an interpretation she wrote of Duvignaud (1968).

19. The appropriation of culture through the consumption of its artifacts, together with the transformation of those artifacts into consumable items, is discussed by Batteau (1984, 104–5); see also Foster (n.d.).

20. As an example of this commoditization of Appalachian culture, consider an advertisement for Appalachia, American Mountain Crafts and Culture, a store located in a shopping center in an affluent suburb of San Francisco:

> For more than 150 years, the people of Appalachia have been making beautiful handicrafts. Practically untouched by today's mechanized world, the people make things today as they have for generations. Come visit us and take a trip to Appalachia through the work of its people: Handstitched quilts and pillows, woodcarvings, hand-tied brooms, oak split and honeysuckle baskets, folk toys and rag dolls, hand-woven rugs and placemats, tinware, ironware, clothing, photos and water colors, records, books, and more.

Placing Appalachians in a positive light and yet phrasing their identity in terms of material culture simultaneously promotes ethnicity and subjects it to commercialization. I have elsewhere discussed this mode of appropriation (see Foster 1977), and a number of other analysts have noted the same process (e.g., Lukács 1968; Batteau 1984; Stephenson 1984). As Batteau (1984, 104) says, by definition, "folk culture exists for consumption by the elite. Basketmaking and handweaving were not folk culture until they were discovered by outside interpreters. They were simply practical necessities." Distinctiveness is articulated only to be placed within the larger framework of exchange, subjecting local culture to the impoverished symbolism of the marketplace. The double bind is thus replicated in this context as well, again characterizing the link between local tradition and mass culture.

21. In questioning the viability of "cultural system" as a coherent and stable analytic construct, at least for the purposes of my interpretation, I generalize from the conclusions of Schneider (1972, 1984) and Geertz and Geertz (1975), who question the viability of "kinship system" as a clearly bounded and delimited *system*.

22. In formulating this section, I have benefited from many discussions with Robert Bellah on the sociology of American culture (see Bellah 1975; Bellah et al. 1985).

# Epilogue

1. The proposal for the Brumley Gap project was reported by Joelle Attinger in *Time,* February 26, 1979, pp. 5–6.

2. Beaver (1986, 145) proposes an interpretation of Appalachian history that recognizes the colonization of the region by outside interests: "Many mountain residents are highly critical of the hillbilly stereotype, the exploitation of mountain resources by eastern and northern 'foreigners,' and the differential treatment of mountain and nonmountain portions of the state [of North Carolina] by both state and federal governments." But she disclaims the relevance of the "colonizing" model of history for the Blue Ridge today: "The residents thus have little reason at present for subscribing to this view of history" (ibid.). I take exception to this diagnosis. The statements of my informants and my argument in Part II clearly indicate the importance of the colonial motif for understanding the history of the present in the Blue Ridge.

3. "Killing Mountains for Coal; Federal Strip Mining Laws Have Not Healed Kentucky's Scars" was written by *Washington Post* staff writer Cass Peterson and appeared in the *Washington Post* (national weekly edition) on June 29, 1987, pp. 6–7. Peterson reports that lax enforcement of weak federal regulations on strip mining has enabled mining companies to renege on promised land-restoration projects after the coal has been extracted.

4. I would like to acknowledge Jeff Boyer's thoughtful comments on this section. He was generous in sharing his many insights with me and in consenting to allow his name and his material to appear in the text.

5. Jeff Boyer's comparison of Latin American peasantry and rural residents in Ashe County should not be discounted as stereotypic. The pattern of rural life in Ashe County is reminiscent of Redfield's (1953, 32–35) view of the relation between peasant and town, city, or market center. The dependency or interdependency intrinsic to Redfield's definition of peasantry is a theme that has come up repeatedly in various guises throughout the present study.

6. I want to acknowledge Paul Rabinow's discussion of cosmopolitans in "Who Are We?" a paper read at the History of the Present conference, held in March 1985 at the University of California, Berkeley, and in "Cosmopolitan Ethnographers," presented in the session "Interlocutors: Edward Said and Representations of the Colonized" at the Eighty-sixth Annual Meeting of the American Anthropological Association in Chicago, November 1987.

# References Cited

Adorno, Theodor
 1976 "Cultural Criticism and Society." In *Critical Sociology,* edited by P. Connerton. New York: Penguin.
Agee, James, and Walker Evans
 1939 *Let Us Now Praise Famous Men.* Cambridge, Mass.: Riverside Press.
Anglin, Mary
 1983 "Experiences of In-Migrants in Appalachia." In *Appalachia and America: Autonomy and Regional Dependence,* edited by Allen Batteau. Lexington: University Press of Kentucky.
Attinger, Joelle
 1979 "In Virginia: Brumley Gap Takes on a Dam Site." *Time,* February 26, 1979, 5–6.
Austin, Richard Cartwright
 1984 "The Battle for Brumley Gap." *Sierra* 69(1):120–24.
Ball, R. A.
 1968 "Poverty Cases: The Analgesic Subculture of the Southern Appalachians." *American Sociological Review* 38:885–95.
Barnett, Stephen A.
 1977 "Identity Choice and Caste Ideology in South India." In *The New Wind: Changing Identities in South Asia,* edited by Kenneth David. World Anthropology Series. The Hague: Mouton.
Barnett, Stephen A., and Martin G. Silverman
 1976 "The Person in Capitalist Ideology." Manuscript.
Bateson, Gregory
 1972 *Steps to an Ecology of Mind.* New York: Ballantine.
 1979 *Mind and Nature, a Necessary Unity.* New York: Dutton.

Batteau, Allen

    1982a    "The Contradictions of a Kinship Community." In *Holding on to the Land and the Lord,* edited by Robert L. Hull and Carol B. Stack. Athens: University of Georgia Press.

    1982b    "Mosbys and Broomsedge: The Semantics of Class in an Appalachian Kinship System." *American Ethnologist* 9(3):445–66.

    1983a    "Appalachia and the Concept of Culture: A Theory of Shared Misunderstandings." In *Appalachia, Social Context Past and Present,* 2d ed., edited by Bruce Ergood and Bruce E. Kuhre. Dubuque, Iowa: Kendall/Hunt.

    1983b    "Rituals of Dependence in Appalachian Kentucky." In *Appalachia and America: Autonomy and Regional Dependence,* edited by Allen Batteau. Lexington: University Press of Kentucky.

    1984    "The Sacrifice of Nature: A Study in the Social Production of Consciousness." In *Cultural Adaptation to Mountain Environments,* edited by Patricia D. Beaver and Burton L. Purrington. Athens: University of Georgia Press.

Beaver, Patricia D.

    1976    "Symbols and Social Organization in an Appalachian Mountain Community." Ph.D. dissertation, Department of Anthropology, Duke University.

    1984    "Appalachian Cultural Adaptations: An Overview." In *Cultural Adaptation to Mountain Environments,* edited by Patricia D. Beaver and Burton L. Purrington. Athens: University of Georgia Press.

    1986    *Rural Community in the Appalachian South.* Lexington: University Press of Kentucky.

Beaver, Patricia D., and Burton L. Purrington, eds.

    1984    *Cultural Adaptation to Mountain Environments.* Athens: University of Georgia Press.

Bellah, Robert N.

    1975    *The Broken Covenant: American Civil Religion in a Time of Trial.* New York: Seabury.

Bellah, Robert N., Richard Madsen, William M. Sullivan, Ann Swidler, and Steven M. Tipton

    1985    *Habits of the Heart.* Berkeley and Los Angeles: University of California Press.

Billings, Dwight

    1982    "Appalachian Studies: Class, Culture and Politics, I." *Appalachian Journal* 9:134–40.

Bingham, Edgar
  1978      "The Impact of Recreational Development on Pioneer Life
            Styles in Southern Appalachia." In *Colonialism in Modern
            America: The Appalachian Case,* edited by Helen Matthews
            Lewis, Linda Johnson, and Donald Askins. Boone, N.C.:
            Appalachian Consortium Press.
Bourdieu, Pierre
  1984      *Distinction: A Social Critique of the Judgement of Taste.* Trans-
            lated by Richard Nice. Cambridge, Mass.: Harvard Uni-
            versity Press.
Bryant, F. Carlene
  1983      "Family Group Organization in a Cumberland Mountain
            Neighborhood." In *Appalachia and America: Autonomy and
            Regional Dependence,* edited by Allen Batteau. Lexington:
            University Press of Kentucky.
Burke, Kenneth
  1950      *A Rhetoric of Motives.* Berkeley and Los Angeles: Univer-
            sity of California Press.
Cain, S. R.
  1970      "Appalachian Analogue: Anthropology and Change."
            *Growth and Change* 1:31–36.
Caldwell, M. F.
  1930      "Change Comes to the Appalachian Mountaineer." *Cur-
            rent History* 31:961–67.
Campbell, John C.
  1921      *The Southern Highlander and His Homeland.* New York:
            Russell Sage Foundation.
Carroll, Vern
  1972      "The Nukuoro Notion of 'Person.'" Paper presented at
            the Symposium on the Cultural Basis of Social Relations:
            Kinship, Person, and Actor. Seventy-first Annual Meeting
            of the American Anthropological Association, Toronto.
Carroll, Vern, ed.
  1970      *Adoption in Eastern Oceania.* Honolulu: University of Ha-
            waii Press.
Caudill, Harry M.
  1962      *Night Comes to the Cumberlands.* Boston: Little, Brown.
  1971      *My Land Is Dying.* New York: Dutton.
  1976      *Watches of the Night.* Boston: Atlantic–Little, Brown.
Caulfield, M. D.
  1972      "Culture and Imperialism: Proposing a New Dialectic." In

*Reinventing Anthropology,* edited by Dell Hymes. New York: Random House.

Clifford, James
  1983        "On Ethnographic Authority." *Representations* 1(2):118–46.

Clifford, James, and George E. Marcus, eds.
  1986        *Writing Culture: The Poetics and Politics of Ethnography.* Berkeley and Los Angeles: University of California Press.

Coles, Robert
  1967        *Migrants, Sharecroppers and Mountaineers.* Boston: Atlantic–Little, Brown.

Crapanzano, Vincent
  1977        "The Writing of Ethnography." *Dialectical Anthropology* 2(1):69–73.

Crocker, J. Christopher
  1977        "The Social Function of Rhetorical Forms." In *The Social Use of Metaphor,* edited by J. David Sapir and J. Christopher Crocker. Philadelphia: University of Pennsylvania Press.

Davis, Angela
  1975        *An Autobiography.* New York: Bantam.

Diamond, Stanley
  1974        *In Search of the Primitive.* New Brunswick, N.J.: Transaction Books.

Dickey, James
  1970        *Deliverance.* New York: Houghton Mifflin.

Dolgin, Janet
  1977        *Jewish Identity and the JDL.* Princeton: Princeton University Press.

Dolgin, J., and J. Magdoff
  1977        "The Invisible Event." In *Symbolic Anthropology,* edited by J. Dolgin, D. Kenmitzer, and D. M. Schneider. New York: Columbia University Press.

Douglas, Mary
  1966        *Purity and Danger.* New York: Penguin.
  1970        *Natural Symbols.* New York: Pantheon.
  1973        *Natural Symbols.* 2d ed. New York: Vintage.

Dreyfus, Hubert L., and Paul Rabinow
  1983        *Michel Foucault: Beyond Structuralism and Hermeneutics.* 2d ed. Chicago: University of Chicago Press.

Dumont, Louis
    1965        "The Modern Conception of the Individual." *Contributions to Indian Sociology* 8:13–61.
    1970        "Religion, Politics and Society in the Individualistic Universe." The Henry Myers Lectures. Photocopy.
    1977        *From Mandeville to Marx: Genesis and Triumph of the Economic Ideology.* Chicago: University of Chicago Press.
    1986        *Essays on Individualism: Modern Ideology in Anthropological Perspective.* Chicago: University of Chicago Press.
Duvignaud, Jean
    1968        *Change at Shebika.* Translated by Frances Frenaye. New York: Vintage.
Erikson, Erik H.
    1968        *Identity, Youth and Crisis.* New York: Norton.
Erikson, Kai T.
    1976        *Everything in Its Path.* New York: Simon and Schuster.
Errington, Frederick K.
    1974        *Karavar.* Ithaca: Cornell University Press.
Evans-Pritchard, E. E.
    1964        "Nuer Modes of Address." In *Language in Culture and Society,* edited by Dell Hymes. New York: Harper and Row.
Fanon, Franz
    1956        *Wretched of the Earth.* New York: Grove Press.
Fetterman, John
    1967        *Stinking Creek.* New York: Dutton.
Fisher, Stephen L.
    1976        "Victim Blaming in Appalachia: Cultural Theories and the Southern Mountaineer." In *Appalachia: Social Context Past and Present,* 2d ed., edited by Bruce Ergood and Bruce E. Kuhre. Dubuque, Iowa: Kendall/Hunt.
Fletcher, Arthur
    1960        *Ashe County, A History.* Jefferson, N.C.: Ashe County Research Association.
Fortes, Meyer
    1971        "On the Concept of the Person Among the Tallensi." *Journal of the Royal Anthropological Institute of Great Britain and Ireland* 101(3):27–58.
Foster, Stephen William
    1973        "Symbolic Alchemy." Manuscript.
    1974        "Stripping the Hopi." Master's thesis, Department of Anthropology, Princeton University.

1976        "The Poetics of Culture." *Reviews in Anthropology* 3(1): 41–51.
1977        "Identity as Symbolic Production." Ph.D. dissertation, Department of Anthropology, Princeton University.
1979        "Rhetoric and the Politics of Culture." Paper presented at the Symposium on Culture, Persuasion, and Power. Kroeber Anthropological Society Meetings, Berkeley, California.
1982a       Review of *The Invisible Minority: Urban Appalachians,* edited by William W. Philliber and Clyde B. McCoy. *American Ethnologist* 9(3):614–15.
1982b       "The Exotic as a Symbolic System." *Dialectical Anthropology* 7(1):21–30.
n.d.        "Appropriating the Primitive." Manuscript.

Foucault, Michel
1980        *Power/Knowledge: Selected Interviews and Other Writings, 1972–1977.* Edited by Colin Gordon. New York: Pantheon.

Freud, Sigmund
1930        *Civilization and Its Discontents.* Translated by J. Riviere. New York: Cape and Smith.

Fruzzetti, L., A. Östör, and S. A. Barnett
1976        "The Cultural Construction of the Person in Bengal and Tamil Nadu." *Contributions to Indian Sociology,* n.s., 10: 157–82.

Gans, Herbert
1974        *Popular Culture and High Culture.* New York: Basic Books.

Gaventa, John
1980        *Power and Powerlessness: Quiescence and Rebellion in an Appalachian Valley.* Urbana: University of Illinois Press.

Geertz, Clifford
1973        *The Interpretation of Cultures.* New York: Basic Books.
1983        "From the Native's Point of View." In *Local Knowledge.* New York: Basic Books.

Geertz, Hildred, and Clifford Geertz
1975        *Kinship in Bali.* Chicago: University of Chicago Press.

Gesler, W. M.
1974        "The Willingness of Farmowners to Sell Land in Ashe County, North Carolina." Master's thesis, Department of Geography, University of North Carolina, Chapel Hill.

Goffman, Erving
1959        *The Presentation of Self in Everyday Life.* New York: Doubleday-Anchor.

Goodman, A. D., et al.

1977    *Rambling Through Ashe.* Ashe County, N.C.: Bicentennial Historical Society.

Goss, Bernard, et al.

1984    *The Heritage of Ashe County, North Carolina.* Vol. 1. Winston-Salem, N.C.: Ashe County Heritage Book Committee and Hunter Publishing.

Graburn, Nelson, ed.

1977    *Ethnic and Tourist Arts.* Berkeley and Los Angeles: University of California Press.

Hallowell, Alfred Irving

1967    "The Ojibway Self and Its Behavioral Environment." In *Culture and Experience.* New York: Schocken.

Hamon, Philippe

1981    "Rhetorical Status of the Descriptive." *Yale French Studies* 61 : 1–26.

Hannum, Alberta Pierson

1969    *Look Back with Love: A Recollection of the Blue Ridge.* New York: Vanguard.

Hartman, Vladimir E.

1957    "A Cultural Study of a Mountain Community in Western North Carolina." Ph.D. dissertation, Department of Sociology and Anthropology, University of North Carolina, Chapel Hill.

Heller, Thomas C., Morton Sosna, and David E. Wellbery, eds.

1986    *Reconstructing Individualism: Autonomy, Individuality and the Self in Western Thought.* Stanford: Stanford University Press.

Herlinger, Elizabeth H.

1972    "A Historical, Cultural and Organizational Analysis of Ozark Ethnic Identity." Ph.D. dissertation, Department of Anthropology, University of Chicago.

Hicks, George L.

1976    *Appalachian Valley.* New York: Holt, Rinehart and Winston.

Higgs, R. J., and A. N. Manning, eds.

1975    *Voices from the Hills: Selected Readings from Southern Appalachia.* New York: Ungar.

Humphrey, Richard

1984    "Religion and Place in Southern Appalachia." In *Cultural Adaptation to Mountain Environments,* edited by Patricia D. Beaver and Burton L. Purrington. Athens: University of Georgia Press.

Janssen, Raymond E.
    1952    "The History of a River." *Scientific American* 186(6):74–80.

Jules-Rosette, Bennetta
    1984    *The Messages of Tourist Art: An African Semiotic System in Comparative Perspective.* New York: Plenum.
    1986a    "Aesthetics and Market Demand: The Structure of the Tourist Art Market in Three African Settings." *African Studies Review* 29(1):41–59.
    1986b    "The Ethnoaesthetics of Tourist Art in Africa: Some Theoretical and Methodological Implications." Paper presented at the Eighty-fifth Annual Meeting of the American Anthropological Association, Philadelphia.

Kahn, Kathy
    1973    *Hillbilly Women.* New York: Doubleday.

Kaplan, Berton H.
    1971    *Blue Ridge: An Appalachian Community in Transition.* Morgantown: Office of Research and Development, Appalachian Center, West Virginia University.

Keesing, Roger M.
    1970    "Toward a Model of Role Analysis." In *Handbook of Method in Cultural Anthropology,* edited by R. Cohen and K. Narroll. New York: Natural History Press.

Kolodny, Annette
    1975    *The Lay of the Land.* Chapel Hill: University of North Carolina Press.

Laycock, George
    1975    "New River, Old Problem." *Audubon* 77(6):58–63.

Leach, Edmund R.
    1961    *Rethinking Anthropology.* New York: Humanities Press.

Lee, Dorothy
    1959    "The Conception of the Self Among the Wintu Indians." In *Freedom and Culture.* Englewood Cliffs, N.J.: Prentice-Hall.

Lefebvre, Henri
    1971    *Everyday Life in the Modern World.* Translated by Sacha Rabinovitch. New York: Harper and Row.

Lévi-Strauss, Claude
    1963a    "The Concept of Archaism in Anthropology." In *Structural Anthropology,* vol. 1, translated by C. Jacobson and B. G. Schoepf. New York: Basic Books.

1963b     "The Effectiveness of Symbols." In *Structural Anthropology,* vol. 1, translated by C. Jacobson and B. G. Schoepf. New York: Basic Books.

Lewis, Helen Matthews

1978     "The Colony of Appalachia." In *Colonialism in Modern America: The Appalachian Case,* edited by Helen Matthews Lewis, Linda Johnson, and Donald Askins. Boone, N.C.: Appalachian Consortium Press.

Lewis, Helen Matthews, and Edward E. Knipe

1978     "The Colonialism Model: The Appalachian Case." In *Colonialism in Modern America: The Appalachian Case,* edited by Helen Matthews Lewis, Linda Johnson, and Donald Askins. Boone, N.C.: Appalachian Consortium Press. [Presented at the annual meeting of the American Anthropological Association, 1970.]

Lieber, Michael D.

1972     "Person, Role, and Relationship on Kapingamarangi." Paper presented at the Symposium on the Cultural Basis of Social Relations: Kinship, Person, and Actor. Seventy-first Annual Meeting of the American Anthropological Association, Toronto.

Lukács, Georg

1968     *History and Class Consciousness.* Cambridge, Mass.: MIT Press.

MacCannell, Dean

1976     *The Tourist: A New Theory of the Leisure Class.* New York: Schocken.

MacClintock, S. S.

1901     "The Kentucky Mountains and Their Feuds." *American Journal of Sociology* 7:1–28, 171–87.

McCoy, Clyde B., and Virginia Watkins

1981     "Stereotypes of Appalachian Migrants." In *The Invisible Minority: Urban Appalachians,* edited by William W. Philliber and Clyde B. McCoy. Lexington: University Press of Kentucky.

Mannoni, O.

1964     *Prospero and Caliban: The Psychology of Colonization.* Translated by Pamela Powesland. New York: Praeger.

Marcus, George E., and Michael M. J. Fischer

1986     *Anthropology as Cultural Critique.* Chicago: University of Chicago Press.

Mathews, Elmora M.
   1965        *Neighbor and Kin.* Nashville: Vanderbilt University Press.
Mauss, M.
   1939        "A Category of the Human Mind: The Notion of Person
                and That of the 'Self.'" *Journal of the Royal Anthropological
                Institute of Great Britain and Ireland* 68(2):263–81.
Mead, George H.
   1956        "Self." In *On Social Psychology,* edited by Anselm Strauss.
                Chicago: University of Chicago Press.
Memmi, Albert
   1985        *Portrait du colonise.* Paris: Gallimard.
Montgomery, B.
   1972        "The Uptown Story." In *Appalachia in the Sixties,* edited
                by D. S. Walls and John B. Stephenson. Lexington: Uni-
                versity of Kentucky Press.
Newcomb, Horace
   1979        "Appalachia on Television: Region as Symbol in American
                Popular Culture." *Appalachian Journal* 7(1–2):155–64.
Obermiller, Phillip J.
   1981        "The Question of Appalachian Ethnicity." In *The Invisible
                Minority: Urban Appalachians,* edited by William W. Phil-
                liber and Clyde B. McCoy. Lexington: University Press of
                Kentucky.
Pearsall, Marion
   1959        *Little Smoky Ridge: The Natural History of a Southern Ap-
                palachian Neighborhood.* University: University of Alabama
                Press.
Philliber, William W., and Clyde B. McCoy, eds.
   1981        *The Invisible Minority: Urban Appalachians.* Lexington:
                University Press of Kentucky.
Pratt, Mary Louise
   1985        "Scratches on the Face of the Country: Or, What Mr. Bar-
                row Saw in the Land of the Bushman." *Critical Inquiry*
                12(1):119–43.
Purrington, Burton L.
   1972        "Revitalizing Rural Cultures: A Case for the Development
                of Rural Ethnicity." *Rural Sociology* 37(2):136–39.
Rabinow, Paul
   1986        "Representations Are Social Facts: Modernity and Post-
                modernity in Anthropology." In *Writing Culture: The Poet-
                ics and Politics of Ethnography,* edited by James Clifford and
                George E. Marcus. Berkeley and Los Angeles: University
                of California Press.

Radcliffe-Brown, A. R.
 1965 "On Joking Relationships." In *Structure and Function in Primitive Society*. New York: Free Press.

Redfield, Robert
 1953 *The Primitive World and Its Transformation*. Ithaca: Cornell University Press.

Reeves, Eleanor Baker
 1986 *A Factual History of Early Ashe County, North Carolina, Its People, Places and Events*. Dallas: Taylor Publishing.

Rosaldo, Renato
 1978 "The Rhetoric of Control: Ilongots Viewed as Natural Bandits and Wild Indians." In *The Reversible World*, edited by Barbara A. Babcock. Ithaca: Cornell University Press.
 1980 *Ilongot Headhunting, 1883–1974*. Stanford: Stanford University Press.

Sartre, Jean-Paul
 1948 *Anti-Semite and Jew*. Translated by G. J. Becker. New York: Schocken.
 1963 *Search for a Method*. Translated by H. E. Barnes. New York: Vintage.

Scheffler, Harold W.
 1976 "The 'Meaning' of Kinship in American Culture." In *Meaning in Anthropology*, edited by K. H. Basso and H. A. Selby. Albuquerque: University of New Mexico Press.

Schneider, David M.
 1967 "Descent and Filiation as Cultural Constructs." *Southwestern Journal of Anthropology* 23:67–73.
 1968a *American Kinship: A Cultural Account*. Englewood Cliffs, N.J.: Prentice-Hall.
 1968b "Rivers and Kroeber in the Study of Kinship." In *Kinship and Social Organization*, edited by W. H. R. Rivers. New York: Humanities Press.
 1969 "Kinship, Nationality and Religion in American Culture." In *Forms of Symbolic Action*, edited by R. F. Spencer. Seattle: University of Washington Press.
 1972 "What Is Kinship All About?" In *Kinship Studies in the Morgan Centennial Year*, edited by P. Reining. Washington, D.C.: Anthropological Society of Washington.
 1976 "Notes Toward a Theory of Culture." In *Meaning in Anthropology*, edited by K. H. Basso and H. A. Selby. Albuquerque: University of New Mexico Press.

1984     *A Critique of the Study of Kinship.* Ann Arbor: University of Michigan Press.

Schneider, David M., and Raymond T. Smith

1973     *Class Differences and Sex Roles in American Kinship and Family Structure.* Englewood Cliffs, N.J.: Prentice-Hall.

Schoenbaum, Thomas J.

1979     *The New River Controversy.* Winston-Salem, N.C.: John F. Blair Publishing.

Schutz, Alfred

1967     *Phenomenology of the Social World.* Translated by G. Walsh and F. Lehnert. Evanston, Ill.: Northwestern University Press.

Schwarzweller, Harry K., James S. Brown, and J. J. Mangalam, eds.

1971     *Mountain Families in Transition.* University Park: Pennsylvania State University Press.

Shapiro, Henry D.

1978     *Appalachia on Our Mind.* Chapel Hill: University of North Carolina Press.

Silverman, Martin G.

1970     "Stereotypes as a Symbolic System." Manuscript.

1971     *Disconcerting Issue.* Chicago: University of Chicago Press.

1972     "Kinship, Person, and Relationship on Rambi Island, Fiji." Paper presented at the Symposium on the Cultural Basis of Social Relations: Kinship, Person, and Actor. Seventy-first Annual Meeting of the American Anthropological Association, Toronto.

1977     "Making Sense: A Study of a Banaban Meeting." In *Symbolic Anthropology,* edited by J. Dolgin, D. Kenmetzer, and D. M. Schneider. New York: Columbia University Press.

Stack, Carol B.

1974     *All Our Kin.* New York: Harper and Row.

Stephenson, John B.

1968     *Shiloh: A Mountain Community.* Lexington: University of Kentucky Press.

1984     "Escape to the Periphery: Commodifying Place in Rural Appalachia." *Appalachian Journal* 11:187–200.

Surface, William

1971     *The Hollow.* New York: Coward-McCann.

Taussig, Michael

1987     *Shamanism, Colonialism and the Wildman.* Chicago: University of Chicago Press.

Taylor, Mildred

n.d.     "Grandpa's River." Manuscript.

Turner, Victor
    1969      *The Ritual Process: Structure and Anti-Structure.* Chicago: Aldine.

U.S. Department of Commerce, Bureau of the Census
    1983      *The County and City Data Book.* Washington, D.C.: Government Printing Office.

Varenne, Herve
    1977      *Americans Together: Structured Diversity in a Midwestern Town.* New York: Teachers College Press.

Wagner, Roy
    1975      *The Invention of Culture.* Englewood Cliffs, N.J.: Prentice-Hall.
    n.d.      "The Negotiable Savage." Manuscript.

Walls, David
    1978      "Internal Colony or Internal Periphery? A Critique of Current Models and an Alternative Formulation." In *Colonialism in Modern America: The Appalachian Case,* edited by Helen Matthews Lewis, Linda Johnson, and Donald Askins. Boone, N.C.: Appalachian Consortium Press.

Warner, W. Lloyd
    1949      *Social Class in America: The Evaluation of Status.* New York: Harper and Row.

Weber, Max
    1968      *On Charisma and Institution Building.* Edited by S. N. Eisenstadt. Chicago: University of Chicago Press.

Weller, Jack
    1965      *Yesterday's People.* Lexington: University of Kentucky Press.

Whisnant, David E.
    1973a      "Ethnicity and the Recovery of Regional Identity in Appalachia: Thoughts upon Entering the Zone of Occult Instability." *Soundings* 56:124–39.
    1973b      "The Craftsman: Some Reflections on Work in America." *The Centennial Review* 17(3):215–36.
    1974      "Growing Old by Being Poor: Some Cautionary Notes About Generalizing from a Class Phenomenon." *Soundings* 57:101–12.
    1980      *Modernizing the Mountaineer: People, Power and Planning in Appalachia.* New York: Burt Franklin & Co.
    1983      *All That Is Native and Fine: The Politics of Culture in an American Region.* Chapel Hill: University of North Carolina Press.

Wiggington, Eliot
    1972      *The Foxfire Book.* Garden City, N.Y.: Doubleday.

Wolfe, Thomas
  1929      *Look Homeward, Angel.* New York: Scribners.
Wolfe, Tom
  1965      "The Last American Hero." In *The Kandy-Kolored Tangerine-Flake Streamline Baby.* New York: Noonday.
Yinger, J. M.
  1960      "Contraculture and Subculture." *American Sociological Review* 25:625–35.

# Index

Abortion, 59

Activism, 3, 153, 183; and the anthropologist, 187, 204; in Appalachia, 215, 218; and resignation, 234n.6. *See also* New River dispute; Politics

Adoption, 59, 67; of the anthropologist, 39; as process of incorporation, 89–91, 109

Adorno, Theodor, 201, 202

Affines, 65. *See also* Kinship

Agee, James, 5–6

Alcohol, 41, 45, 58, 61, 65; sales of, in Ashe County, 22, 216

Alienation, 60, 188, 202, 232n.3; and change, 19, 179; urban, 223–24

American Electric Power Company, 125, 131, 132. *See also* New River dispute

American kinship, 68, 70, 229n.5. *See also* Kinship; Schneider, David M.

American values, 147, 161, 184; autonomy, 13, 169, 179; egalitarianism, 51; freedom of choice, 2; pragmatism, 165; self-sufficiency, 3, 169. *See also* Democracy; Independence; Property; Self-determination

Ancestry, 63, 70, 74–75, 210; of county population, 78; and family histories, 83–84; and land, 167

Anderson, Stella, 145

Anglin, Mary, 231n.12

Anthropologist, 39–44, 61, 203–4; as activist, 187; on Appalachians, 45; in Ashe County, xiii, 19, 221–22; and cultural domains, 92; in ethnographic writing, xv; journal of, 42; as marginal, 43; and mountaineers, 21; as outsider, 118–19; as student of local history, 36

Anthropology, 209; as critique, 10, 162, 191, 196–98, 201–2; interpretive, xiv, 42–43. *See also* Ethnography

Appalachia (region): as colony, 195–96; community studies of, 5, 67; cultural domination in, 179; culture of, xiv, 198, 202, 227n.9; development in, 6; and fatalism, 116, 221; history of, 172, 203; kinship in, 75; political struggle in, 4, 215, 220; representation of, 161–63, 223. *See also* Development; Domination; Strip mining

Appalachian Power Company (APC), 125–31, 133, 150, 173; and Brumley Gap proposal, 207–8; determination of, 155, 156; land acquisition by, 181

Appalachian Regional Commission, 174, 196, 226n.6

Appalachians: ethnicity of, 47; as ethnic minority, 52; as illiterate, 45; as impoverished, 46. *See also* Stereotypes

Appalachian State University, 33, 40, 42, 144, 192. *See also* Education

Archeological sites: at Brumley Gap, 207; on New River, 131

Architecture: in Ashe County, 55–56; church, 100

Armed forces, 30–31, 36, 59, 209

Art, 100, 161, 186, 210–11; and politics of culture, 186–88. *See also* Commoditization; Frescoes; Handicrafts

Ashe County, North Carolina: education in, 25; history of, 19; population of, 21

Ashe County Library, 23, 42, 69, 132

Authenticity, cultural, 150, 183, 201; of handicrafts, 187–88; and politics, 197

Autonomy. *See* American values

Compositor: G & S Typesetters, Inc.
Printer: Braun-Brumfield, Inc.
Binder: Braun-Brumfield, Inc.
Text: 11/13 Bembo
Display: Bembo